Grow
YOUR OWN

Grow

YOUR OWN

Angus Stewart & Simon Leake

CONTENTS

INTRODUCTION TO URBAN FARMING

1

INTRODUCTION FROM ANGUS AND SIMON

Mechanisation is gradually changing the way we live and work, freeing up our busy lives for more productive pursuits. Urban dwellers now have a fabulous opportunity to spend more time growing a proportion of their own fresh produce, while also significantly reducing their carbon footprint and organic-waste stream. As well as allowing us the satisfaction of eating homegrown food, urban farming enables us to reconnect with the agricultural world and teaches our kids where food comes from.

Grow Your Own: How to be an Urban Farmer is an insightful guide to cultivating nutritious food crops in city environments. As trained horticulturists and communicators with plenty of experience in growing our own food, we have a lot of wisdom that we are keen to share with you. We explain how soils and other growing media work, the needs of plants and how urban environments differ from traditional farms. We reveal how to improve and maintain soils in a sustainable way as well as the principles of using composts, fertilisers and mulches in the urban environment. In addition, we also show you how to manage weeds, pests and diseases with little to no use of artificial chemicals.

As the world's human population increases, and cities continue to get bigger and bigger, it is imperative that we explore more economical and environmentally friendly ways to feed those living in high-density situations. *Grow Your Own: How to be an Urban Farmer* examines the importance of producing a diverse supply of fresh food that has not travelled for thousands of miles, and utilising small spaces and innovative ideas to make the most of every urban surface.

LOOKING TO THE PAST

Not so long ago, most householders had some kind of productive garden. I (Simon) remember going to Britain to see my grandparents when I was about six years old. We arrived in winter, and it was very cold. Grandad took me out into the frosty garden to pick brussels sprouts. I can

still hear the 'plonk-plonk-plonk' as he snapped off the hard, white sprouts and dropped them into the metal bucket I held. To this day, I still love brussels sprouts covered with warm butter, salt and pepper.

My mother always had a few things in the garden – at an absolute minimum there was parsley and mint, essential for a Sunday roast. Our neighbour, who had a very big garden with fruit trees and vegetables, would give us chokos when they were in season. He also kept Sussex chooks, and we didn't mind about the roosters crowing – you had to get up anyway. Most houses in the street had a vegetable garden, and many people swapped and traded produce with each other.

For me (Angus), my childhood often took me to my grandparents' vegetable gardens. My paternal grandfather, Roy Stewart, was a magistrate who had fought in the First World War, and his weekends were all about growing 'Grosse Lisse' tomatoes in homemade compost that had been carefully sieved. I enjoyed helping him make liquid fertiliser using the ready supply of chicken manure from the family chook run.

OPPOSITE Simon Leake (left) and Angus Stewart are both well-regarded horticulturists who know how to grow healthy edible plants in city environments.

LEFT Growing a diverse range of vegetables and fruits on your urban farm is one of the best ways to reduce your environmental footprint.

Angus recalls: 'My maternal grandparents were farmers in Victoria, so at their place there was always a ready supply of fresh dairy products and homegrown vegetables. As a child gardener, I could never see the point of growing flowers when the space could be used to cultivate an edible crop. That view has softened somewhat over the years, but I still delight in growing anything edible. In recent times, I have taken to exploring the diversity of Australian bush foods.'

HEADING TOWARDS THE FUTURE

In the 1960s, it was reasonably common for Aussie families – especially postwar immigrants from Europe – to have a vegie patch. By the 1980s, however, it was increasingly rare. The rise in materialism and the convenience of driving to a supermarket to buy food overwhelmed any desire to obtain food by performing backbreaking agricultural labour. There are still some big fruit and vegie gardens in suburbs with large immigrant populations, but they are few and far between.

Recently in the Western world, there has been a revival in interest in how food is produced and an eagerness to return to the simplicity of our pastoral past. An extension of this ethos has been the birth and development of permaculture, which espouses a much more ecological approach to food farming than the extraordinary crop monocultures of industrial-scale agriculture. In most of the rest of the world, particularly the developing world, urban farming is a basic necessity and has not been forgotten or discarded.

Today, around 20 per cent of the world's food production occurs in urban environments. Our aim with this book is to make sure this proportion rises, as the number of people living in urban environments irrevocably increases. We emphasise the ease with which you can grow a multitude of crops in the tiniest of urban areas, using everything from vertical gardens to clever containers. Even on a small balcony, you can turn your kitchen scraps into fertiliser that will help you grow a lifetime's supply of fresh herbs and salad greens.

ABOVE Traditional Australian 'quarter-acre block' gardens of the twentieth century almost always featured an extensive backyard vegetable patch complete with at least one citrus tree.

OPPOSITE Follow permaculture ideals by recycling your kitchen scraps into a well-balanced organic fertiliser that completes the environmental loop on your urban farm.

PHENOMENAL PERMACULTURE

A philosophy for a more sustainable way of life for humanity, permaculture is well suited to urban farming at any scale. It is all about observing the principles of natural ecosystems that have evolved over countless aeons, and then applying them to various aspects of human society and environment. It is a broad philosophy that not only relates to food production, but also to things such as energy and water usage. The concept was first developed in Tasmania by Bill Mollison and David Holmgren, who were concerned with the unsustainable nature of modern industrial agriculture and its detrimental effects on the environment – in particular, on biodiversity. The concept has since become a worldwide phenomenon.

Permaculture design principles can be used to create eminently sustainable urban farms that produce as wide a variety of crops and animal products as possible in a given environment. *Grow Your Own: How to be an Urban Farmer* highlights the scientific principles that underpin organic farming, and will help you create permaculture systems on your urban farm. By using methods such as worm farming and composting to recycle nutrients and organic matter back into the soil, and other growing media, we can devise systems that readily mimic the nutrient cycling and soil building that happens in the natural world.

Our chapter entitled Choosing the Right Crops is designed to get you thinking about food plants from a much broader perspective, so that you are aware of why particular species first came to be food crops and how their wild relatives fit into their natural ecosystems (for example, potatoes and other root crops function as water and nutrient storage, and legumes add extra nitrogen to the soil via their symbiotic relationship with bacteria in their roots). Using this information, you can choose a biodiverse range of crops that will provide a seasonal range of fresh produce – this is totally compatible with general permaculture principles.

Sustainable water use is another key permaculture principle. As we show within our Water and Drainage chapter, harvesting stormwater that might otherwise have gone to waste (or worse, created environmental damage) is a no-brainer. Simply using storage tanks or altering the topography of growing areas to utilise surface run-off keeps perfectly good water resources on your urban farm. While this book is not about permaculture per se, it is all about providing you with the building blocks that allow you to understand how to apply the same natural ecological principles to your urban farm.

WHAT DO WE MEAN BY URBAN FARMING?

Lots of people have gardens, but how is urban farming different from gardening? 'Urban' usually refers to cities, suburbs or various areas not considered to be strictly rural in nature, while 'farming' relates to cultivating the land and, usually, the growing of crop plants (as opposed to gardening, which implies the growing of purely ornamental plants). Put the two words together, however, and they can mean different things to each person.

We believe that the term 'urban' can be applied to any populated area. It could describe, for example, a small kitchen garden, a house garden on a large property, a council allotment on the fringe of a small English village or the Chinese market gardens that were once common around many major cities. The word 'farming' conjures up images of commercial operations with extensive plantings, their purpose being to sell produce for profit. However, for us, 'farming' is an activity that can provide useful and valuable produce on any scale. Private vegetable gardens are much better defined as urban farming because of the considerable tangible and intangible 'wealth' created. It is ironic that most economic statistics do not consider the wealth generated by urban farmers who grow crops for their own consumption.

For us, urban farming involves some kind of useful produce being grown in inhabited areas. This is usually vegetables, herbs and fruits, but also sometimes cereal crops such as maize. Cut-flower production or even creating potted plants for sale might also be considered under the umbrella term 'urban farming'.

ASPECTS OF URBAN FARMING

Urban farming has, of course, been carried out for centuries. However, in a modern context with a globalised society, urban farming is all about reconnecting with the basics of how food is produced. Most urban farmers will not ever be able to grow enough food to completely supply their needs, but what we can do is learn to place a higher value on food production generally.

Growing your own food enables you to control its quality, reduce or eliminate the use of pesticides and reduce the 'food miles' (in other words, the energy required to ship food from far-flung destinations).

Naturally, you will be satisfying your own needs and wants from your urban farm, but there are many other creative possibilities – such as swapping, bartering or selling your produce at local farmers' markets. Urban farming is typically practised on either private or public land; the cooperative nature of community and school gardening allows those of us with very limited space to utilise public land, but we certainly won't exclude those who want the tranquillity of their own private urban farm. Small animal husbandry can be integrated with fruit and vegetable operations if there

THE MAGIC OF MICRO-GARDENS

Micro-gardens make use of small spaces, such as on rooftops or balconies, and can be managed by people both young and old. Studies by the Food and Agriculture Organization of the United Nations (FAO) revealed that a micro-garden of just one square metre could produce any one of the following:

- around 200 tomatoes (30 kg) a year
- 36 heads of lettuce every 60 days
- 10 cabbages every 90 days
- 100 onions every 120 days.

is sufficient space, with chickens being the most practical option in urban areas. Aquaponics is an increasingly popular form of urban farming that combines raising fish with growing crops.

AN ENVIRONMENTAL PERSPECTIVE

Urban farming is all about cultivating food crops in built-up, heavily populated areas rather than growing it well outside cities and transporting it long distances to reach the eventual consumer, a complex process that is often costly to both the environment and the individual. It makes a lot of sense, therefore, to look at growing as much fresh food as we can in urban areas.

Discarded food and kitchen scraps are often regarded as waste and find their way into rubbish dumps. If we recycle the large quantities of nutrients and organic matter from scraps by using them on the urban farm, then we are not only saving money by not buying commercial composts and fertilisers, but we are also solving a costly municipal waste-disposal problem – one that results in further economic damage through the environmental degradation that it causes. This is clearly an issue where each and every person can contribute in some small (or large) way by utilising the organics they generate each day in an environmentally friendly way.

Food security for the cities of the world is also a concern that has only just received overdue recognition in recent years. While it would require our cities to be seriously reorganised in order to provide the bulk of our food from urban farming, it is certainly a worthwhile objective to dramatically increase the amount we are growing using currently available space. History tells us that in times of crisis it is possible to make a big difference through urban farming. During the Second World War, the 'Dig for Victory' campaign in England galvanised extraordinary support from the masses to replace the food supplies that had been cut off from mainland Europe and the rural areas of the United Kingdom. Urban farming often becomes much more common during times of distress and poverty – but why wait for the bad times? We should encourage urban farming now, in preparation for any economic and environmental crises that may befall our cities in the future.

KEY FACTS ABOUT URBAN FARMING

According to the website of the Food and Agriculture Organization of the United Nations (www.fao.org):

- There are some 200 million urban farmers in the world, supplying food to 700 million people – about 12 per cent of the world's population.
- Urban farming provides for 30 per cent of vegetable consumption in Kathmandu, 50 per cent in Karachi and 85 per cent in Shanghai.
- Some 50 per cent of Asian urban households farm.
- Small livestock are an important part of city farming. For example, livestock are raised by 17 per cent of urban households in Kenya.
- The average Latin American urban family spends 1–1.5 working days a week on its urban garden and saves 10–30 per cent on its food bill.

Urban farming has taken many forms throughout the history of civilisation, from a survival necessity to a pleasurable pastime. It has Its roots deep in human history, and in fact was the first form of farming in the Middle East's ancient Fertile Crescent region.

But let's go back even further than that. Well known in Australia are Queensland's Bunya Mountains, which were named after the majestic bunya pines. These trees grow huge cones weighing up to 10 kilograms, which are packed with highly nutritious nuts. Like many plants, bunya pines tend to bear heavily every second or third year. From ancient times, Aboriginal people would put out the word that a good season was coming, and men, women and children would come from hundreds of kilometres around to gather for the feast. The remains of the steps they cut in the trees to harvest the cones can still be seen to this day.

Until the harvest was done, the Aboriginal people would remain sedentary – abandoning the need for constant movement in search of food. They were 'urban' – collecting together in a 'village' camp to swap stories and enrich their lives. Rumour has it they ensured some seeds remained so there were bunya pines around for future generations. Is this one of the roots of urban farming? There is a great deal of evidence to suggest that Aboriginal people were 'farming' in other ways, such as burning grasslands to promote plant growth in order to subsequently harvest the grain from the native grasses.

The first farmers

From excavations of ancient hamlets in Palestine, Syria and southern Turkey, we know that the first farms were close to – indeed, immediately next to – the houses where the people lived. Dating to around 7000 years ago, these sites feature the seeds of emmer wheat as well as the seeds and pollen of many different flowers, wild herbs and early vegetables. These were urban farms, not commercial ones, but over time the excess of food that they created led to the growth of larger and larger 'villages', then towns and very soon cities.

Early farmers of the Middle East were the world's first plant breeders, as they started to select plants with larger fruits, seeds and roots to create better and more productive crops. The archaeological record shows clearly that, with time, the grain size of wheat became bigger and plants held their seeds a lot longer, making wheat much easier to harvest. Today, building on the breeding work of several

LEFT This Aztec petroglyph of maize is an elegant record of the crop that allowed early cities to flourish.

OPPOSITE Many extensive kitchen gardens beside old European houses and villas have been farmed successfully for centuries.

thousand years, we now have large-grained, nutritious wheat plants that do not shatter at all, but sit upright as they wait to be harvested.

Meanwhile in pre-European America, the early Mayans were dealing with the rather infertile soils of Mexico's Yucatán Peninsula. They gradually changed their slash-and-burn rainforest farming into a form of crop rotation of maize, beans and squash, a system known as milpa. The beans built up soil nitrogen levels, a nutrient vital for the maize in the next rotation, while the squash also used the nitrogen and could climb and scramble to maximise the use of space. Milpa was more than a system of farming – it was also a method of uniting the urban community.

Roman model

Every Roman villa had a house garden that supplied all the things the great staple, wheat, could not: flavoursome food, essential vitamins and meat protein (derived from fowls and rabbits). The garden frescoes in the renowned Villa of Livia in Rome feature vivid renditions of fruits, flowers and vegetables, revealing not only what highborn Romans ate, but also the things that they most valued in life.

The Roman villa model of urban farming most closely resembles the situation in modern industrialised countries. Staples such as wheat, rice, maize and millet are grown on large-scale farms, whereas house, village or community gardens provide essential complementary foods, gainful employment, recreational enjoyment and a sense of control of our destinies. Agriculture makes life possible, but horticulture makes it worthwhile.

The ties that bind

Urban farming, in all its forms, is remarkably resilient. The satisfaction our forefathers obtained from growing food and feeding their families is increasingly attractive to many people living in urban spaces, and they strive to reconnect with their past. Many of us are finding that we have to relearn the gardening skills and rebuild the plant knowledge that have been lost in the last two or three generations — but we take on these tasks with great joy.

In Adelaide, South Australia, this coveted link to the past is celebrated every year during the annual olive harvest. Olive trees grow well in the alkaline soils and Mediterranean climate of Adelaide, and the early city planners had the foresight to plant these tough and useful trees throughout the city's parklands and along roadsides. The city council has found it necessary to manage the harvest by issuing permits to pick olives, which prevents turf wars and the trampling of garden beds.

THE BENEFITS OF URBAN FARMING

This type of farming offers many different advantages, which range from small to large scale.

HELPING PEOPLE

Urban farming provides an enormous swag of social, health and therapeutic benefits for the individual. Growing your own food will save you money if it is done efficiently, especially if you use the nutrients found in kitchen scraps to feed your garden. It provides much-needed physical exercise and superb mental stimulation, and in community gardens there is the added advantage of social interaction – including the satisfaction of swapping and bartering away produce you have grown.

Your produce is fresher and will generally have a better taste because it can be harvested when it has fully ripened and it can be eaten straight away. You can also grow edible plants that may not be readily available from retail outlets, such as heirloom vegetables and rare herbs. If you are environmentally conscious, then urban farming is also a great way to reduce your carbon footprint in an enjoyable and viable way.

PROTECTING THE ENVIRONMENT

Urban farming is a potent tool with which we can all get involved to create better environmental outcomes, and this will lead to cities around the world being much more sustainable. A decline in freight as well as decreased energy consumption during food production will curtail the demand for fossil fuels. Utilising local recycled water and organic wastes as fertiliser will reduce expenditure, as well as promote carbon sequestration on urban farms. Large numbers of individual urban farmers are also willing and able to grow a much greater variety of crops and heirloom species, thus ensuring there is genetic diversity among plants for future urban farmers who are likely to be operating in very different climatic conditions.

Growing your own food will save you money if it is done efficiently, especially if you use ... kitchen scraps to feed your garden.

CREATING GREEN CITIES

On a broader scale, urban farming can bring significant benefits to whole neighbourhoods. Community gardens link diverse groups of people together, and this often reduces crime rates. School gardens empower students to be physically and mentally active, and they teach children lifelong skills in nutrition and growing food. Urban farming can also help to buffer microclimates within cities, reducing the 'heat island' effect that cities create due to their energy usage.

ABOVE Freshly picked produce from the urban farm reaches the table quickly, ensuring ripeness and great flavour.

OPPOSITE Working in community gardens provides demonstrable benefits for both physical and mental health.

WHERE CAN WE DO URBAN FARMING?

The human race is a very inventive species that is defined by its use of tools and technology, and this remarkable trait has long been applied to urban farming. While many urban farmers have traditional backyard plots or participate in community gardens, others are constantly refining and developing methods for utilising vertical and rooftop gardens as well as very small spaces, such as balconies and courtyards. Indoor cultivation is also a reality, through the use of artificial lighting and hydroponics – and technology is evolving rapidly to make these specialised techniques more environmentally and economically viable.

In addition to parcels of spare land in highly populated cities, we are also looking to utilise peri-urban areas (regions that are destined for urban development in the future). All around our cities there are spaces that can – and already are – being used to grow food in a sustainable way.

URBAN FARMING IN SOIL

Most urban farming occurs in soil, but this soil can be vastly different from its natural state. In fact, soil scientists have a name for soils that have been greatly altered by human activities: anthroposols. Regardless of whether they have a tiny patch of land or they are part of a larger enterprise, urban farmers work to improve the fertility of their soil through the use of compost, fertiliser and mulch, hence adding to the area of anthroposols in the world. This is not a bad thing. Urban soils can be much more fertile than their rural cousins.

ABOVE Specially designed potting mixes are now lightweight enough to make rooftop urban farming a far more feasible idea.

With population densities increasing, yards are getting smaller and smaller in cities around the world. Clever urban farmers are thinking outside the square when it comes to growing areas, utilising the leftover space next to driveways, planting vertical gardens along fences and incorporating raised beds in paved areas and courtyards.

On a broader scale, Europe is the home of allotment gardening. Public spaces have been turned into collective urban farms, where citizens have their own 'allotment' or plot of land on which they can grow whatever they want. In more recent times across the Western world, school and community gardens have followed this trend, setting aside tracts of land for students and community members to cultivate their own food.

There are many unexplored opportunities in the urban areas of the world with respect to suitable spots for urban farming. Some of the most underutilised spaces are those along transport corridors, such as 'rail trails' and road verges. Parklands and old bowling greens are only now being considered as possible locations for urban farms.

URBAN FARMING WITHOUT SOIL

The advent of commercially available potting mixes and soil-less growing media – such as perlite and coconut coir – means that having no soil (or poor soil) is no longer a barrier for the urban farmer. 'Protected environment' houses (commonly known as greenhouses, glasshouses or poly-tunnels) enable urban farmers to extend the growing season of plants cultivated in soil-less media.

In high-rise and heavily built-up areas, focus has shifted to using rooftops, balconies, patios and walls for food production. This requires the use of specialised containers, growing media and fertiliser programs that suit the unique microclimates found in cities and address the specific light constraints and wind issues of metropolitan regions. Whether you are growing crops in a bathtub or a sophisticated wicking bed, the use of pots and other containers allows you to grow edible plants in all sorts of cramped places.

Taking soil-less cultivation to a whole new level is hydroponics, a system whereby plants are grown in an inert medium (such as pure sand or perlite), and the nutrients that would normally come from soil are supplied to the plants via a balanced liquid feed. This type of system is dominating the commercial production of fast-turnover crops, such as salad greens (for example, lettuce) and soft-leaf herbs (for example, basil and coriander). There are many advantages to hydroponics, not the least of which is that nutrition is not dependent on soil condition so it can be carefully controlled, and crops grown in hydroponic 'humidicribs' can be better protected from pests and diseases. However, running a successful hydroponic system requires an acute understanding of fertilisers, and there is often tension between the advocates of 'organic' growing and the heavy reliance on synthetic mineral fertilisers in commercial hydroponics.

BELOW Most local councils approve of the use of road verges for urban farming, which is a great way to utilise land that usually lies dormant.

NEXT PAGES As long as crops have access to sunlight, water and plenty of nutrients, they will thrive on urban farms of any size.

THE ENVIRONMENT FOR URBAN FARMING

② 2

LOOKING AT YOUR SURROUNDINGS

The environment created by urban areas has a profound effect on farming in various ways, both good and bad. A basic understanding of what affects plant growth can enable you to adapt your conditions for optimum growth and maximise your crop productivity. Take some time to assess your growing environment for the following factors.

TEMPERATURE

The length of your growing season is largely determined by latitude, topography and proximity to the modifying effects of oceans. The further inland we go, and the higher the altitude we ascend, the greater the variation in temperatures between day and night, and the greater the potential for colder temperatures and frost. Topography is an important influence, as localised low spots in an area will tend to be more frost prone, given that cold air drains to lower-lying areas.

Cities are generally much warmer than surrounding countryside. A major reason for this is that there are less plants evaporating water in urban areas. As water is evaporated, it causes a cooling effect known as the 'latent heat of vaporisation'. Since water absorbs heat when it moves from being a liquid to being a gas, this consumes a lot of the solar energy falling on the plant, and cools it. A similar process was used in the days before the invention of the refrigerator to keep butter from melting in a meat safe – wet canvas surrounding the meat safe kept it cool as the water evaporated.

In urban environments, less of the incoming heat from the sun is used to evaporate water via plants, and more of it ends up heating hard surfaces and the atmosphere. The reflection of solar radiation energy off light-coloured concrete or metal – it seems that every architect wants their building to be white or, worse, silver – heats the air above the surface. Energy that

BELOW Stonework and pavers can be used in cooler climates to absorb and store heat during the day. This helps to moderate temperatures.

OPPOSITE Plants thrive in the warm conditions found in urban situations. Light-coloured buildings reflect sunlight, while dark-hued asphalt draws in daytime heat and slowly releases it at night.

isn't reflected off heats the material it hits, warming it so it then radiates its heat off during the night. This is not all bad news, however, as food plants usually love warmth and will grow very quickly in the warmer environments of cities.

Crops and temperature range

Provided they have enough water to evaporate, plants do best in warm environments – as demonstrated by the luxuriance of a tropical rainforest. Most food plants appreciate the warmth of our cities, and do very well in them. Growing seasons are often longer, and you can even grow subtropical species in cities as far south as Melbourne, Hobart and Adelaide. With a bit of protection, microclimates can be created anywhere in Australia.

Each crop has an optimum temperature range, so comparing the monthly averages for your area to the growing requirements of the crops in which you are interested will give you a starting point. As well as average temperatures, you will also need to look at maxima and minima, because certain crops – such as pome fruits (for example, pears) and blueberries – need a certain amount of 'chilling' (the number of hours below 7°C, depending on the variety you are growing). Consequently, high-chill crops may not be a good choice in warm cities. Also, some crops may suffer if maximum temperatures exceed certain limits, and there can be damage to yields.

LIGHT

Everyone knows that plants need light. But how much light does your growing area receive throughout the day, and also during the different seasons as the position of the sun changes between summer and winter? If you are on a slope, what is the aspect of your growing area? In the Southern Hemisphere, the north side of a hill, or a house, will be warmer and sunnier than the south side.

Most people have observed that plants growing in low-light conditions are spindly and tall. This phenomenon is called 'etiolation'. The tendency to grow tall in search of sunlight is a response to conditions in a forest, but it doesn't always help the plant in a concrete jungle.

Plants can grow with less than full sunlight, provided they get a few hours of direct sunlight a day, preferably towards the middle of the day. Below about 50 per cent of full sunlight – depending on where you live and how much sunlight there is – productivity starts to decline. Very few plants can live if they receive below about 10 per cent of full sunlight, and those that do live will not produce useful food crops.

The main problem within urban areas is shadowing by buildings, which is sometimes referred to as the 'canyon effect'. Picture yourself with a skyscraper to the east and another to the north (or to the south, if you're in the Northern Hemisphere). The sun comes up, but you don't see it. You get one or two hours before the other building shadow falls, and then you get three to five hours of full sun all afternoon – except if your neighbour to the west has a row of tall, thick trees, in which case

ABOVE Pear trees require hundreds of hours of temperatures below 12°C to produce a crop of fruits each year.

Plants can grow with less than full sunlight, provided they get a few hours of direct sunlight a day, preferably towards the middle of the day.

you only get one or two hours in the afternoon. Your plants will get just enough sun to live, but they won't thrive and yield well – and they will be weak and spindly, no matter how fertile the soil.

On the right wavelength

Did you know that plants only use part of the sunlight that falls on them? 'White' light from the sun can be split up into its constituent wavelengths by water in the air (a rainbow) or a glass prism. Remember your rainbow colours: red, orange, yellow, green, blue, indigo and violet? Plants have two kinds of pigments (chlorophylls) that are responsible for photosynthesis, namely chlorophyll a and b. Chlorophyll a uses light mostly in the blue–violet range, and chlorophyll b mostly in the red–yellow range. Both reflect green light, which is why plants appear green – they don't need green light to photosynthesise. The human eye sees white light very well, but it is not always the best judge of the correct wavelengths or strength of light necessary for photosynthesis.

A camera light meter is a useful guide to available light, but note that photosynthetically active wavelengths are not fully detected by these meters. Simon once used one to demonstrate that a failing indoor plant was receiving only about 2 per cent of total light input in winter, which was not enough to support growth. It goes to show that the eye is not really a good measure of available light for plants. You can see perfectly well at 2 per cent of natural light, but it would starve a plant.

What is important about light is the total amount received in a day. For example, if a plant gets four hours of full sun at around midday in winter, but was in full shadow both morning and evening, this would represent about 70 per cent of total solar input for the day, since the sun is at its most powerful around midday. This is quite sufficient for most plants. If, however, a plant receives two hours of full sun in the early morning and two hours in the late afternoon, this would only represent around 20 per cent of total solar input, as the sun is weakest at the beginning and end of the day. This is insufficient

for most productive plants, but may be enough for various herbs, or, alternatively, a pretty display of ferns. If light levels are likely to be limited for an extended time, then foliage plants such as salad greens may be the best crop option.

If you have doubts about how much sun your garden is getting, use a camera light meter. In the area where you want to grow plants, point the meter towards the sun and take a reading. Then go to a location close by that is in full sun, and take another reading. Now compare the reading from the area of interest with that from the full-sun position. For the highest productivity, you want to see a result that is better than 70 per cent of full sun in winter and 50 per cent in summer. With a result that is below these numbers, productivity will fall. Ideally you would take six readings spread over the day, from sunrise to sunset (on a clear day), and repeat the exercise four times a year, as the sun strength and day length obviously change with the seasons. It should be noted that this method doesn't work in areas of heavy atmospheric pollution or smog, because the full sun readings are likely to be adversely affected.

ABOVE Light levels in high-density urban areas should be assessed when planning a site's suitability for urban farming.

OPPOSITE, TOP Crop protection, such as shade cloth, can greatly mitigate the detrimental effects of wind tunnels in urban areas.

OPPOSITE, BOTTOM Water tanks now come in many shapes and sizes to facilitate water harvesting in a wide variety of urban situations.

As well as not enough light, we can also be faced with the situation of too much light (and therefore heat) when growing on rooftops in cities. Full sun all day plus strong winds, particularly during summer, can lead to environments that cause plants to suffer from water stress. The solution is to shield the plants with shade cloth.

WATER

The total amount as well as the distribution of rain throughout the year will affect what crops you can grow. It is always worth trying to select crops that will suit your natural rainfall pattern, as supplementary irrigation can be an added cost as opposed to the free stuff from the sky. However, most high-yielding vegetables are not drought tolerant and need supplementary water.

Surprisingly, most cities (with the exception of desert cities) have excess run-off water and should be able to support urban farming without the need to use town (potable) water supplies. This occurs because of the high percentage of sealed concrete and asphalt surfaces that results in an almost 100 per cent run-off of rainfall. In fact, due to our fear of stormwater and flooding, we have deliberately engineered vast systems to ensure that stormwater gets off our streets and into rivers and oceans as fast as possible, leaving nothing behind. This is a tragic waste, given that we have the technology to capture, store and utilise all of this water for useful purposes such as growing food.

Thankfully, water harvesting is becoming increasingly popular in cities, and most local government areas now encourage the installation of rainwater tanks. A vision for the future involves more regionally based schemes, where run-off from roads and suburb-wide catchments is collected for redistribution as irrigation water.

There are many different water-storage systems that can be incorporated into urban buildings to facilitate the collection of stormwater. In addition to the traditionally round above-ground tanks, there are now all sorts of other options in various shapes and sizes that can fit into the small and often-awkward spaces found in medium- to high-density urban areas. Tanks and storage structures can also be situated underneath outdoor urban areas.

GONE WITH THE WIND

A major problem in urban environments is the wind-tunnel effect. Buildings deflect wind, and some growing situations may suffer thanks to the high winds that are channelled their way. As well as the physical damage that high winds can cause, they can also greatly elevate transpiration. It is worth spending some time assessing your site for any potential wind-tunnel effects. Windbreaks can be used to mitigate winds; plant sturdy hedges, or use materials such as shade cloth to create a barrier.

CASE STUDY: ROOFTOP FARMING

Wendy's Garden

Wendy Siu-Chew Lee is a great example of an urban farmer who is exploring ways of producing food in the small spaces on top of buildings. These areas have their problems – particularly with wind, light and lack of soil – however, Wendy is determined to overcome these hurdles to cultivate as much organically grown produce as possible in her rooftop garden located in a leafy northern Sydney suburb.

Having recently taken up the challenge of gardening with edible plants, Wendy freely admits that she is still on a steep learning curve. However, she is clearly invested in the project, and has spent considerable time experimenting with a range of growing systems and a relatively wide range of crops. This has already brought her a reasonable degree of success, as well as the odd learning experience.

Wendy has found tremendous variation in the performance of various systems, and one of her biggest issues has been finding a potting mix that will give her reliable performance over an extended period of time. Modern potting mixes are often based on large proportions of organic components, such as composted pine bark, which continue to break down and collapse in the pot, leading to a lack of aeration. We suggested to Wendy that she should find a mix with a greater percentage of mineral components, such as horticultural ash, perlite and coarse sand, which will not collapse over time.

Wendy uses a hungry bin worm farm to generate liquid fertiliser and solid castings that she adds to her mixes as an organic 'tonic' that both conditions and feeds her potting mixes. One of her recent 'learning experiences' was overloading her worm farm with a large quantity of overripe fruits that overwhelmed the worm population – the subsequent 'rotten-egg gas' smell of her unit told her that something had gone badly wrong. She has since replenished the worm population and is now careful to ensure that moist food scraps are balanced with dry, carbon-rich materials, such as shredded cardboard. Otherwise, she is enthusiastic about the sustainable loop that is created by using worm farming to recycle the nutrients and carbon she and her partner generate each day in the kitchen.

There are several things that Wendy has found are particularly well adapted to rooftop gardening:

- Wicking beds in the form of the Vegepod system – this is a self-contained system that has a large well of water, which means it does not need as much watering as non-wicking beds. See pages 218–19 in the Water and Drainage chapter for more information on wicking beds.
- Grow bags – flexible bags of potting mix with collapsible support frames for climbing vegetables, such as tomatoes and cucumbers, have proven to be an excellent way to maximise production in her limited space.
- Various containers – these are placed on castors to enable Wendy to easily move them around.
- An espaliered olive tree – this is an excellent ornamental/ edible plant for one of her walls.
- A vertical garden system – this has proven to be a useful way to grow strawberries.

The take-home message from Wendy's garden is that experimenting with a range of growing systems is a useful way to figure out what will work in your particular rooftop, balcony or courtyard area.

CLOCKWISE, FROM OPPOSITE An espaliered olive tree maximises the use of limited space; experimentation with various growing systems is ongoing; the hungry bin worm farm is perfect for generating both liquid and solid organic fertiliser from Wendy's kitchen scraps; vertical gardening is ideal for crops, such as strawberries, which benefit from being off the ground.

Quality and quantity

Water quality is a vital consideration, and supply must meet several criteria if sustainable production is to be achieved. Salinity must be within the limits of the species you want to grow. Salts can come from various places, depending on the source of your water. Bore and recycled water can both contain significant levels of salts that may be damaging to plant growth, and can also build up in the soil over time. Background salts can also be an issue if you want to liquid feed your plants, as fertilisers (both organic and inorganic) will further elevate the salinity of your irrigation water. On the other hand, town water and captured rainwater almost never contain excessive salt levels.

Human pathogens can sometimes be present in recycled and harvested water supplies, and this can be a problem if you are growing crops such as salad greens. This is not because the pathogens are taken up by plants – they are not – but because salad vegetables aren't cooked, so there is a chance that harmful microbes such as *Salmonella* can be ingested from the surface of the leaf. If pathogenic microbes are a problem, there are various sterilisation systems that can be used, such as ultraviolet radiation and chlorination.

Most urban areas will be connected to a town water supply that potentially provides a source of unlimited water. However, town water is likely to be expensive, and water restrictions due to drought are increasingly common and can seriously affect water supply for plant production. It is therefore highly advisable to explore alternative water sources that can reduce dependency on town water supply.

One of the essential roles that water plays in plants is that of carrying dissolved nutrients up through the roots to the plant. If the plant is starved of water, it will also be starved of nutrients. Conversely, waterlogged soil leads to an exclusion of air, and the roots die – literally by drowning. The issues of supplying water to your urban farm, estimating watering needs, and having sensible watering practices to avoid stressing plant-growth processes is discussed in Water and Drainage (see pages 212–27).

GET SOME AIR

The atmosphere supplies three gases that are essential for plant growth: oxygen, carbon dioxide and nitrogen. Oxygen, at roughly 21 per cent of Earth's atmosphere, is never a limiting factor for plant growth. In many urban areas, carbon dioxide is often elevated because of atmospheric pollution, as are other gases potentially advantageous to plants, such as sulphur dioxide. Atmospheric pollution is therefore likely to be more beneficial than harmful for urban farms, and in particular extra carbon dioxide from the burning of fossil fuels can stimulate extra photosynthesis and plant growth. Consequently, urban farming is a great way for city dwellers to mitigate their carbon footprints.

OTHER ENVIRONMENTAL FACTORS

The choice of crops for your urban farm will also be influenced by these impacts on the growing environment.

♠ **Climatic extremes** The potential for extreme weather events should be a part of your crop selection thinking. Hailstorms, severe frost events, windstorms and droughts are all risks that need to be managed, particularly for long-term crops such as fruit and nut trees.

♠ **Soil type** It is always a good idea to select crops that suit your soil type, otherwise you will be potentially encouraging problems such as root-rot diseases.

♠ **Growing conditions** Ensure the drainage and water- and nutrient-holding capacity of your soil is appropriate.

♠ **Prevalence of pests and diseases** For instance, the presence of fruit flies in your area may make it very difficult to grow particular fruit crops, such as stone fruits.

ABOVE Elevated carbon dioxide levels in cities actually help accelerate the development of fast-growing plants, such as vegetables.

OPPOSITE Collecting rain in a tank is an excellent way of sourcing high-quality irrigation water for your urban farm.

CHOOSING THE RIGHT CROPS ③

WHAT TO GROW ON YOUR URBAN FARM

Deciding which crops to produce is an extremely important consideration for any farm, but is particularly so for the urban farm where space is at a premium. The overall growing environment must obviously be taken into account, and decisions need to be made about whether to work with the existing conditions or to modify them to overcome environmental extremes such as frost.

The end use of your produce will also be a factor: is it to be sold or used domestically, or a combination of the two? If you are primarily aiming at producing your own food, then the widest diversity of crops possible will give you plenty of scope for producing some food in every month of the year, while also minimising the risks of losses through pests and diseases. If, however, you are producing crops for sale, then narrowing the range down to a few crops will ensure that commercial-scale production is far more cost effective.

FOOD FAMILIES

The botanical world is divided into plant families based on similarities between different species, and it is no coincidence that particular families have been selected by urban farmers for millennia because of their palatability, ease of growth and adaptability to a range of growing environments. Thus, it makes sense to look at our crop choices family by family to decide what is best for our own unique urban-farm environment.

Crop rotation is another critical concept to understand in selecting what to grow, as members of the same plant family will tend to be susceptible to the same or similar pests and diseases. Growing a variety of crops from different families and then rotating the positions in which they are grown within the urban farm helps to prevent the build-up of pests and diseases, something that is particularly important for soil-borne diseases (see pages 60–1 for more detailed information on crop rotation). In this context, knowledge of the major plant families that are used for food production is very useful, so let us look at them in order of their importance.

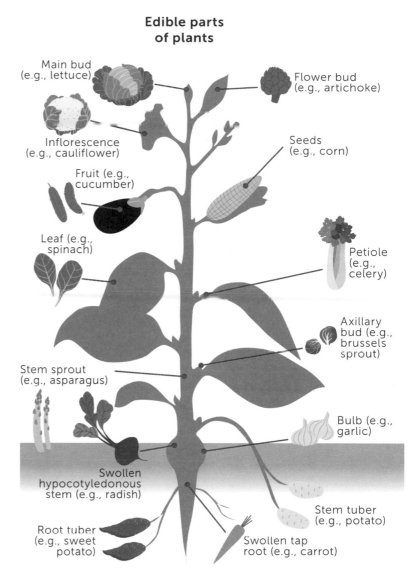

Edible parts of plants

Main bud (e.g., lettuce)

Flower bud (e.g., artichoke)

Inflorescence (e.g., cauliflower)

Seeds (e.g., corn)

Fruit (e.g., cucumber)

Leaf (e.g., spinach)

Petiole (e.g., celery)

Axillary bud (e.g., brussels sprout)

Stem sprout (e.g., asparagus)

Bulb (e.g., garlic)

Swollen hypocotyledonous stem (e.g., radish)

Stem tuber (e.g., potato)

Root tuber (e.g., sweet potato)

Swollen tap root (e.g., carrot)

Fabaceae (Papilionaceae) – the legume family

♠ **Origins** With more than 19,000 species, this is the world's third-largest plant family (after orchids and daisies). It can be found as a dominant component of virtually all types of plant communities on every continent of the planet (barring Antarctica), from tropical rainforests to dry deserts. Many of our most economically important legumes have evolved with humanity over the millennia, and they provide not only tasty food but also useful

OPPOSITE
Knowing your plant families well and rotating crops between growing beds are both critical for pest and disease management.

The choice of what crops to grow will be governed by the overall objectives of your urban farm. The rise and rise in the popularity of farmers' markets in recent times has created opportunities for urban farmers to obtain much higher returns for their crops than through wholesale-market channels. Specialisation in one or a few crops for sale allows for a more efficient use of resources and for some economies of scale in marketing as well as growing. The downside of this strategy is that specialising in one or a few crops tends to entrench the pests and diseases associated with them on your farm. However, an appropriate integrated pest management strategy as discussed in the Pest and Disease Management section (see pages 230–6) is a sustainable way to meet such challenges.

On the other hand, if the sole aim of the farm is to provide produce for the home (and to perhaps barter or donate excess yield to the local community), then our suggestion would be to grow as large a range of crops and livestock as possible. This strategy will provide the widest possible nutritional balance of major food groups for family and friends, and will also help to minimise the risk of particular plant pathogens or pests from becoming established on your urban farm.

medicines (such as gum arabic), timber, dyes and natural pesticides (such as rotenone).

♠ **Characteristics** The various members of the legume family are extraordinarily diverse in growth habit. They range from small, herbaceous, bushy plants and vigorous climbers to shrubs and trees such as carob (*Ceratonia siliqua*), the long pods of which are used to make a chocolate substitute. This huge group of plants is arguably the most important of all for human survival, given its role in providing non-animal protein through beans and peas of various types. Pulses are a group of legumes that are harvested for their dried seeds, such as chickpeas and lentils, which are a particularly easy-to-store source of protein.

The defining features of plants in the legume family are a seed pod that splits down two sides, which is usually the harvestable part of the plant, and an amazing symbiotic relationship with *Rhizobium* bacteria in their roots. This relationship enables each plant to take nitrogen from the air and turn it into nitrate, which feeds the plant. Effectively, the plants are able to produce their own fertiliser from thin air!

All members of the legume family play a significant role in the ecology of wild-plant communities as pioneer species that can grow in all sorts of difficult environments, and this is most likely a factor in why they were adopted by early farmers as crop plants. Another application of their 'pioneering' ability is their use as green-manure crops. They are grown to the flowering stage and then ploughed back into the earth, where they break down and add extra nitrogen and other nutrients, as well as organic matter, to the soil – making this an extremely useful fertilising technique for large areas. The practical aspects of green-manure cropping are covered in the Fertilisers chapter (see pages 150–75).

♠ **Examples** There are many different types of edible beans, but the archetypal ones belong to the species *Phaseolus vulgaris* that originated in the Americas and was a staple of indigenous agriculture in the central region of the Americas.

This species has numerous common names, including French bean, kidney bean, string bean and haricot, and features a huge range of varieties, which can either have a bushy or climbing growth habit. It is one of the easiest vegetables to grow; its large seeds can be direct sown into the soil, where they germinate quickly, and the plant grows and bears pods in a matter of weeks. Other important legumes include broad bean (*Vicia faba*), garden pea (*Pisum sativum*), peanut (*Arachis hypogaea*), mung bean (*Vigna radiata*), pigeon pea (*Cajanus cajan*), scarlet runner bean (*Phaseolus coccineus*) and soya bean (*Glycine max*). A couple of particularly fascinating examples of legume crops are the lentil and wattles.

Lentil (*Lens culinaris*) is one of the earliest plants domesticated by humans. Evidence of its consumption by humans goes back to Neolithic times in the western Asian region now encompassing Turkey, Iraq and Syria. There are many different varieties of this incredibly useful pulse, which have been selected over the thousands of years these plants have been in cultivation, and seed colours now range from yellow to orange, green and black.

Wattles (*Acacia* species) are very important Australian legumes. Edible seeds from many different species, such as golden wreath wattle (*Acacia saligna*) and golden wattle (*Acacia pycnantha*), formed a staple part of the diet of Aboriginal people. Mulga (*Acacia aneura*) is found throughout many parts of inland Australia, and the tree's wood was used by Aboriginal people for a variety of purposes, such as firewood and to create tools. Dozens of other wattle species have been recorded in historical documents as also being utilised for a multitude of non-culinary purposes.

♠ **Cultivation requirements** Legumes need near neutral to slightly alkaline soil, as many of them – such as beans and peas – are not well suited to acid soil. Most legumes are rather

OPPOSITE Your choice of crops will be determined somewhat by whether they are to be eaten at home or sold to other people.

ABOVE LEFT The characteristic flowers and pods of legumes are the key identifying features of this very important food family.

ABOVE Also known as fava bean, broad bean produces pods that are up to 30 centimetres in length.

intolerant of waterlogging and soil salinity, so a well-drained, friable soil enriched with a base dressing of well-rotted manure or compost will give the crops a flying start. Climbers such as peas require staking or trellising.

Because of their ability to fix their own nitrogen, most legumes will grow better than other plant families in low-nitrogen conditions. However, it is important that they have a ready supply of the various other essential nutrients if crops are to reach their full potential. For nitrogen fixation by the root nodules to occur, it is essential that the right strain of *Rhizobium* bacteria is present. Usually the process happens thanks to natural bacterial populations in healthy garden soil; however, it is also possible to obtain cultured strains of the optimum type of *Rhizobium* and inoculate the seeds before they are sown. This is routinely done in large-scale agriculture and horticulture.

♦ **Pests and diseases** Most legumes are propagated from seed, and it is important to ensure that your seed supply (whether purchased or self-collected) is free of systemic problems such as bean blight (caused by the bacterium *Xanthomonas axonopodis*) and mosaic viral disease – both of which can drastically reduce yields. Sap-sucking pests such as bean flower thrips, white flies and two-spotted mites can build up rapidly once the crop is underway, and it is vital that they are managed as soon as they start to appear so you can avoid major crop losses (for helpful strategies, see the Pest and Disease Management section on pages 230–6).

Solanaceae – the nightshade family
♦ **Origins** There are over 2500 species in the nightshade family, which have provided many of the world's tastiest and most important vegetable crops as well as medicinal and spice plants. Most of the important food species come from the Americas, and in particular the Andes Mountains.

♦ **Characteristics** This fascinating family includes herbaceous plants, climbers, shrubs and trees. Species from this family are often recognised by their (generally) small, tubular

flowers with five petals and five stamens. Various species produce chemicals called alkaloids, which often give the foliage and/or flowers a pungent smell. These chemicals are not an essential part of plant metabolism, but appear to have evolved as a defence mechanism to make the plants unpalatable to grazing animals. Perhaps the most famous alkaloid is nicotine, which is obtained from tobacco (*Nicotiana tabacum*). Weeds from this family often have names that should be taken literally – such as deadly nightshade – as the alkaloids they produce are toxic and definitely should not be consumed.

♦ **Examples** Members of the family, such as tomatoes (*Solanum lycopersicum*) and potatoes (*Solanum tuberosum*), have been bred and selected for thousands of years so that the

ABOVE Eggplant fruits are a good example of the edible part of solanaceous crops, and their pretty purple colour contrasts well with the green foliage.

edible parts have lost any toxic properties that their wild relatives might have had. The tubers of potatoes have become one of the world's largest sources of carbohydrates, in the form of starch. Other members of this family include eggplant or aubergine (*Solanum melongena*), capsicum and chilli pepper (*Capsicum annuum*), tamarillo (*Solanum betaceum*), pepino (*Solanum muricatum*), wild gooseberry (*Physalis angulata*), Cape gooseberry or Inca berry (*Physalis peruviana*) and goji berry or wolfberry (*Lycium barbarum* and *Lycium chinense*).

Australia has over 100 species in this family, with the most interesting being the *Solanum* species, such as kutjera or desert raisin (*Solanum centrale*), the fruits of which Aboriginal people dried and ate. Various other species of *Solanum* have edible fruits when ripe, but due to the toxic nature of this family generally, most of these plants are not commonly grown as food plants and should be regarded with caution.

♠ **Cultivation requirements** The wild members of the nightshade family tend to be colonisers of disturbed areas of soil, such as after a bushfire or when a tree falls over, or along roadside verges that have recently been bulldozed. They germinate easily from seed and grow rapidly to maturity, so they need a high level of nutrition and relatively well-drained soil. Many solanaceous plants prefer acid soil.

♠ **Pests and diseases** The lush nature of plant growth in this family tends to be very attractive to a wide variety of pests and disease-causing organisms. Caterpillars such as cutworm are a big problem when establishing the crop, while sap suckers such as aphids, thrips and white flies are very common pests throughout the life of the plants. Fungal, bacterial and viral diseases that affect the foliage, fruits and vascular (conducting) tissues are also very common at various stages of the plant's life cycle and will sometimes cause utter

ABOVE LEFT
The five-petalled flowers of the nightshade family are very distinctive and a highly useful characteristic for identification.

ABOVE The fruits of tomatoes come in various shapes and sizes. They can also be a variety of colours, from red and orange to green and purple.

devastation to crops. It is well worth researching varieties that are best suited to your growing environment, as they will hopefully suffer from fewer pest and disease issues.

Rosaceae – the rose family

♠ **Origins** Many of the food plants in this family were developed from wild species in Eurasia and North America, and they have been in cultivation for many centuries. Various fruit trees are the product of either deliberate or chance hybridisation, so they have a rather complex parentage. The upshot of this is that there are many different cultivars available that require vastly different climatic conditions, so it is important to research the best cultivar for your local growing conditions.

♠ **Characteristics** Interestingly, many of our favourite fruits come from the same family as roses. The flowers are a defining feature of the family, with five sepals, five petals and numerous spirally arranged stamens. These flowers contain the female parts that give rise to soft and fleshy fruits.

♠ **Examples** Family members include apple and crabapple (*Malus pumila*), pear (*Pyrus communis*), medlar (*Mespilus germanica*), quince (*Cydonia oblonga*), cherry (*Prunus avium*), peach and nectarine (*Prunus persica*), plum (*Prunus domestica*), apricot (*Prunus armeniaca*), raspberry (*Rubus idaeus*), strawberry (*Fragaria* species), blackberry (*Rubus fruticosus*) and almond (*Prunus dulcis*). Rose hep or rose hip is the fruit of various rose (*Rosa*) species, and is often made into tea. A valuable Australian contribution to this family is the native raspberry, of which there are several useful species, such as *Rubus parvifolius*.

♠ **Cultivation requirements** Climatic considerations are especially important when selecting the right cultivars for your operation. Many members of this family originate in cool climates, where the 'chill factor' is vital to the success of crops such as apples, cherries and pears (the 'chill factor' refers to the number

of hours below 7°C that the plant experiences throughout the cold or winter season, and requirements can vary from 150 to 1400 hours). Pollination is an important consideration for good fruit set in all types, and access to pollinators such as bees is vital to success. Peaches, nectarines and apricots are largely self-fertile and can be grown in isolation, but other fruits – such as plums and cherries – require cross-pollination and therefore need a mixture of different varieties to be grown near to each other to provide pollen and to ensure good fruit set.

ABOVE The strawberry is an important edible member of the rose family that holds its seeds on the outside of its fleshy fruits.

◆ **Pests and diseases** Queensland fruit flies, red spider mites and pear and cherry slugs are all devastating pests that can cause major economic damage to fruit yields. In addition, bacterial and fungal problems such as Phytophthora root rot and fire blight strike the roots and foliage of many species, reducing the plant's ability to take up nutrients and water.

Apiaceae – the carrot family

◆ **Origins** This family contains over 3500 species that are found across most of the globe, with the majority of edible and useful species coming from Eurasia. Given the success of this family, it would seem that there are many other potentially useful species in countries such as Australia.

◆ **Characteristics** The umbrella-like shape of its flower heads and seed heads distinguishes this family; an interesting bit of botanical trivia is that the family was once called Umbelliferae. The foliage is often divided into sections and usually contains essential oils that give off a pungent aroma, especially when crushed, which makes many species particularly useful as herbs. The seeds, roots, leaves and stems of various species are utilised as flavouring and food sources, while other species have medicinal properties.

◆ **Examples** As well as some of the classic root vegetables, such as carrot (*Daucus carota*) and parsnip (*Pastinaca sativa*), there are also herbaceous vegetables such as celery and celeriac (*Apium graveolens*), and herbs such as dill (*Anthemum graveolens*), coriander (*Coriandrum sativum*), caraway (*Carum carvi*), fennel (*Foeniculum vulgare*) and curly parsley (*Petroselinum crispum*). An Australian contribution to this famous food family is a relative of celery known as sea parsley or sea celery (*Apium prostratum*), which is very easy to grow and has a very strong flavour.

◆ **Cultivation requirements** The food crops from this family are mainly annuals and biennials that grow easily from seed, which, for many species, can be readily collected from the urban farm, provided the crop is disease free. Indeed, many of the herbs from this family, such as curly and Italian parsley, will often produce volunteer seedlings in vegetable plots where they are being grown. Most members of the family are fast-growing plants with short life cycles, and they respond extremely well to extra soil fertility in fairly neutral pH conditions. For the root crops in this family, it is vital to have friable topsoil to a depth of at least 500 millimetres; the

LEFT As with other grains in the grass family, sweet corn (which is also often known as maize) is one of the world's most important food crops.

domesticated maize in the Americas. The aforementioned plants form a huge proportion of the world's food and have proven to be the most economically important crops developed by humanity.

◆ **Characteristics** Grasses all feature more or less linear leaves that have parallel venation, which distinguishes them from the majority of other edible plant families. The flowers are generally inconspicuous, so the plants are normally pollinated by the wind rather than by insects such as bees. The edible portion is usually the seeds; however, vegetative parts such as leaves and shoots are sometimes consumed (for example, with bamboos).

◆ **Examples** As well as wheat (*Triticum aestivum*), rice (*Oryza sativa*) and maize (*Zea mays*), other grains such as barley (*Hordeum vulgare*), oats (*Avena sativa*), sorghum (*Sorghum bicolor*), millet (*Panicum miliaceum*) and rye (*Secale cereale*) are also widely used. Bamboos (*Bambusa* species) provide young shoot tips as a food throughout Asia, while sugar cane (*Saccharum officinarum*) is a source of sweetener across the globe. Given the ease of large-scale production, grain crops are not usually an important crop for urban farms. The grasses that are more likely to be found in the urban farm are maize (*Zea mays*) as the vegie sweet corn, or lemongrass (*Cymbopogon citratus*) as a culinary herb. Aboriginal people collected seeds from various native grasses, but these were apparently never grown as intensively cultivated crops. However, there is evidence that grasslands were 'cultivated' in a different sense, through the use of fire to spur growth. This growth provided seeds for harvesting and plants for grazing animals, such as kangaroos, which were then more easily hunted.

◆ **Cultivation requirements** With the exception of rice, which is grown in paddies with copious volumes of water, most edible grasses are fairly adaptable to a variety of soil and climatic conditions. However, they require relatively high levels of fertility to reach their full cropping potential.

various herbs will grow in a variety of soil types across a wide range of climatic conditions.

◆ **Pests and diseases** Soil-borne fungal diseases and pathogenic nematodes tend to cause the most damage to this family, as many of its members – such as carrots and parsnips – are harvested for their edible roots. Root-knot nematodes, black root rot, Sclerotinia rot and bacterial soft rot can affect crops at any stage between sowing and harvest. Notes on dealing with these various problems can be found in the Pest and Disease Management section (see pages 230–6); however, crop rotation (see pages 60–1) helps to avoid these problems and is a particularly important practice when growing this family.

Poaceae – the grass family

◆ **Origins** Grasses are very cosmopolitan and are found across all but the coldest parts of the globe. Crops such as wheat and barley were first cultivated in the Middle East, rice originated in Southeast Asia, and indigenous peoples

● **Pests and diseases** Fungal diseases of foliage, crown and roots are the most common problems found in cereal crops. Corn crops are particularly susceptible to stem borers, which are the caterpillars (larvae) of several species of moths. Although cereal and other grass crops are generally not going to be a major part of the average urban farm crop mix, the general principles of controlling fungal diseases within them can be found in the Pest and Disease Management section (see pages 230–6).

Rutaceae – the citrus family

● **Origins** Most of the edible plants in this family originated in Southeast Asia and Australia; however, they have been in cultivation for so long that many of the commonly grown citrus cultivars have arisen in cultivation, often as chance seedlings. For hundreds of years, citrus plants were grown in special greenhouses called orangeries to get them through harsh European winters.

● **Characteristics** The feature that all members of this family have in common is that most parts of the plant contain essential oils that are usually very readily detected, particularly when the fruits or foliage are crushed. These oils produce the flavours and aromas that we have come to know and love from this family. Most of the useful members of this family are trees and shrubs that can be used to create habitat for wildlife such as birds, which can help to control insect pests. A good example of this is the rather thorny native Australian finger lime (*Citrus australasica*) that not only has delicious fruits, but will also provide nesting opportunities for small insect-feeding birds.

● **Examples** Citrus trees are by far the most important members of this family, and include orange, grapefruit and tangelo (which are various forms of *Citrus aurantium*), lemon (*Citrus limon*), mandarin or tangerine (*Citrus reticulata*), cumquat (*Citrus japonica*), pomelo (*Citrus maxima*), citron (*Citrus medica*) and lime (both the exotic, *Citrus x aurantiifolia*, and

native Australian types). The herb rue (*Ruta graveolens*) is also a readily grown member of this aromatic group.

● **Cultivation requirements** This popular plant family will benefit greatly from careful attention to soil preparation and selection of the most appropriate varieties for your particular environment. For instance, citrus plants vary greatly in their adaptability to frost, with cultivars such as the 'Eureka' lemon being much more tolerant of heavy frost than many other cultivars. Very good drainage is a particularly vital soil characteristic, as is slightly acidic conditions, because one of

ABOVE The citrus family is characterised by perfumed flowers and the numerous translucent oil glands found in the foliage and fruits.

the most common problems in citrus is a deficiency in trace elements (such as iron and manganese) caused by alkaline conditions. Amendments of sulphur and iron sulphate are particularly important for correcting alkaline soil conditions, and the provision of extra nitrogen, phosphorus and potassium is also important as the plants in this family are generally very heavy feeders.

♠ **Pests and diseases** Aphids and thrips are particularly attracted to new growth and need to be managed as much for the viral diseases they may be spreading as for the damage they do by sucking the sap of the plant. A variety of insect pests, such as citrus gall wasps, stink bugs and leaf miners, can all cause damage in various seasons throughout the year, so maintain vigilance to prevent crop losses. Fungal root diseases, such as Armillaria and Phytophthora, can potentially cause plant loss if trees are waterlogged for prolonged periods.

Brassicaceae – the crucifer or mustard family

♠ **Origins** The members of this family are often referred to as 'brassicas'. There are more than 4000 wild species in this family, with a particular centre of diversity in both Europe and Asia. Indeed, most of the important brassicas have been developed from the wild plants of Eurasia. These plants have been cultivated for centuries, and this has led to an extraordinary diversity of form and function in the various vegetables that have arisen.

♠ **Characteristics** The unifying feature of this family is the crucifix-shaped four-petalled flowers (interestingly, the family was once called Cruciferae). Among the thousands of species there are not only important food plants, but also common and rather insidious weeds of disturbed areas such as roadsides and train tracks. Harvestable parts of the species include leaves, stems, flowers and seeds. Some brassicas, such as the various mustard varieties (*Brassica juncea*), contain significant quantities of pungent essential oils that are important condiments, but they are also grown because

they exude chemicals that can control soil-borne pests such as nematodes.

Brassicas are notorious for accumulating sulphur compounds, and this can cause excessively odorous flatulence for people who overindulge in vegetables such as broccoli or cabbage. On the upside, mustard compounds are reputedly antibacterial, and mustard dressings have been used throughout history to cure wound infections.

♠ **Examples** This is one of the most important vegetable families, with particular species giving rise to multiple crops. For instance, the species *Brassica oleracea* has given the world brussels sprouts, broccoli, cauliflower, cabbage, kohlrabi and kale. The species *Brassica rapa* offers vegetables as diverse as turnip, bok choy (pak choi) and tatsoi. Yet another such

ABOVE Something a little different from the standard lemon tree, the native Australian finger lime is now readily available as a crop plant for urban farmers.

OPPOSITE The cabbage shows the typical form of clumping edible foliage for which Brassicaceae plants are renowned.

multifaceted species is *Brassica juncea*, which provides canola, mustard and mizuna. Wasabi (*Eutrema japonicum*), horseradish (*Armoracia rusticana*) and radish (*Raphanus sativus*) are other useful members of this family.

♦ **Cultivation requirements** Most brassicas are annuals that benefit from the supply of high levels of nutrition to fuel their rapid growth. They are generally propagated from seed and are classic cool-weather crops that should be grown throughout the autumn and winter months in most areas. As a guide, an average day temperature of 20–25°C and night temperature of 10–15°C are about right for optimum flowering and production of a wide range of brassicas. If temperatures are too warm, brassicas often run to flower before the plant fills out, a process known as bolting.

♦ **Pests and diseases** Brassicas tend to be particularly susceptible to common pests such as aphids, thrips, white flies and especially white cabbage moths. Viral diseases such as cauliflower mosaic virus can be easily transferred from weedy brassica species (such as hedge mustard, *Sisymbrium officinale*) to vegetable crops by sucking pests such as thrips and aphids. Hungry snails and slugs are also a major problem at the seedling stage of the crops. Detailed information on dealing with these issues can be found in the Pest and Disease Management section (see pages 230–6).

Cucurbitaceae – the pumpkin or gourd family

♦ **Origins** There are close to 1000 wild species – which are often known as cucurbits – in this well-known family. They are found throughout the tropical and warm-temperate regions of the world, from Africa and Europe to Asia and the Americas. The cucurbits were one of the first plant groups to be domesticated for agriculture, and they remain one of the most fascinating and important groups for the urban farmer,

ABOVE The crucifix-like flower shape is characteristic of Brassicaceae plants, and it gives rise to one of the common names for the family, crucifer.

not least because they are very adaptable climbing plants (albeit ones that hate frost).

♦ **Characteristics** This family is characterised by large, fleshy fruits (for example, melons and gourds). They are often scrambling or climbing plants with large, fleshy leaves; their showy yellow flowers are often either exclusively male or female.

♦ **Examples** The family includes pumpkin, squash and gourd (*Cucurbita maxima*), butternut (*Cucurbita moschata*), zucchini or courgette (*Cucurbita pepo*), cucumber (*Cucumis sativus*), choko (*Sechium edule*) and various fruits, such as rockmelon and honeydew melon (*Cucumis melo*) and watermelon (*Citrullus lanatus*).

♦ **Cultivation requirements** Given that they tend to have long runners, these plants need plenty of space and are best situated in spots where they can be allowed to 'run free'. They need full sun and plenty of nutrition to reach their full potential, and they are usually susceptible to frost damage and require a protected spot in colder climates. An interesting footnote to the cultivation of cucurbits is illustrated by the competitions held to grow 'giant pumpkins', where specimens in excess of 200 kilograms have been recorded. This has been achieved by methods such as drip feeding the plants with the liquid from worm farming.

♦ **Pests and diseases** Most species of cucurbits are susceptible to powdery mildew fungus, which needs to be carefully managed if it appears because it can often end the life of the plant. Good air movement around the plant will help stop the appearance of powdery mildew fungus in the first place. Other fungal diseases, such as Fusarium wilt, can cause the sudden death of plants, and bacterial soft rot is a threat once fruiting begins. As far as pests go, sap suckers such as white flies, melon thrips, red spider mites and aphids tend to congregate under the large, fleshy leaves and in the crevices at the base of the leaves and flower stalks – vigilance is important to ensure early intervention.

ABOVE Fruits of Cucurbitaceae plants form at the base of the showy female flowers.

LEFT Like many of the fleshy fruits that are the edible part of the cucurbits, pumpkins come in all sorts of interesting colours.

The cucurbits were one of the first plant groups to be domesticated for agriculture ... because they are very adaptable.

Johnstone's Kitchen Gardens

Tim and Liz Johnstone are part of a new breed of urban farmers who utilise small parcels of land on the immediate outskirts of cities (peri-urban areas). They supply a wide range of organically grown produce – mainly rare and heirloom vegetables, herbs and garnishes – direct to urban customers at farmers' markets and to restaurants.

Situated in Richmond, on the north-west outskirts of Sydney, the Johnstones' farm comprises several hectares of river flats with particularly sandy alluvial soil for the most part. Mushroom compost is used liberally, both as a soil conditioner and fertiliser, and does a very good job on both counts. It transforms the structureless grains of sand into a fairly rich, well-aggregated soil that holds adequate moisture and nutrients for the fast-growing mainly annual crops that Tim and Liz find to be in high demand.

Tim is particularly keen on seeking out unusual crops, from interesting heirloom varieties such as rainbow beetroot to multicoloured *Amaranthus tricolor*. He also looks for rare vegetables, such as the Mexican sour gherkin (*Melothria scabra*), salty ice plant (*Mesembryanthemum crystallinum*), mizuna (*Brassica juncea* var. *japonica*) and golden purslane (*Portulaca*

oleracea). Seeds and other planting materials are sourced from overseas as well as local suppliers. Quality is emphasised over quantity, and this has won over a loyal clientele.

Another important feature of the farm is the use of protected environments and other cultural methods to extend the season for many of the crops. Poly-tunnels are utilised to modify climatic conditions in winter, when frosts can play havoc with crops grown in the open ground. In summer, covers are used to minimise the heat stress suffered by plants during the extreme maximum temperatures that prevail. Drip irrigation is the preferred method of applying moisture, as the soil tends to repel water (it becomes hydrophobic when it dries out), and a slow application rate is far better for deep penetration than using spray irrigation.

Johnstone's Kitchen Gardens is an excellent example of a small business that is capitalising on the demand for fresh, novel, locally grown produce. People are increasingly keen on purchasing their produce at farmers' markets, where they can deal directly with and establish a personal relationship with growers. Buyers can then be sure that they are getting truly organic produce every time.

CLOCKWISE, FROM OPPOSITE Colourful gourds create ornamental interest on urban farms; Thai basil is one of several varieties the Johnstones grow; mizuna (*Brassica juncea* var. *japonica*) has a wonderful texture; Malabar spinach (*Basella alba*) is an unusual climbing leafy green vegetable; Mexican sour gherkin (*Melothria scabra*) is a miniature relative of the cucumber; the edible foliage of *Amaranthus tricolor* can add vibrant colour to salads.

Minor food families

As well as the major plant families listed earlier, there are many minor contributors that are incredibly important in providing diversity in the planet's food supply. Our advice is to experiment with and grow as wide a variety of crops as possible in your urban farm, including plants from both major and minor food families. Here is an abbreviated rundown of some of the minor plant families and their more important species that provide valuable biodiversity among crops.

⧫ **Orchidaceae — the orchid family** This family encompasses around 28,000 species, but surprisingly contributes only a handful of edible species to agriculture and horticulture. The seed pod of the vanilla orchid (*Vanilla planifolia*) is the most important crop, but the

HEIRLOOM CROP VARIETIES VS MODERN PLANT BREEDS

Agriculture and horticulture evolved through the selection of genetically improved plants and animals, leading to established 'breeds' that have been handed down for generations. These are now often referred to as 'heirloom' or traditional varieties because of their long history in cultivation. Modern industrial-scale agriculture and horticulture has (very sadly in our view) led to the demise of many traditional 'breeds' of plants and animals that were often very well adapted to the specialised environments in particular regions.

F1 hybrids are a particular type of hybrid seed that is produced by crossing inbred seed lines. This complicated process is usually only feasible for large commercial seed companies because of the expensive hand-pollination methods involved. Such hybrids show more vigour than their parents, but they do not breed true. Seeds from them will either be sterile or will produce offspring with characteristics like their parents.

One of the more controversial subjects regarding food production in recent times has been the introduction of GMOs (genetically modified organisms) to large-scale farming. The term GMO is usually reserved for a plant or animal that has been produced through genetic engineering, where particular genes are transferred from one organism to another.

Our view on GMOs is that the jury is still out on their long-term effects on the environment and consumers. However, their widespread use in industrial-scale agriculture and horticulture means that a worldwide experiment is already underway that will tell the story one way or another over the longer term. In the meantime, the urban farmer has an abundant biodiversity of crop choices, and, as such, we should be exploring all the options that help to preserve the amazing genetic diversity that we have built up over thousands of years. It is an absolute certainty that climate change will require us to increasingly employ traditional techniques of plant selection and breeding; if we allow heirloom varieties and undeveloped and potential wild-food plants to disappear from the planet, it will be at our peril.

We would encourage urban farmers everywhere to look at heirloom varieties first, but also to consider modern plant varieties — because many of these have been bred by traditional techniques that have served humanity well for thousands of years. In other words, consider each plant variety on its origins and merits when choosing what to grow. And, wherever possible, introduce a mixture of crops and varieties to help preserve genetic diversity in our food crops for the benefit of future generations.

plant requires tropical growing conditions. Aboriginal people ate the tuberous roots of a number of native ground orchids, but these plants are probably a bridge too far for growing in urban farms.

♠ **Asteraceae – the daisy family** With over 32,000 species, this family has contributed a few very useful edible plants. Lettuce (*Lactuca sativa*) and sunflower (*Helianthus annuus*) – and their close relative, the Jerusalem artichoke (*Helianthus tuberosus*) – are the stand-out crops, despite the latter's ability to cause a great deal of flatulence in people after the delicious tubers are consumed. Herbs from the family – such as yarrow (*Achillea millefolium*), purple coneflower (*Echinacea purpurea*) and dandelion (*Taraxacum officinale*) are easily grown – and they are excellent choices for attracting pollinators such as bees to production areas.

♠ **Lamiaceae – the mint family** It is instantly familiar because most of its members are rich in essential oils. The plants also feature square stems and distinctively tubular-shaped 'labiate' flowers that have a prominent lip at the bottom. The family includes many of our most popular culinary and medicinal herbs, such as peppermint (*Mentha x piperita*), thyme (*Thymus vulgaris*), sage (*Salvia officinalis*) and oregano (*Origanum vulgare*). Found all over the world, particularly in moist environments such as riverbanks, this family has numerous Australian members – not the least of which is river mint (*Mentha australis*), which was used by Aboriginal people for both culinary and medicinal purposes.

Although it provides very little bulk in our food supply, the mint family is nonetheless one of the most useful of all food plant groups for the urban farmer. The plants take up very little space and are very good at attracting pollinators. Many are long-term perennials that propagate very easily by division of the clumping or running stems. It is a good idea with some of the more rampant species, such as the mints, to contain them in beds where they cannot spread at will.

♠ **Amaryllidaceae – the amaryllis family** This is an interesting group, because the plants in it feature true bulbs (as opposed to tubers or other underground plant parts). The largest group of edible bulbs in the botanical world, it includes the following species: onion (*Allium cepa*), chives (*Allium schoenoprasum*), garlic (*Allium sativum*) and leek (*Allium ampeloprasum*). All of them form clumps with pungent, linear, grey–green leaves and terminal clusters of mauve or purple lily-like flowers.

The amaryllis family is very easy to grow and is great for frosty climates, as the bulbs can be planted deep enough so that they are insulated against the worst of the cold. Usually the bulbs or seeds of the crops are planted in autumn and harvested in late spring or early summer, but in milder climates most species

OPPOSITE The globe artichoke is a particularly ornamental edible member of the daisy family.

ABOVE The distinctively shaped flowers of the mint family are instantly recognisable.

can be grown throughout the year. The family is generally free of pest and disease problems, but does require deep, well-drained soil to optimise the yield and to prevent rotting if wet periods are experienced.

♠ **Zingiberaceae – the ginger family** As well as ginger (*Zingiber officinale*), other very useful edible members of this family that are readily grown on urban farms include galangal (*Alpinia galanga*), turmeric (*Curcuma longa*) and cardamom (*Elettaria cardamomum*), whose seeds provide one of the world's most sought-after spices. The family is spread across tropical and subtropical areas of the world, but the various edible members can be grown successfully in warm-temperate climates as well. For most species, the edible rhizomes (underground stems) grow actively throughout the warmer months of the year and are then harvested in autumn. As well as a warm, frost-free climate, the plants generally require a free-draining situation and a high level of nutrition during their growing season (spring to early autumn).

♠ **Myrtaceae – the myrtle family** It is perhaps best known for its essential oils, a characteristic of the family that can often be observed as translucent oil glands when a leaf is held up to the light. Oils obtained from the leaves of gum trees (*Eucalyptus* species) and tea-trees (*Melaleuca* species) are some of the world's best botanical disinfectants, and they also provide unique culinary flavours. In addition to the essential oil-producing members of the family, there are also a number of species that produce beautiful fruits, including various lilly pillies (*Syzygium* species) from Australia and Southeast Asia, and the feijoa (*Acca sellowiana*) from South America.

All of these plants come from tropical or subtropical climates, and they are not particularly well suited to frosty gardens. For cooler climates, there are some excellent Australian bush-food plants that have appeared in nurseries recently, including muntries (*Kunzea pomifera*), midgen berry (*Austromyrtus dulcis*) and narrow-leaf myrtle (*Austromyrtus tenuifolia*). Generally, the myrtaceous plants

with edible parts are shrubs or trees that are adaptable and easy to grow provided they are in a warm climate. The most serious problem they face is myrtle rust, a fungal disease that reduces the yield by infecting both the foliage and flower buds.

♠ **Moraceae – the fig family** This is a large and cosmopolitan family of over 1000 species, many of which are edible. The genus *Ficus* contains dozens of edible species beyond the common fig (*Ficus carica*); Australia has many native figs that were prized by Aboriginal people for their edible fruits. The other major edible group in this family is the mulberries (*Morus* species), of which there are several very useful species that might find a place on larger urban-farm blocks. Last but not least is the tropical genus *Artocarpus*, which provides two incredibly useful fruits for

ABOVE Pigface has brightly coloured flowers that catch the eye, but it's the plant's fruits that are edible – they taste somewhat like salty custard.

tropical regions: breadfruit (*Artocarpus altilis*) and jackfruit (*Artocarpus heterophyllus*).

All of the edible members of this family are trees, and as such they are only suitable for large urban farms. However, growing techniques such as espaliering plants against a wall can make them a more practical option in smaller spaces. The members of this family are generally easy to grow in warmer climates and have relatively few problems apart from birds stealing the fruits!

♦ **Aizoaceae – the ice-plant family** A truly fascinating family of succulents, these plants have edible foliage – and, in some cases, edible flowers. The Australian plants Warrigal greens (*Tetragonia tetragonioides*) and rounded noon-flower (*Disphyma crassifolium*) are becoming popular as a source of greens for various culinary pursuits. Pigface is the common name for various species within the genus *Carpobrotus* that are found in coastal areas around the world. In Australia, karkalla is the Indigenous name for the species *Carpobrotus rossii*, and Aboriginal people ate the fruits of this plant. All species in this family are very easy to grow as well as being salt tolerant, making them suitable for both coastal and inland areas that have saline soil. Most of the species are readily propagated from cuttings and can be used as ground covers; they are ideal as fire-retardant plantings near buildings.

♦ **Amaranthaceae – the amaranth family** This has been an important group of edible plants in South America for thousands of years. Quinoa (*Chenopodium quinoa*) is a good example of this, and it is ironic that it has been recently 'unearthed' as a so-called 'superfood' given its long history in cultivation. Australia has a number of native *Chenopodium* species, known as saltbushes, which have a long history of use as food plants by Aboriginal people, and these are now being discovered by modern chefs. Various species in the genus *Amaranthus* have also had a long history as food plants, including the blood amaranth (*Amaranthus cruentus*), love-lies-bleeding (*Amaranthus caudatus*) and Prince-of-Wales feather (*Amaranthus hypochondriacus*). Another fascinating group in this family is the samphires, such as various *Sarcocornia* species. Amaranths are relatively easy to grow from seed, in the case of the annual types, or cuttings from the perennial types, such as the samphires. Many species are also salt tolerant, making them suitable for coastal areas and saline soil elsewhere.

BELOW LEFT Figs were one of the first edible plants to be domesticated for horticulture, and they remain popular with urban farmers today.

FOLIAGE FOR FOOD

For those just starting out in urban farming, one of the simplest and most successful strategies is to concentrate on crops where the harvestable part of the plant is foliage. Crops such as lettuce (*Lactuca sativa*), curly parsley (*Petroselinum crispum*), silverbeet (*Beta vulgaris*) and Warrigal greens (*Tetragonia tetragonioides*) are very rewarding plants to grow, because there is less potential for crop losses. Even if some damage is done to foliage crops, they can still generally be used. Foliage crops are often very simple to propagate and very fast to produce. By contrast, where the final harvestable item is a fruit (including nuts, pumpkins and tomatoes, as well as sweet fruits), there is more room for damage to occur, as the plant has to produce both foliage and fruits before it can be harvested. Fruit and nut trees are often long-term crops that take up a lot more space and require more specialist growing knowledge than foliage crops.

♦ **Cactaceae – the cactus family** A famous family of succulents, these plants often feature spiny foliage. They grow well in challenging conditions, such as in arid areas or saline soil. The fleshy fruits of many cacti are edible, but not many species have been domesticated because of their relatively slow growth rates and the specialised growing conditions required. However, they certainly deserve consideration where water supplies are limited. Prickly pear (*Opuntia ficus-indica*) is probably the most important food crop among the cacti, with both edible fruits and foliage. The climbing cactus *Hylocereus undatus* is commonly marketed under the name dragon fruit, and features rather spectacular-looking fruits with a dramatic red and green colouration. Edible cacti are readily propagated from cuttings and are easily grown as long as they are not exposed to wet conditions and waterlogged soil for prolonged periods.

Miscellaneous plant families

There are so many more crop plants from small and unusual plant families that we could examine, particularly those from tropical and subtropical regions where plant biodiversity is at its greatest. This subject would fill a whole book on its own, and it is beyond our scope to fully explore it here. Suffice it to say that hunter–gatherer cultures all over the world spent many millennia experimenting with the plants they encountered. A relatively small proportion of the many thousands of species that have been used as food have been fully domesticated for food production. It is our view that the world needs as much genetic diversity as possible in its food-crop options. We encourage you to research this topic at every opportunity and to experiment with all the options that cross your farm-gate trail.

CROP ROTATION

It is generally not a good idea to grow plants that are closely related to each other in the same place year after year, as this can cause problems with pests and diseases as well as soil fertility. Read the Food Families section earlier in this chapter to see which plants are closely related. For example, tomato, eggplant, capsicum and potato are all part of the Solanaceae family and are therefore closely related to each other, but they are not closely related to the brassicas (for example, cabbage, cauliflower and broccoli) or to the cucurbits (for example, cucumber, squash and pumpkin). So ideally make a plan to rotate plants from different families around the various beds.

Avoiding outbreaks

We particularly recommend crop rotation for the management of pests and diseases, especially to prevent their build-up. In particular, crop rotation principles can be used to mitigate certain soil-borne problems, such as root-knot nematodes, fungal root rots and some insect pests. Particular issues are often unique to specific plant families; by rotating crops from the same plant family around different locations in the urban farm, you will greatly minimise the incidence of problems.

Root-knot nematodes severely affect a wide range of crops, including tomato, potato and sweet potato, and it is difficult to control nematode populations where these crops are grown continuously without rotation. Maize, onion, cabbage and cauliflower are relatively resistant to root-knot nematodes, so they are excellent crops to rotate with other less-resistant plants. Grasses are also highly resistant, so lemongrass or green-manure crops of sorghum, for example, also work to reduce nematode numbers. Marigold is known to deter nematodes; it is often utilised as a companion plant, but it certainly could be used as a rotation crop.

Crop rotation is not usually successful at controlling flying insect pests, especially in the relatively small plots used in urban farming. Nor is it appropriate for perennial crops such as fruit trees. In orchards, maintain a healthy level of organic-matter content in the soil by adding compost; alternatively, plant annual green-manure crops among the trees in winter, and cut them down in early spring so they decay and feed the soil, producing disease-suppressive organic matter at the same time.

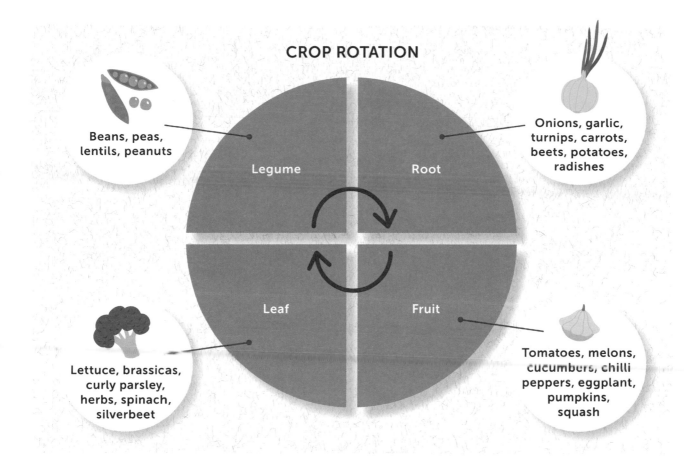

CROP ROTATION

Beans, peas, lentils, peanuts → Legume

Root ← **Onions, garlic, turnips, carrots, beets, potatoes, radishes**

Lettuce, brassicas, curly parsley, herbs, spinach, silverbeet → Leaf

Fruit → **Tomatoes, melons, cucumbers, chilli peppers, eggplant, pumpkins, squash**

Boosting productivity

Another important reason for crop rotation – especially in broadacre farming – is to allow the soil to build up much-needed fertility again, particularly nitrogen fertility, by planting legume crops or clover pasture after a nitrogen-hungry crop such as maize, for example, has been grown and harvested. This consideration does not always apply in urban farming if, as we recommend, composted organic matter and fertiliser is applied as pre-plant and side-dressing applications. However, if you do not have access to these materials, then legumes are another tool in a natural-fertiliser strategy for your urban farm if you need it.

Rotating crops allows organic matter to accumulate, for example under a pasture or green-manure crop, to help improve soil structure and physical fertility. Again, if we add composted organics regularly, this is not usually necessary in urban farms.

Rotation is often essential in traditional zero-input farming methods, such as slash-and-burn farming and the milpa rotation system that alternates beans with squash and maize to try to slow the decline in soil fertility. The beans fix nitrogen, which is then used as mulch to improve yields of the next crop of maize or squash.

In intensive horticulture, and particularly in urban farming, space is often very limited and rotation is not always possible, or it occurs at very considerable cost in lost production time. From a soil-fertility viewpoint, this is not a problem as compost and other organic inputs replace the necessity to build soil fertility by rotation. By importing compost, we can ensure physical fertility (including structure, organic matter and porosity) does not decline but gets better with time, and if we use nutrient-rich organic matter such as manure, or we use fertilisers intelligently, chemical fertility will not decline either.

THE NEEDS
OF PLANTS

4

NUTRIENTS FOR PLANT HEALTH

Plants require just three things to grow: sunlight and water to fuel photosynthesis, and access to a handful of elements (about 15 of the 92 naturally occurring elements). These elements are the building blocks of plants, and are classed as either macronutrients (elements that plants require in large quantities) or micronutrients (trace elements that plants require in tiny amounts). Carbon, hydrogen and oxygen are all absorbed from the atmosphere or from water; nutrients found in soil, such as nitrogen and phosphorus, are taken up by the plant through its roots, along with water.

PHOTOSYNTHESIS – A REMARKABLE REACTION

Carbon and one of its gases, carbon dioxide, have been getting a lot of bad press lately, but we need to rethink their importance – we must never forget that all life on Earth cannot exist without them. Through the process of photosynthesis, plants use solar energy to convert carbon dioxide from the atmosphere into carbohydrates. These carbohydrates are then used to create an astonishing array of carbon-based biochemicals, such as oils and proteins.

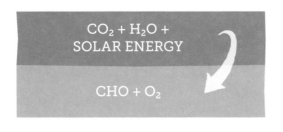

$$CO_2 + H_2O + \text{SOLAR ENERGY}$$
$$CHO + O_2$$

The above equation for photosynthesis shows that a plant utilises the energy of the sun to force carbon dioxide and water to combine into sugars (carbohydrates), giving off oxygen as a waste product. Carbohydrates can then be used to produce the thousands of organic chemicals that make up plant bodies, or they can simply be stored (as sugar in the case of sugar cane, or as starch in potatoes).

At night, of course, there is no solar energy, so the plant then uses the stored carbohydrates in an opposite reaction called 'respiration':

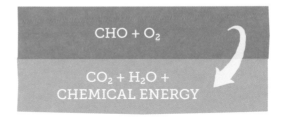

$$CHO + O_2$$
$$CO_2 + H_2O + \text{CHEMICAL ENERGY}$$

Alternatively, an animal can eat the plant and use the same respiration reaction to liberate the plant's sugars. These are then used to fuel the animal's body, as animals cannot make their own carbohydrates through a photosynthetic process.

A plant grows because – as long as it has adequate sunlight – it can utilise photosynthesis to create and store more carbohydrates during the day than it uses in respiration at night. If a plant's access to sunlight is not adequate, then the plant may not produce enough carbohydrates to allow growth.

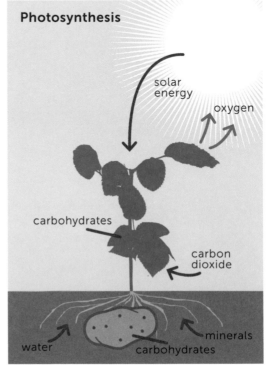

Photosynthesis

solar energy

oxygen

carbohydrates

carbon dioxide

water

carbohydrates

minerals

OPPOSITE Carbon dioxide and water are both essential nutrients for photosynthesis. For maximum growth, however, sunlight needs to be freely available as well.

Atmospheric gases and the urban farm

As far as we know, Earth is the only planet where the processes of photosynthesis and respiration have been developed by living organisms. Photosynthesis supplies every living thing on the planet with food, and it is responsible for increasing the amount of oxygen in our atmosphere from none to 21 per cent. It is also responsible for all the carbon-based fossil fuels (oil, coal and gas) on Earth that we are now burning and returning to the atmosphere at a rapid rate. Urban farming is a great way to take advantage of elevated carbon dioxide levels, and it helps the planet, too.

In practice, two of the essential nutrients needed by plants – carbon and oxygen – come from the atmosphere and cannot be manipulated by farmers. We don't really think of water as a nutrient, but it does provide the hydrogen needed to make carbohydrates during the photosynthetic reaction – so it could indeed be considered a nutrient. While we can't easily manipulate the atmosphere and its gases, making water readily available to plants is possibly the farmer's most important job, and it's called 'irrigation'. Vast effort is put into irrigation by all human societies that farm. See the Water and Drainage chapter (pages 212–27) for more information about irrigation.

WASTE NOT, WANT NOT

Carbon dioxide (CO_2) is the waste product from the burning of fossil fuels, and its accumulation in the atmosphere is contributing to global warming. Fortunately for us, plants love it! Many greenhouse experiments show that if you enrich the air with carbon dioxide, the growth of plants will accelerate. It is not usually economically viable, given the cost of compressed carbon dioxide, to use this product in urban farms. However, we can take advantage of heightened levels of this gas in the atmosphere to fuel plant growth and hopefully bring a bit more balance to our planet.

NUTRIENTS SUPPLIED BY THE SOIL

The remaining chemical elements that are essential for plant growth are all obtained from the soil (or other growing media) via the plant's roots. In descending order of abundance, these elements are:

- nitrogen (N)
- potassium (K)
- calcium (Ca)
- phosphorus (P)
- magnesium (Mg)
- sulphur (S)
- iron (Fe)
- manganese (Mn)
- zinc (Zn)
- copper (Cu)
- boron (B)
- molybdenum (Mo).

The essential elements for plant growth are broken down into two categories, according to the relative amounts required: macronutrients and micronutrients. It is worthwhile to consider some of the basic facts about each individual element.

ABOVE Plants in protected environments need good ventilation to ensure that the carbon dioxide supply is constantly replenished.

FAR LEFT A general yellowing of foliage is often a sign of nitrogen deficiency.

LEFT ABOVE Plants that have a purplish tinge on the older leaves may be deficient in phosphorus.

LEFT BELOW Blossom end rot of tomatoes is usually the result of major calcium deficiency.

Macronutrients

♦ **Nitrogen (N)** is essential for green vegetative growth. A highly soluble element that is present in two forms (ammonium and nitrate), it is also one of the most expensive fertiliser elements. Nitrogen deficiency is the single most common deficiency in plants, and it is the greatest limitation to worldwide agriculture. An excess of nitrogen causes tall, floppy growth as well as poor flowering.

♦ **Potassium (K)** is particularly important for maintaining cell pressure in plants and for flowering. It is a highly soluble element sometimes called potash that is easily washed or leached from the soil by rainfall and irrigation. Wood ash is rich in potash, but it should only be used sparingly on soil because it also has quite an alkaline pH level.

♦ **Calcium (Ca)** is especially important for shoot and root-cell growth. Many native soils are low in calcium, but urban soils often have high levels – thanks in part to the calcium-rich mortar that is sometimes left behind after building activities. As it is not particularly

THE 'BIG THREE'

Nitrogen, phosphorus and potassium together make up the 'Big Three' fertiliser requirements, and their relative proportions are given on fertiliser labels as the NPK ratio. Many fertilisers contain only these three elements, relying on the soil to supply the remaining nutrients needed by plants. These fertilisers are ideal for leafy green vegetables, which need a higher proportion of nitrogen than flowering and fruiting edible plants.

soluble, calcium can be a difficult element to correct if it is deficient – it is usually applied as lime or gypsum.

♦ **Phosphorus (P)** is vital for root growth and strong stems. Most natural Australian soils are low in phosphorus; while many of our native plants have adapted to these soils, they are often insufficient for productive farming and need to be improved. Great gains in agricultural productivity were made when the application of superphosphate became widespread.

♦ **Magnesium (Mg)** is important in photosynthesis and – like calcium – also plays a vital role in regulating the pH level of the soil. Magnesium may be applied as a solid (for example, as dolomite), which is not soluble, or in soluble form (as Epsom salts).

♦ **Sulphur (S)** is important for protein synthesis, and it is usually supplied in combination with other elements as sulphates – for example, gypsum (calcium sulphate). In its elemental form, sulphur is used to acidify soil. Some plants, such as brassicas, have high sulphur needs, hence the 'sulphurous' smell of cabbages.

Micronutrients

♦ **Iron (Fe)** is essential during chlorophyll production. It is insoluble, and its availability to plants is dependent on soil pH, as it becomes unavailable when the soil is alkaline.

LEFT Yellowing between the leaf veins of new leaf growth is often caused by iron deficiency in the plant.

ELEMENT LEVELS IN PLANTS

ELEMENT	DEFICIENCY SYMPTOMS	APPROXIMATE CONCENTRATION*
Nitrogen (N)	General paleness, overall yellowing of leaves, browning starting with oldest leaves, stunted growth	2–4 %
Potassium (K)	Lacklustre growth and flowering, yellowing then browning of leaf margins of oldest leaves, low wear tolerance in turf	1.8–4 %
Calcium (Ca)	Blackened and distorted stem and root tips, abnormal development of flowers and fruits, 'end rot' of flowers and fruits, poor root growth	0.3–0.5 %
Phosphorus (P)	Stunting, poor branching, overall lacklustre growth, red or purple tinges on leaves and stems	0.25–0.6 %
Magnesium (Mg)	Mottled yellowing on leaves	0.2–0.4 %
Sulphur (S)	Overall yellowing of leaves, slow growth	0.2–0.4 %
Iron (Fe)	Yellowing between veins of youngest leaves	100–300 mg/kg
Manganese (Mn)	Yellowing between veins of youngest leaves, deformity of growing tips	50–500 mg/kg
Zinc (Zn)	Yellowing between veins of leaves, deformity of growing tips	15–50 mg/kg
Copper (Cu)	Yellowing between veins of leaves, deformity of growing tips	5–20 mg/kg
Boron (B)	Deformity of growing tips, 'hollow stem' in brassicas, stem and tuber browning	10–50 mg/kg
Molybdenum (Mo)	Yellowing of leaves, 'whiptail' in brassicas	0.03–0.1 mg/kg

Note: We usually measure macronutrients as a percentage by dry weight. Micronutrients are present in much lower amounts, however, so we express these as milligrams per kilogram, which is a more sensitive unit of measurement.

♦ **Manganese (Mn)** is very much like iron – it is necessary for manufacturing chlorophyll, and its availability is dependent on pH levels. To some extent these two elements can substitute for one another (for example, iron deficiency can be alleviated somewhat by adding manganese, but not completely). An excess can be toxic to many species, such as clover; manganese toxicity is common on acid soils in manganese-sensitive plants.

♦ **Zinc (Zn) and Copper (Cu)** are essential to many enzyme pathways, synthesising myriad organic compounds that make up plants. Generally, they are less available when the soil has a high pH level. They are often deficient in rural soils, but rarely deficient in urban soils due to pollution with metals. Sometimes this pollution rises to levels that are toxic to plants.

♦ **Boron (B)** is vital for growing cells. Deficiency is more common in certain groups of plants, such as brassicas (for example, cabbage, broccoli and cauliflower). However, deficiencies are uncommon in urban soils.

♦ **Molybdenum (Mo)** is required by plants for nitrogen metabolism, such as turning nitrates into proteins. Fortunately, due to human activity, obvious molybdenum deficiency is very rare in urban soils; it is really only seen in legumes, such as clovers, that are growing in pasture soil. Organic fertilisers and composts contain all the molybdenum you will need for your urban farm.

NUTRIENT DEFICIENCIES

Plants need about 15 elements from the soil to live and grow. An inadequate supply of one or more of these elements leads to an array of problems, from discolouration of foliage to distortion of growth. The Element Levels in Plants table on the opposite page summarises the symptoms of nutrient deficiencies in plants and gives an estimate of the concentration of nutrients within living plant tissue. The last column provides other vital information, because it tells us the best ratio of nutrients we need to put back into the soil after we have removed them by harvesting a crop.

An important principle in feeding your plants is that of the most limiting nutrient. A plant will only grow as well as the most limiting nutrient allows. For example, if a soil is high in all nutrients except nitrogen, any plants growing in that soil are likely to be pale and sickly – despite having most of the nutrients they need, they still will not thrive. If we add nitrogen to the soil, the plants will respond rapidly without the need to apply any other nutrient. The same issue can happen with trace elements such as iron, where an application of iron will often cure yellowing of the new vegetative growth.

DOES YOUR PLANT HAVE A NUTRIENT DISORDER?

Most people are quick to blame poor nutrition when things go wrong with their plants, but it's important to eliminate other possible causes first. Here's a list of things to check.

☐ **Water content** Dig a hole to about 150 millimetres deep near a struggling plant. Does the soil look right for the desired moisture content? Or is it too wet or too dry?

☐ **Root problems** Have a look at the plant roots that are protruding into the hole. Are there signs of galls or swellings that could be due to nematodes? Are the roots black and mushy, which is an indication of root disease?

If the plant is healthy, then the roots should be fleshy and white.

☐ **Foliage issues** Examine the leaves for grubs, aphids and scale insects.

☐ **Stem trouble** If you find holes in the stem, and frass (which looks like fine sawdust) around the holes, then you may have borers.

If you have checked the above list and you have not discovered any obvious problems, then you can start to think about possible nutrient disorders. Some of the most frequently seen disorders are given in the table on page 70. If issues persist or symptoms are not clear, you should have your soil or plant foliage tested by experts.

COMMON PLANT NUTRIENT AND OTHER DISORDERS

APPEARANCE	SYMPTOMS	LIKELY CAUSES	CURE
	Wilting and dieback, perhaps with marginal burn on leaves	Root-rot diseases	Try a fungicide drench
		Waterlogging	Stop watering, and dry out soil
		Excessive fertiliser or salts	Leach heavily to remove soluble ions
	Pale spindly plants, poor growth	Nitrogen deficiency	Apply a high-nitrogen side dressing
		Multiple nitrogen/ phosphorus/ potassium deficiency	Apply composted manure tea, liquid fertiliser from a worm farm or mineral NPK fertiliser
	Marginal yellowing or burn on leaves, poor growth, poor fruit set	Potassium deficiency	Water with compost tea, worm juice or sulphate of potash (2 g/L)
	Stunting, yellowing and reddish colours on leaves	Phosphorus deficiency	Use a high-phosphorus organic fertiliser or water with monoammonium phosphate (1 g/L)
	Yellowing between veins of leaves, usually worst on youngest leaves	Iron and/or manganese deficiency due to high pH level, excessive phosphorus or both	Spray foliage with chelated* iron and manganese

*Note: 'Chelated' means the element is bound to an organic molecule that acts as a carrier and keeps the element in solution (otherwise it would precipitate because it is not very soluble). Chelated elements can be purchased from many nurseries and garden centres; sometimes they are sold as part of balanced mixtures containing a number of micronutrients (trace elements).

NUTRIENT CYCLES

In the wild, essential plant nutrients are accumulated and efficiently recycled in natural soil/vegetation systems. This is achieved via the all-important litter layer on top of the soil in forests, and the 'thatch' layer at the base of plants in grasslands. In many forests around the world (and especially within Australia), nutrients are released back into the soil by fire followed by rain; the water dissolves the nutrients and washes them back into the soil, thereby completing the nutrient cycle and fertilising the plants.

In human farming systems, these natural nutrient cycles need to be replaced or mimicked in order to maintain the correct balance of soil nutrients for optimum plant growth. Large farms use inputs of fertiliser and the rotation of crops to help maintain fertility, but even these farms will eventually need to address the inevitable run-down of organic matter and physical fertility if they are to maintain soil productivity. In intensively used urban-farming land, these nutrient cycles are even further interrupted – there is no forest litter or thatch layer, and seldom do we have the space to rotate crops.

We can grow crops purely on synthetic fertiliser inputs – as hydroponic culture proves – but, fortunately, urban environments also produce a lot of waste organic materials that we can use for composting and worm farming. This returns precious nutrients and organic matter to soil, thus creating, preserving and even restoring fertility. Many of these inputs are so cheap that we often find urban soils actually increase in fertility over time. Read the Composting and Mulching chapter (see pages 176–211) for information about the composting process that substitutes for natural cycling and the many ways it can be adapted to create superbly sustainable urban farms.

SOILS AND SOIL
FERTILITY ⑤

WORKING FROM THE GROUND UP

Soil can be thought of – especially in a farming context – as a delivery system for the minerals and gases that plants need to grow. Plants can also grow in the complete absence of soil, as long as the nutrient minerals are carefully balanced in the proportions that the plant needs, by either creating fully balanced organic fertilisers or by using purchased mineral fertilisers dissolved in water (see the section on Hydroponics on pages 122–3). The principles discussed in this chapter relate to the fertility of all growing media, from natural soils to lightweight potting mixes for rooftop gardens.

Depending on your urban farm's particular circumstances, you will most likely use either natural or artificially constructed soils for your garden beds. The first preference is to utilise your on-site soil if at all possible, as this is the cheapest and easiest option. Well-managed natural soil is very forgiving of our mistakes and the imbalances we can create in soil fertility, and it helps to 'even out' nutrient supply. We can do many things to boost this 'buffering' capacity of soil, so that most of us can grow healthy urban produce without having to fully understand all the technicalities of soil science.

NATURAL SOILS

Most people have heard of topsoil and subsoil, but few know that there are three basic soil horizons, or layers: A, B and C. Technically, there are actually five horizons – the O horizon comprises the organic matter that lies on top of any healthy natural soil, and the R horizon is the bottom layer of rock (this horizon is more accurately called 'parent material', as it's not always rock). The Soil Profile diagram on the opposite page shows the different soil horizons.

In natural systems, the weathering of the rock (parent material) releases dissolved nutrients; the vegetation takes up the nutrients it requires and discards any elements it does not need. As plants die and decay, the nutrients that they have bioaccumulated are returned

to the soil in roughly the same proportion as the plants took them up. Nutrients released by the decomposing vegetation in the O horizon make their way into the topsoil, where plants take them up; this nutrient cycle repeats again and again. Over time, the important plant nutrients accumulate in the topsoil, improving its fertility relative to that of the original parent material. This is the essential basis of nutrient cycling or bioaccumulation in natural soil systems.

In urban soils, we don't have the decomposing vegetation to allow nutrient cycling – or do we? Mulches are a human-created O horizon, and some – such as pea straw or lucerne hay – will break down and enrich the topsoil in an urban farm. In the absence of mulch, compost becomes an urban farmer's best friend. Composting is an artificial

ABOVE Urban soils can have very different profiles to the normal A, B and C horizons of natural soils.

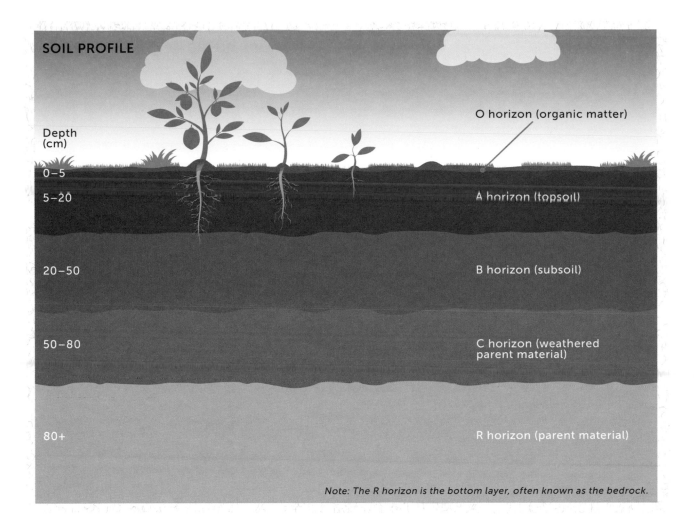

SOIL PROFILE

Depth (cm)

O horizon (organic matter)

0–5

5–20
A horizon (topsoil)

20–50
B horizon (subsoil)

50–80
C horizon (weathered parent material)

80+
R horizon (parent material)

Note: The R horizon is the bottom layer, often known as the bedrock.

way of cycling nutrients, and it is vital to maintaining the high level of soil fertility required to grow extremely productive and nutrient-dense horticultural crops. It circumvents the need for natural bioaccumulation to maintain the fertility of soil, and it does not take thousands of years. In a very real sense, composting allows us to create our own topsoil.

Preservation and enhancement of the precious existing bioaccumulated topsoil should be a priority for every farmer and gardener. However, thanks to our current knowledge of soil chemistry and plant needs, we now have the means to quickly improve a soil's fertility and productivity if necessary. In order to understand how to do this, we need to look at the concept of soil fertility and how it relates to our urban farm.

NOT ALL ROCKS ARE EQUAL

I once heard a NASA astronaut talking about the soil samples he obtained from the moon. He was quite wrong to use the word 'soil', because there is no soil on the moon – only powdered rock. You need living things – including microbes, plants and animals – to work on powdered rock before you get soil to form. Because of bioaccumulation, we find that soils all over the world show remarkably similar properties, although it is certainly true that parent materials with better levels of the essential nutrients (such as igneous rocks created by volcanic activity) form better and more productive soils more quickly than those with poorer geology.

LEFT If your topsoil has a high level of fertility, it will be dark in colour and loamy in texture.

SOIL FERTILITY

In The Needs of Plants chapter (see pages 62–71), we saw that plants absorb carbon, hydrogen and oxygen from the atmosphere, but they obtain the great majority of their nutrients from the soil – the nutrients are dissolved in water and taken up by the roots. Because plant roots need elements both in gaseous and liquid form, it is useful to divide soil fertility into three parts:

1 **Physical fertility** – the soil has optimum amounts of air and water.
2 **Chemical fertility** – the nutrients are in the right amount and balance.
3 **Biological fertility** – this is important for particular plants that form symbiotic relationships with microbes (for example, legumes and *Rhizobium* bacteria).

If a soil has excellent physical fertility, then it is able to provide the physical support, water and aeration that plant roots need. Note this focus on the role of the roots – they must remain healthy so they can support the plant in an (often) upright position, allowing the leaves to get maximum sunlight, and take up water that is needed for both nutrient uptake and photosynthesis. Also, the uptake of water is an active process that requires energy from respiration, so therefore the roots need oxygen. No oxygen, no root function – and the plant wilts, as it is unable to transport water and nutrients to the leaves. Thus, somewhat ironically, the first sign of waterlogging in plants is wilting!

The chemical fertility of a soil is its ability to supply the elemental nutrients that plants require, in the ratios and proportions they need them (The Needs of Plants chapter discusses in detail the essential plant nutrients and the amounts needed for healthy growth). This chemical fertility can be supplied from either organic or inorganic sources, and nutrients such as nitrogen are often derived from both. Thus, we can build chemical fertility with different fertilising strategies.

Physical and chemical fertility are intimately related. Plant roots take up their chemical elements dissolved in water. The oxygen needed by roots to do this is in itself a chemical, and it could be thought of as an essential plant nutrient. Cut off the oxygen to the roots, and there is no water or nutrient uptake. Therefore, physical fertility is the most important consideration when it comes to soils, because plants will die much faster from a lack of water or oxygen in the soil than from any nutrient deficiency. A soil with good physical and chemical fertility will usually also show good biological fertility.

If a soil has excellent physical fertility, then it is able to provide the physical support, water and aeration that plant roots need.

PHYSICAL FERTILITY

This is possibly the easiest thing for urban farmers to judge for themselves – you just have to answer the question, 'What does a root need?'. In a nutshell, a root requires:

- physical support
- water
- oxygen (gaseous exchange)
- ease of penetration (the more energy it takes to penetrate the soil, the less energy is available for production of edible structures)
- a nutrient supply (again, the harder a root has to work for this, the less energy is available for producing a useful yield).

To assess whether your soil has physical fertility, you just need a nose, an eye and a hand, and maybe a couple of tools. Use all your senses to examine your soil, and you will soon learn about its density, structure and texture.

Soil density

The first issue to consider is soil density. Compression of a soil by either foot or machinery traffic in urban environments causes compaction and an increase in soil density, and this is the great enemy of root expansion. The denser the soil, the harder the roots have to work to penetrate it, and to access water and nutrients.

Use a hand trowel or spade to obtain a soil sample – the very act of digging will tell you plenty about the soil's density. Now look at the topsoil. Is it dry, yellowish powder, or dark and crumbly aggregate? Dark soil indicates that organic-matter levels are high (which is usually good), while pale yellow or red soil with no peds signifies a poor structure and low organic-matter levels (which is bad, unless you have a sandy soil that naturally drains well). The Soil Density table below describes various levels of soil density, and how to use each soil type.

Soil structure

Grab a handful of soil, and loosely crumble it in your hand. Can you see little grains or big chunks of soil? Structure is concerned with the size and shape of soil particles, and how well they bind together into crumbs (which are known as peds or aggregates). These peds have different shapes – such as 'granular', 'blocky',

SOIL DENSITY

OBSERVATION	DENSITY	SUITABLE FOR
Soil can be scooped up easily by hand	Very low, fine state of tilth	All forms of annual horticulture, root and other vegetables, floristry and seedlings
A hand trowel can be pushed in easily	Low	Most forms of annual horticulture, fruit and nut trees
A hand trowel can be pushed in with some effort	Low to moderate	Long-lived annuals and perennials, fruit and nut trees
A spade can be pushed in with some assistance from the foot	Moderate	Perennial crops, fruit and nut trees
A spade can only be pushed in by jumping on it	Moderate to high	Fruit and nut trees, shade trees, lawns
A fork can be pushed in with some assistance from the foot	High	Shade trees, windbreaks, rough grasses
A fork cannot be pushed in except with extreme effort	Extreme	Rough grasses, weedy forbs, highly tolerant trees

'platy' and 'prismatic' – and inside them are small pores in which water is held. In the spaces between the peds are large pores through which water drains by the force of gravity, allowing air to enter. A well-structured soil has a balance between the two types of pores, making it both free draining yet able to retain a good amount of moisture for plant growth. The soil is similar to a good sponge cake: light, fluffy and full of air.

If there is no combining of soil particles into peds, then the soil exists as single grains and is said to be without structure, or 'apedal'. Loose sand is the perfect example of this, as it has very good aeration but an extremely poor water-holding capacity.

In heavy clay with very small particle sizes, the only way air can get into the soil is if the clay is structured, allowing cracks and larger pore spaces. The more cracks and pores the clay has, the better the aeration will be. Clays with no structure are among the worst for erosion and the restriction of plant roots, while well-structured clays, such as the black earths of the Darling Downs in Queensland, are among the very best growing soils in the world. Well-structured clays combine the good aeration of sand with the water-holding capacity of clay, providing the perfect mix of air, water and solid support.

An unstructured growing medium such as mangrove mud has no air at all. Mangroves can live in it because they put up little snorkel-like roots (called pneumatophores) to allow air to enter the rest of their root systems. Other plants that grow in unstructured waterlogged soils, such as rice, have an aerated structure along their roots, like foam rubber, that allows air to get to their roots. It's not that these plants tolerate low oxygen levels – they just have ingenious ways of getting oxygen to their roots other than through soil pores.

BELOW Vegetable crops derive their nutrients largely from the topsoil, where water, oxygen and mineral levels are optimal.

Stability and dispersion

A well-structured soil is useful, as it admits air and water into the profile, but how stable is the structure? Will it collapse easily into sludge when you start working and wetting it to create your urban farm? This is a common problem in new housing estates, where natural soil has been disturbed and poorly structured clay is brought to the surface.

The collapse of soil structure upon wetting is known as 'slaking'. When unstable soil is cultivated and then receives rainfall or irrigation, it turns into mud that won't conduct air and water. Even worse is 'dispersion', where fine particles of clay become suspended in water and won't settle out. A muddy brown river or dam indicates dispersive clay. This is one of the worst soil scenarios to encounter, because once the soil disperses it will set hard upon drying and be difficult to transform back into a well-structured soil.

Testing a soil for the stability of its structure is not difficult, particularly with loams, clay loams and clays. Take some air-dried peds that are 5–10 millimetres in diameter, and place them carefully in a jar of clean water. Observe their behaviour in the first minute or two.

- **Classes 1–6 peds slake** – they fall apart into a little pyramid of mud.
- **Class 7 peds are stable** – they swell but don't fall apart much.
- **Class 8 peds are highly stable** – there is no observable change except in colour.

Slaking is undesirable, as it indicates that a soil is prone to collapse when wetted, but most soils will slake at this stage. Classes 7 and 8 are the most desirable form of peds, and they are usually associated with high organic matter, which binds soil particles together.

Now leave the peds in the water for half an hour. What changes have occurred?

- **Class 1** – the water surrounding the ped is completely muddy. This indicates highly dispersive soil.
- **Class 2** – there is a muddy 'halo' around the ped. This indicates an unstable dispersive soil.

ABOVE Soil structure can be seen by grabbing a handful of soil and shaking it a little – it should fall apart into aggregates.

SOIL PORES

Water is held more firmly by the soil in fine pores and is released more easily from coarser pores. The finer the pores, the higher the water will rise up in the soil from a water table. This is easily demonstrated by purchasing two sponges from the supermarket, one with coarse pores and the other with fine pores. Wet them up with some coloured water, and then place them on their side to drain. The finer sponge retains more coloured water – showing a higher water table or 'capillary fringe' – than the coarser sponge. Remember also that the coarser the pores, the more air will enter once the water has drained. This is called 'air-filled porosity'.

LEFT In the middle is dispersive clay. As seen on the left, organic matter coagulates clay particles; on the right, gypsum does the same. The most fertile soils combine organic matter and calcium to create structure.

CLAY, CLAY – GO AWAY!

If your urban farm has a clay soil, don't despair! It is often said that clay soils are difficult to work with, but in reality all the world's most fertile agricultural soils are well-structured (well-aggregated) clays or clay loams that combine the magnificent water-holding capacity of clay with the perfect drainage of sand. The secret is well-behaved clay. A badly behaved dispersive clay soil sets like concrete, while a well-behaved one – which is full of organic matter and plenty of calcium – breaks up or crumbles into aggregates. This means the soil allows in air but also retains moisture. If you have a badly behaved clay soil, assess its structure and then work out a plan to improve it.

Dispersion of clay is undesirable, as it indicates a soil that is highly prone to erosion. Such dispersive clay soil will usually be low in organic matter and light in colour (commonly either white, yellow or yellow–brown). Dispersive soils will respond to gypsum.

If the water around the peds in the jar is not muddy after half an hour, move on to the next step in the testing process. Shake the jar hard, then set it down and let it settle for 10 minutes.

- **Classes 3–5** – a significant proportion of the soil remains dispersed, leaving the water muddy. This means the soil will be dispersive in running or high-energy water. These kinds of soils are likely to seal up during periods of rainfall or irrigation.
- **Class 6** – the water clarifies completely. The soil may slake, but it is not naturally dispersive even if provoked.

Dispersion is caused by too much sodium and not enough calcium in the soil. Sodium causes clay particles to repel each other when suspended in water.

Garden soils should always be Class 6 or higher. A little slaking is acceptable, but they should never disperse, even if vigorously shaken in water. These soils are always dark in colour, with plenty of organic matter 'gluing' the soil particles together. They should never be sodic (in other words, full of sodium), and will always contain sufficient calcium to prevent dispersion.

Basically, dispersion is caused by too much sodium and not enough calcium in the soil. Sodium causes clay particles to repel each other when suspended in water, whereas calcium causes them to coagulate together and drop out of suspension. This is why gypsum (calcium sulphate) – affectionately known as the 'clay breaker' – is used to improve dispersive soils. It displaces the sodium and causes the clay particles to coagulate. Highly organic soils are very unlikely to respond to gypsum, because the organic matter prevents the clay from dispersing.

Test for gypsum responsiveness

If your soil shows any dispersion (Classes 1–5), then you should establish if it would respond to gypsum. Take two jars, and place a tablespoon of soil in each one. Drop a small pinch of gypsum (or plaster of Paris) in one jar, and fill both jars with water. Place a lid on both jars, and then shake them vigorously for about 5 minutes or until the soil is thoroughly dispersed. Set them aside for an hour.

If, after an hour, the soil in the gypsum-treated jar has completely coagulated and the water is clear, but the untreated jar is still muddy, then the soil is gypsum responsive. If the untreated jar is only slightly muddy, use around 100 grams of gypsum for every square metre of soil in your garden.

If the untreated jar is so muddy that you can't see through it at all, then you will likely need up to 500 grams of gypsum for every square metre of soil. If the untreated jar is muddy but you can see through it, then you will likely need between 100 and 500 grams per square metre. Gypsum is best dug in, but it is not entirely useless if it is left on the surface to incorporate slowly.

STRUCTURE IN ARTIFICIAL SOILS

Even when making artificial soil mixes for rooftop gardens and containers, we need to consider the basic principles of physical soil fertility. Therefore, we have to design the mix so that it has highly granular components, which – despite having no structure – are very well aerated. Ingredients such as pine bark, sphagnum moss, perlite and horticultural ashes (with a large particle size) all hold water well within the particles, but allow water to drain out and air to enter between the particles. In this respect, we are mimicking a strongly structured soil with its good balance of fine and coarse pore spaces.

Encouraging good structure

In natural soils, good structure develops if you have the following situations:

- wetting and drying cycles that cause shrinking and swelling, thereby creating cracks and structure
- high organic-matter levels that also cause shrinking and swelling, and bind soil particles together to form peds
- the right balance of clay minerals that shrink and swell (if you don't, then you can amend your clay to improve its behaviour)
- the correct level of calcium (see the test for gypsum responsiveness on page 81)
- restricted traffic and compaction.

Most important of all is a regular application of organic matter that stimulates biological activity as well as the soil organisms (such as worms and ants) that create pore space in the soil. This will greatly reduce your need to cultivate your soil (a practice that tends to destroy structure).

The structure of soils can be ruined or diminished by bad practices. The following situations do not encourage good structure and porosity:

- compaction by stock, traffic and pedestrians
- waterlogging that prevents the much-desired shrink–swell cycle that leads to cracking and structure
- low organic-matter content that also reduces shrinking and swelling, which in turn decreases biological activity
- constant or repeated vigorous ploughing (excessive rotary hoeing is a common culprit here).

Ploughing or digging to fix the density and 'fluff up' a soil creates a temporary increase in pore space. However, if it is repeated too often – especially when there is insufficient organic matter, so there is a tendency for the soil to disperse – then the soil structure collapses like a failed soufflé.

Soil texture

The mineral fraction of a soil consists of three different particle types differentiated by size: sand, silt and clay. Soil texture is a way to quantify what sort of soil particles you have and in what balance they are found.

It's important to know the texture of a soil, because middle-of-the-road textures such as loam and clay loam tend to be the easiest soils to manage. This does depend on the structure, of course, as only well-structured soils have the necessary range of pore sizes for good aeration and drainage as well as good water-holding capacity. Consequently, soil texture combined with structure is a measure of the mix of pore sizes and the proportion of water and air that is held.

Texture is linked to a soil's ability to hold water (for example, sands hold little water and clays hold a lot). However, when it comes to growing plants, it gets a bit more complicated, because some soil textures won't release their water to plants readily even though there is a lot of water in the soil. Clay, for example, holds up to 60 per cent water by volume, but it won't release all its water to any plant growing in it because it has such fine pore spaces (capillaries). As plants start to extract water, the difficulty of obtaining more water increases until it gets to the point where the plant cannot get any more. This is called the 'Permanent Wilting Point' for a pretty obvious reason – the plant wilts and won't recover. Think of squeezing out a wet sponge. The first gentle squeeze releases most of the water, a firm squeeze discharges some more, and by twisting it tightly between two hands you can get the last drops out – but you will never get it completely dry by squeezing. There is water there, but you – like the plant in clay soil – simply haven't got the strength to get it out.

In natural soils, the texture of the subsoil will be 'heavier' (in other words, more clay) and less well structured than that of the topsoil, because fine clay particles easily leach out of the topsoil. This is true for all but the deepest coastal sands, where there is no clay. So, if you have a natural soil with crumbly clay loam in the topsoil, you might expect to have a fairly heavy, plastic and poorly drained subsoil.

To see the textures of your soil layers, dig down to a depth of around 600 millimetres (if your soil is deep enough). This is not easy; a post-hole digger will help, otherwise dig a 600-millimetre square pit to get to the 600 millimetres in depth. This is all the soil depth most crop plants will need, fruit trees included. Note any changes in colour and texture, or if rocks appear.

As you dig down into natural soils, you will usually see less of the dark colours and more of the ochre colours of iron oxide emerging. The structure will be less obvious, and there will be none of the fine crumbs we usually see in our topsoil. This lower part of the soil profile may even form into coarse blocks or lumps of clay. This is not good, and may need correction. Remember, texture will nearly always get 'heavier' with depth in natural soils.

LEFT Colour is a guide to a number of important soil properties. On the left, the yellow hue of this subsoil indicates poor aeration at depth. In the middle, this bright reddish subsoil has good drainage. On the right, this topsoil has a darker grey colour due to its superb organic-matter content.

In urban soils, you might not find the normal profile of A, B and C horizons. There might be layers of clay alternating with layers of sand and loam. This is evidence of human impact, and it often occurs on building sites. Layering in this way is not good for water movement in the soil profile. If the layering is severe enough, consider homogenising the top 300 millimetres of soil by deep digging.

Tests for soil texture

The simplest and, with a little experience, the most accurate way to assess soil texture is the hand-texture method. Obtain about a cupful of the soil layer being tested, remove any obvious stones, sticks and foreign matter, and then proceed as follows:

1 Take a small handful of your soil, and wet it slowly. Add just enough water so that the soil does not stick to your fingers but is moist enough to glisten to the eye. If it becomes sloppy and wet, add more soil until you get the mixture right.
2 Work the soil with the palm and fingers of one hand to form a ball of soil, or bolus, that is evenly mixed with no lumps remaining. This may take a few minutes of working. Hold the bolus up to your ear while working it – can you hear the grinding of sand?

3 Try pulling out a ribbon of soil between your forefinger and thumb. How long can you make it?

Use the information in the Soil Texture Guide table on the opposite page to assess your soil type by its texture.

If you can hear particles rubbing together as you work the bolus, and if it is also quite hard to make a ribbon of any length, it's sand. If it feels smooth and silky, and you can easily make ribbons over 5 centimetres in length, it's in the clay-texture category. Most people can tell sand from clay, but it's the in-between textures that are a bit harder. The basic texture divisions are sands, loams, clay loams and clays, but we can have degrees of these as well, such as 'loamy sand' (sand with a bit of loam in it) and 'sandy clay' (clay with a bit of sand in it). Sands are said to be 'light', while clays are 'heavy' in texture.

Another common method you can use to determine your soil type is known as the jar test. Take a handful of soil, place it into a jar of water, replace the lid and then vigorously shake the jar until the soil has completely broken down. This may take some time with heavy clay.

The large particles of sand will settle first, followed by silt and finally clay. You

the soil is well drained or not. Organic matter is always dark brown or black, and it is darker when the soil is wet. Dry topsoil with high organic matter might be dark grey, but it will go almost black when it is wet. Topsoils are nearly always darker than subsoils.

Iron minerals often dictate the colour of natural subsoils. Indigenous people used these bright oxides and hydroxides for millennia as red and orange pigments for cave painting and body art. Today they are utilised in cosmetics (rouge and lipsticks), paints, cement colouring and medicines. This is because they are very stable, and a tiny bit goes a long way.

As well as playing a fascinating role in human cultural activities, the colours of iron oxides are interesting because they change depending on how wet the oxides are. This can tell us a lot about how well drained our subsoil is. Basically, the sequence is:

- **Grey/olive/greenish** – permanently saturated, very poor drainage, completely anaerobic.
- **Light grey/yellowish** – mostly saturated, poor drainage, moderately anaerobic.
- **Yellow/orange** – intermittently saturated, reasonable drainage, periodically anaerobic.
- **Orangey red** – mostly dry, good drainage, mostly oxidised.
- **Bright red** – never saturated, extremely good drainage, always oxidised.

LEFT During the soil texture test, a bolus of moistened soil is squeezed out to make a ribbon. The length of the ribbon indicates the texture, from sand to clay.

will then be able to see the bands of the different soil particles, thus allowing you to estimate their relative proportions in your soil. This method offers a crude breakdown of your soil; however, we feel that the best way of identifying and understanding your soil is the hand-texture method.

Soil colour

A skilled gardener or soil scientist uses colour to make observations about soil behaviour. The two most important things that colour can tell us is the organic-matter content and whether

SOIL TEXTURE GUIDE

TEXTURE	RIBBON LENGTH	COMMENTS
Sand	No ribbon can be made	Gritty, coarse or fine sand; can't be moulded
Loamy or clayey sand	0–1.5 cm	Slight coherence, gritty
Sandy loam	1.5–2.5 cm	Coherent but gritty
Loam	2.5–3.5 cm	Smooth and coherent but not gritty; may be spongy if high in organic matter
Clay loam	3.5–5.0 cm	Feels plastic and smooth; some fine sand may be present
Clay	5.0 cm or longer	Like plasticine; some sand may be present

COPING WITH POOR TEXTURE

The fact that loams usually have the best balance of pore size for holding a good amount of water and air is not to say that sandy soils do not give good results provided that water can be kept up to the plants, or that clays cannot form the basis of an excellent garden. The art of turning a poor natural soil into one that is great for horticulture (a 'hortic' soil) essentially involves deepening the soil to increase rooting depth. A layer of heavy clay subsoil, for example, can be slowly turned into a highly porous, well-structured clay loam or cracking clay that allows water and oxygen – and subsequently roots – to enter. One of the classic strategies for achieving this is to add gypsum to the subsoil, which helps it to aggregate, thereby improving its structure. As a rule, clays are only useful when they are well structured, and the gardener with clay soil will need to keep up the organic matter and not over-cultivate the soil to assist in maintaining structure.

Desert soils are bright red in colour because they are almost never anaerobic (without oxygen), while mangrove mud or swamp soil is grey because it is permanently saturated. You may find that the top of your subsoil is bright red, but as you go down the profile and it becomes moister, the subsoil becomes more yellow or even mottled yellow and light grey. It's all about the amount of air versus the amount of water. Consequently, it is worth digging a hole in your soil to check out the colours of the iron minerals in the various soil horizons, particularly the subsoil.

Moisture content

It is important to be able to assess a soil's moisture content in order to judge when it needs irrigating. Most people irrigate based on gut feelings or the dry appearance of the

surface of the soil, which very often leads to either insufficient or excessive water and wastage of water. Most professional farmers use soil-moisture sensors and Bureau of Meteorology evaporation and rainfall data to accurately determine how much water to apply to their soil.

When measuring soil moisture, there are two extremes:

1 The upper end is called the Field Capacity, which is the amount of water the soil holds about 48 hours after it was completely saturated then allowed to drain.
2 The lower end is called the Permanent Wilting Point, which is the moisture content below which the plant cannot get any more water and wilts beyond the point of recovery.

ABOVE If the soil looks dry and is not cool to the touch, it is approaching Permanent Wilting Point.

The best farmers know the texture and water-holding capacity of their soil, so they allow their soil to dry to about halfway between Field Capacity and Permanent Wilting Point before irrigating. They apply just enough water to bring it up to Field Capacity again, so they do not use more water than the soil can hold.

In practice, of course, the average urban farmer is not going to get out the calculator and consult the Bureau of Meteorology evaporation records every time they irrigate. However, like professional farmers, they need to get to know the particular moisture-holding characteristics of their soil and how much water they need to apply to wet the soil down to the bottom of the root zone.

There are all sorts of fancy electronic devices that measure soil moisture, but – with a little training – the human senses are very good at judging moisture content. The number one mistake people make is judging moisture by the condition of the soil surface, so ensure you dig down about 100 millimetres, pick up a handful of soil and observe it in good light; also touch the newly exposed soil with the back of your hand. Use the Assessing Soil Moisture table on page 88 to help you work out the moisture content of your soil.

The next issue to deal with is how much water to apply. If your soil is about halfway between Field Capacity and Permanent Wilting Point, then the approximate amount of water to apply to the top 300 millimetres of the topsoil (the root zone) is shown in the Water Application table on page 89.

Note that the amounts of water added are in millimetres of depth, and they are quite significant. This emphasises the fact that it is more efficient and better for plants if you water them deeply and infrequently rather than lightly and often, as the latter situation will allow water to evaporate from the surface and encourage shallow root growth. Deep watering to bring the whole root zone up to Field Capacity encourages deeper rooting and allows the surface to dry out between waterings. This dry surface layer acts as mulch and prevents surface evaporation, reducing the net amount of water needed.

ABOVE Make sure you dig down to at least 100 millimetres below the surface to assess soil moisture; ignore the surface.

FOLLOW YOUR NOSE

Smell is a very reliable guide to the balance of air and water in your soil. In the presence of oxygen, soil smells earthy. In its absence, it smells like old socks or the water at the bottom of a vase of long-dead flowers. If soil has a particularly nasty aroma, then it has probably 'gone bad' and something needs to be done about it. The classic smell of waterlogged swampy soil is 'rotten-egg gas', or hydrogen sulphide – sulphur in its reduced form. While generating hydrogen sulphide in the science lab has long amused schoolchildren, in an urban soil it is no laughing matter – as your crops will quickly object to such toxic growing conditions.

There are cases where farmers want to cause their crop some moisture stress by allowing it to approach – if not actually reach – the Permanent Wilting Point. Called 'regulated deficit irrigation', it is common when growing wine grapes as it concentrates the juice and leads to the production of superior-quality wines. It is also used for stone fruits, such as peaches and figs, where excess water is disastrous for the ripening fruits. The fruits will 'blow up' or split if too much rain or irrigation occurs at this time. The urban farmer may like to experiment with encouraging ripening and concentrating the nutrients and flavours in common vegetables by keeping them a little on the dry side before harvest.

CHEMICAL FERTILITY

As we saw in The Needs of Plants chapter (see pages 62–71), plants require 12 elements (or nutrients) from the soil to grow and thrive – this is the chemical fertility of the soil. We could argue that there are actually 14 essential elements, because there are two others whose necessity remains debatable: sodium and

ASSESSING SOIL MOISTURE

OBSERVATION	MOISTURE CONTENT	CONSEQUENCE
Dark, glossy, shining wet, sodden; feels cold to the back of the hand	Above Field Capacity	Exclusion of air, waterlogging and root death by asphyxiation
Dark, matt, obviously moist; feels cool to the back of the hand	About Field Capacity	Usually about right, adequate balance of air and water content
Dark, matt; feels relatively cool to the back of the hand	Around or below Field Capacity	Still good, don't need to water
Dark, matt; feels just cool to the back of the hand	About halfway between Field Capacity and Permanent Wilting Point	Might need to water soon
Lighter in colour, matt; neutral temperature to the back of the hand	Approaching Permanent Wilting Point	Need to water, as yield is starting to seriously decline
Light, matt; feels warm to the back of the hand	About Permanent Wilting Point	Water now, as you have suffered yield decline
Very light, matt; bone-dry powder that feels warm to the back of the hand	Below Permanent Wilting Point	Only the toughest plants are alive, only succulents give better than zero yield

chlorine, which together make sodium chloride (common salt). These elements are present in all plants, but only a few plants seem to respond positively when they are applied to soil. Small amounts of common salt are certainly necessary for animals, but plant deficiencies of common salt are effectively unknown. Generally speaking, there will be enough common salt in any soil for you not to have to worry about applying it.

All 12 elements supplied from the soil are taken up by the plant's root system in a simple (ionic) form after they have dissolved in water. This is the same regardless of whether the elements are derived from an organic source (such as compost and manure) or an inorganic (mineral) source (such as lime and gypsum). The elements are present in the soil water (soil solution) as salts – but we don't just mean common salt (although sodium chloride is one of the salts found in soils), as there are many others (such as magnesium sulphate and sulphate of potash). A salt is a substance that dissolves in water by separating into a positively charged part (a cation) and a negatively charged part (an anion). For example, sodium chloride or common salt (NaCl) separates into $Na^+ + Cl^-$, where sodium (Na) is the cation and chloride (Cl) is the anion.

It follows then that plants in a dry soil won't have enough water not only for photosynthesis, but also for nutrient uptake – they actually starve from lack of water! Hence the expression we hear used sometimes: 'Water is the best fertiliser.' A crucial point about the delivery of nutrients to plant roots is that not all salts (nutrients) dissolve as readily as each other in water. Thus, delivery of some nutrients is much easier than others. Being highly soluble, nitrogen and potassium are much easier to deliver to plants in liquid form while they are in active growth. But calcium has low to moderate solubility, and it is therefore very important to ensure there is adequate calcium present in the soil before you start a crop. The Plant Elements and Their Solubility table on page 90 shows the dissolvability of the essential plant elements.

If we remember that the number of cations always has to be balanced with the same

WATER APPLICATION	
SOIL TEXTURE	WATER TO APPLY (MM)
Sand	23
Fine sand	30
Sandy loam	27
Fine sandy loam	33
Loam	26
Organic loam	35
Clay loam	27

OPPOSITE Once crop plants start to wilt, there is a good chance that you have lost significant yield.

ABOVE All *Prunus* species (such as peaches and plums) are prone to fruit splitting if excessive water is applied close to ripening time.

A SPECIAL CASE

In general, all the compost and organic forms of nutrients that we apply to our plants must break down to their ultimate ionic forms for the plant to take them up. However, there is an exception to this rule. Some simple organic 'chelating' compounds, such as sugars and amino acids, are small enough to pass through the walls of the root cells. Insoluble elements that have been 'chelated' to improve their availability to plant roots can be purchased to correct specific deficiencies. You may have seen chelated iron in garden centres, as it's a useful way of overcoming iron deficiency in plants growing on alkaline soils. There are also chelated forms of other trace elements that are commercially available, such as zinc and copper, as well as blends that combine various trace elements into a single fertiliser.

number of anions, you can start to mix and match nutrients to make up all sorts of fertiliser salts that can be used to improve the chemical fertility of your soil. There are several common combinations:

- calcium sulphate (gypsum) – $CaSO_4$
- ammonium sulphate – $(NH_4)_2SO_4$
- iron sulphate – $FeSO_4$
- magnesium sulphate (Epsom salts) – $MgSO_4$
- sulphate of potash – K_2SO_4
- calcium carbonate (lime) – $CaCO_3$.

BIOLOGICAL FERTILITY

Healthy soils contain huge numbers and varieties of macroorganisms and microorganisms, and research has shown that the larger the number and diversity of organisms, the more fertile the soil usually is. Biological fertility is the ability of a soil to support an array of beneficial organisms.

Populations of soil organisms will vary dramatically from soil to soil, and even from

OPPOSITE Organic matter of all kinds is the fuel for a soil's microbial life, and it helps to increase biological fertility.

PLANT ELEMENTS AND THEIR SOLUBILITY

ESSENTIAL ELEMENT	CATION	ANION	SOLUBILITY
Nitrogen (N)	Ammonium: NH_4^+	Nitrate: NO_3^-	Very high
Potassium (K)	K^+		Very high
Calcium (Ca)	Ca^{2+}		Low to moderate
Magnesium (Mg)	Mg^{2+}		Moderate to high
Iron (Fe)	Fe^{3+}		Moderate to very low
Manganese (Mn)	Mn^{2+}		Moderate to very low
Zinc (Zn)	Zn^{2+}		Low
Copper (Cu)	Cu^{2+}		Low
Phosphorus (P)		PO_4^{3-}	Low to very low
Sulphur (S)		SO_4^{2-}	Moderate to high
Boron (B)		BO_4^{2-}	High
Molybdenum (Mo)		MoO_4^{3-}	Low
Carbonate		CO_3^{2-}	Very low

day to day within the same soil, depending on how much food (organic matter) for growth and reproduction there is, the moisture content and the temperature of the soil. These organisms benefit from the same physical fertility factors as plants – they need a balance of nutrients, as well as access to air and water in the soil – and they offer many benefits in return. For example, soil organisms exude a range of soluble organic compounds that are known to stimulate root growth and hence nutrient uptake.

Some people claim that they can tell the 'health' of a soil by analysing the proportions of various microbes (for instance, fungi versus bacteria), but in our opinion there is very little evidence that this is of any real use. In fact, soil microbiology provides the most fertile ground for all kinds of unproven (and unprovable) claims, which has led to a raft of 'cures' being peddled to the unwary. While we are great advocates for creating your own healthy living soil by using homemade compost and worm-farm castings to bring all the beneficial organisms you need to your urban farm, we have seen many commercial products aimed at aiding soil biology that appear to be a complete waste of money.

Commercial potions abound that are said to contain microbes that will 'unlock' soil fertility.

SALTS AND PH

SALTS DISSOLVING IN WATER

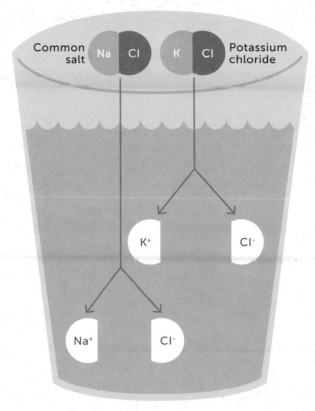

A salt is a substance that dissolves in water, but did you know that water is actually a salt? It dissolves to a small degree in itself:

$H_2O \rightarrow H^+ + OH^-$

This is the basis of pH, or acid/alkali chemistry. H^+ cations cause acidity, while OH^- anions cause alkalinity. Note that water has an equal number of acid (H^+) and alkali (OH^-) ions. This makes water pH neutral: neither acid nor alkaline.

Now let's add hydrogen chloride (HCl) to the water to make the salt hydrochloric acid (which is commonly used to lower the pH of swimming-pool water):

$HCl \rightarrow H^+ + Cl^-$

There is now an excess of the acid H^+ ions, and the water into which the hydrogen chloride is dissolved is said to be acidic.

If we mix sodium hydroxide, otherwise known as caustic soda (NaOH), with water:

$NaOH \rightarrow Na^+ + OH^-$

There is now an excess of the alkali OH^- ions, and the water into which the sodium hydroxide is dissolved is said to be alkaline.

Regardless of the fertiliser you are using, it must first dissolve into an ionic form before plant roots can take up its nutrients. But what stops the nutrients from simply being washed away by rainfall? Soil has a very elegant system for storing nutrients.

Humus (fully decomposed compost) and clay particles in the soil act like a sponge to soak up and store both water and nutrients. The way they do this is that both carry an overall negative electrical charge, which attracts positively charged ions (cations). The nutrients are thus held in the soil so that they do not leach out. The cation exchange capacity (CEC) of a clay or organic particle refers to the negative electrical charge that it carries, which allows it to attract cations. Plant roots have to 'exchange' one cation for another to get the nutrients they need from the soil particles, and they do this by exuding a hydrogen ion (H^+).

The higher the CEC, the greater the soil's capacity to store nutrients – and the higher the level of fertility of the soil. All the best soils have a high clay and organic-matter content to maximise the CEC. In horticulture, we usually increase the CEC by adding organic matter such as well-rotted compost to the soil, but you can also use clays such as bentonite and vermiculite.

The major cations present in soils – sodium, hydrogen, aluminium, potassium, calcium and magnesium – balance on the CEC. It just happens that the best balance of the major cations for plant growth and soil structure is:

- sodium – less than 5 per cent
- hydrogen and aluminium – less than 2 per cent
- potassium – 5–15 per cent
- calcium – 60–75 per cent
- magnesium – 15–25 per cent.

If your soil shows any dispersion (see Stability and dispersion, pages 79–81), chances are that it is deficient in exchangeable calcium and has excessive amounts of sodium or magnesium on the CEC; in other words, the soil is sodic, magnesic or both. This is very common in clay subsoils and results in them being poorly structured, sticky (or 'cloying', the origin word of 'clay'), hard setting and badly behaved. Such soils will respond to gypsum.

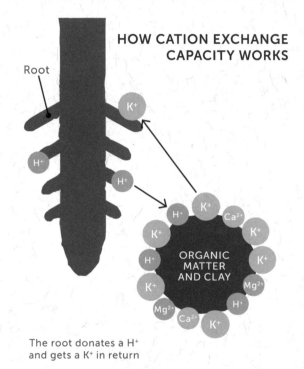

HOW CATION EXCHANGE CAPACITY WORKS

Root

ORGANIC MATTER AND CLAY

The root donates a H^+ and gets a K^+ in return

Adding compost, worm castings and fresh organic matter to your soil ... greatly encourages the beneficial microbes that are already present in the soil to multiply. Nothing else is needed.

'Probiotics' that list benefits such as 'increases root mass' and 'activates and restores your soil' are increasingly being stocked in garden centres. When asked to produce any objective evidence of their claims, a deathly silence often follows. Indeed, it would seem somewhat illogical to assert that adding a little bottle of microbial solution to a soil that already contains trillions upon trillions of the same organisms would change anything.

Other suspicious preparations (usually involving microbes or organic humus extracts) claim to 'unlock' nutrients that are tied up in the soil. You can't replace the 30 kilograms of phosphorus and 300 kilograms of potassium per hectare taken out of the soil every year during crop cultivation by 'unlocking' more nutrients – you need to add more nutrients to the soil. Even if these preparations did work (which they don't), it would be, in effect, nutrient 'mining' and not sustainable. Our philosophy is simple, and it works: what we take out of the soil, we must put back into the soil.

Our advice? With the exception of *Rhizobium* and some strains of fungi (mycorrhizae), there is no evidence to suggest that there is any benefit to manipulating soil microbes by adding any particular strain of them to soils. Rather, incorporate what microbes need to live on, and they will soon colonise the soil in their millions. Adding compost, worm castings and fresh organic matter to your soil on a regular basis is not only good for the plants, but it also greatly encourages the beneficial microbes that are already present in the soil to multiply. Nothing else is needed.

Facts about soil microbiology

The particular form of organic matter added to the soil influences the types of microbes that are present. Put cheese or milk (protein) in a soil, and more likely than not you'll get penicillin-like fungi growing in it; straw (cellulose) invites a different kind of fungi to colonise your soil. Place meat in soil, and you'll get all kinds of smelly bacteria. Each type of organism has a complex range of dietary preferences, and organisms will proliferate when their needs are met.

There is good evidence that well-composted organic matter contains a wide spectrum of microbes that seem to suppress certain root diseases of plants. We conducted a trial once using compost on root rot of beets. Our

In the world of soil biology, always remember: there is a lot of muck and magic. If it sounds too good to be true, it probably is. And, even more importantly, making and using your own organic composts and worm castings is the cheapest, best and simplest way to introduce beneficial microbes into your garden.

ASSESSING SOIL PH

The level of acidity or alkalinity (as measured by the pH) in a soil is a fundamentally important property that affects a soil's physical, chemical and biological fertility. There are three main reasons for this:

1 Some plants and their roots simply cannot survive outside a narrow pH range.
2 The level of acidity influences chemical reactions in the soil and determines how available most nutrients are to plant roots.
3 The vast majority of microorganisms that are vital for maintaining a living and productive soil environment require a certain level of acidity to be active.

Soil pH is a good indicator of the general state of health of your soil, so measuring it is like a doctor taking your blood pressure – it will give a pretty good idea of whether there is a balanced, healthy environment below the surface. Various factors, including the long-term use of fertilisers such as ammonium sulphate, can gradually alter pH over time, so testing your soil's pH every few years is a good 'check-up' for your soil.

The pH scale ranges from 1 (highly acid) to 14 (highly alkaline). An extreme pH at either end of the scale (think battery acid at one end, and caustic soda at the other) equates to a very corrosive situation that will kill any plant exposed to it. The vast majority of soils fall within the range of 4 to 8, and most plants prefer a pH of between 5 and 7. Most natural Australian soils are acid, except in coastal areas of South Australia and Western Australia and pockets of New South Wales and Victoria, where basalt and limestone occur. Granites and most sedimentary rocks such as sandstone give rise to acid soils.

ABOVE Compost heaps don't have to be pretty to be useful soil microbe farms – they just have to be well fed with kitchen scraps and green matter!

OPPOSITE, LEFT If a plant's veins are green but the cells between the veins are yellow (known as interveinal chlorosis), this is a sure sign of iron deficiency due to alkaline soil.

compost treatment controlled the disease at least as well as using twice the recommended rate of the strongest fungicide.

There are two types of microbes for which the benefit to plant growth has been very well documented. Bacteria in the *Rhizobium* genus fix nitrogen in legume roots, while mycorrhizae live in plant roots and help the roots to extract nutrients such as phosphorus by greatly increasing the surface area of the roots. Both varieties of microbes are very choosy when it comes to their plant friends; a particular strain will only usually benefit one plant genus, or even just a single plant species. The bottom line with these beneficial microbes is that they can only be introduced to your soil in specific circumstances, so research the subject very carefully before spending any money on these organisms.

Problems caused by incorrect soil pH

Nutrient availability is strongly affected by pH level. This is because the solubility of some ionic nutrients is dependent on pH. The classic example is iron, which forms very insoluble iron oxide in soil with an alkaline pH level. This makes it unavailable to plants that are not specifically adapted to alkaline soil. A deficiency of iron results in severe yellowing of a plant's new leaves (which is known as interveinal chlorosis). Interestingly, the same symptom shows up in plants with manganese deficiency thanks to alkaline soils.

Plants that are intolerant of alkaline soils have traditionally been known as acid-loving plants, and they include:

- Rutaceae: pretty much every *Citrus* species
- Rosaceae: raspberries (*Rubus* species) and strawberries (*Fragaria* species)
- Proteaceae: macadamia nut (*Macadamia integrifolia*)
- Ericaceae: blueberries (*Vaccinium* species).

However, rather than calling them acid-loving plants, it would be better to describe them as 'iron-inefficient' plants because of their inability to take up iron when soil pH is alkaline. On the other hand, some plants – formerly known as 'lime lovers', but now called 'iron-efficient' plants – have mechanisms that allow them

TESTING THE PH OF YOUR SOIL

There are two products within the urban farmer's reach for testing pH. One is a small colour-test kit, which is relatively inexpensive and can give accurate results if the instructions are followed. **(1)** A small amount of moist soil is placed onto a white tile. **(2)** Drops of indicator solution are added until the soil is just saturated. **(3)** Special white powder is sprinkled on top of the wet soil, and the powder changes colour based on the soil's pH. **(4)** The powder colour is then measured against the colour chart provided.

Another tool for testing pH is a small battery-operated pH meter. The only ones that are of any real value are those with glass bulb probes. These give very accurate readings and cost around $200 each. This may sound like a lot of money, but not in comparison to losing all your produce due to an acid or alkaline soil. We are continually confronted by commercial growers who are reluctant to spend $200 on a pH meter and yet will spend $2000 a year on lime and dolomite that they may not need.

to obtain iron even from alkaline soils. They do this by exuding acids that convert the insoluble iron oxide into a soluble form. Plants in this group include:

- Lamiaceae: rosemary (*Rosmarinus officinalis*), lavenders (*Lavandula* species) and thyme (*Thymus vulgaris*)
- Fabaceae: garden pea (*Pisum sativum*), beans (*Phaseolus* species) and lucerne (*Medicago sativa*).

In very acid soils, with a pH below 5.5, two very important ions can rise to toxic levels: manganese and aluminium. Some plants are tolerant of high levels of these two ions, but most are not – excess manganese and aluminium depresses plants' productivity or kills them. Plants susceptible to toxicity from these two elements include most species in the Fabaceae (legume) family, one of the most important of all food families. This is why you are commonly advised to put lime on the soil before planting peas and beans, although this will only be necessary if the pH is 6 or less.

Raising soil pH

Often known as sweetening or liming the soil, raising a soil's pH to reduce acidity is accomplished with liming agents. There are a number of different liming agents, which vary both in their mineral composition and their liming strength (see the Liming Agents to Raise pH table on page 99).

The two most common liming agents are lime (calcium carbonate) and dolomite (calcium magnesium carbonate). Rarely is builder's lime used, but its great advantage over lime is that it's more soluble and hence reacts faster. It can also be applied to the surface and washed in, but be careful – it is very caustic and can burn your eyes. Note that it is much stronger than lime, so you don't need as much.

Which liming agent you should use depends on the amount of calcium relative to magnesium in your soil. Ideally there is about three to five times more calcium than magnesium. Note that liming agents should not be utilised unless a pH test shows that they are needed. Excess

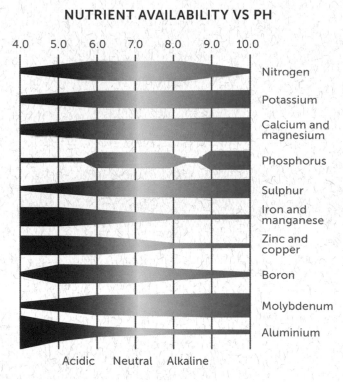

NUTRIENT AVAILABILITY VS PH

4.0 5.0 6.0 7.0 8.0 9.0 10.0

Nitrogen
Potassium
Calcium and magnesium
Phosphorus
Sulphur
Iron and manganese
Zinc and copper
Boron
Molybdenum
Aluminium

Acidic   Neutral   Alkaline

TESTING FOR TOO MUCH LIME

Overliming the soil is a common problem. Often people are told by 'experts' that the soil in their area is acid and needs lime, and many seed packets suggest the addition of lime at sowing. If this is done regularly for many years, lime levels will build up and the soil's pH will rise. This is disastrous for acid-loving plants, as they will be forever affected by iron deficiency. They will have distorted leaves and stunted plant growth.

To test for lime, place a small amount of soil on a dish or in a glass jar, and add a few drops of a diluted acid, such as one part hydrochloric acid (sold as swimming-pool or brickie's acid) and five parts water. Fizzing or bubbling indicates the presence of calcium carbonate (lime), as the carbonate reacts with the acid to produce carbon dioxide gas. The more violent the fizzing, the greater the lime content and the harder it will be to acidify the soil. Consider growing alkaline-tolerant plants.

ABOVE The width of the colour band is an indication of the availability of the nutrient at a given pH – the wider the better.

OPPOSITE Members of Fabaceae (such as peas and beans) are intolerant of acid soils. They will need lime if the pH is below about 6.5.

lime has its own set of problems, which are even more difficult to correct than an acid soil.

The use of lime is appropriate for many unimproved acid soils when they are first brought into cultivation, as they often have enough magnesium but insufficient calcium. For long-term maintenance, however, always utilise a mixture of equal parts lime and dolomite. This provides two important nutrients, calcium and magnesium, in exactly the right balance.

Some common fertilisers acidify soils, and the worst offenders are the ammonium forms of nitrogen: urea, ammonium phosphate and ammonium sulphate. Continued use of these will cause a gradual drop in pH, and this will need to be offset periodically (possibly every two to five years) with a liming agent.

The amount of lime or dolomite needed to raise a soil's pH depends on soil texture and the starting pH. Clays need much more than sands to obtain a given pH rise. The Using Lime or Dolomite to Raise pH table on the opposite page will help you work out the approximate amount of lime or dolomite required per square metre to raise the pH in the top 100 millimetres of your soil. And remember: the importance of testing your soil's pH regularly cannot be stressed enough.

RANGE OF PH IN NATURE

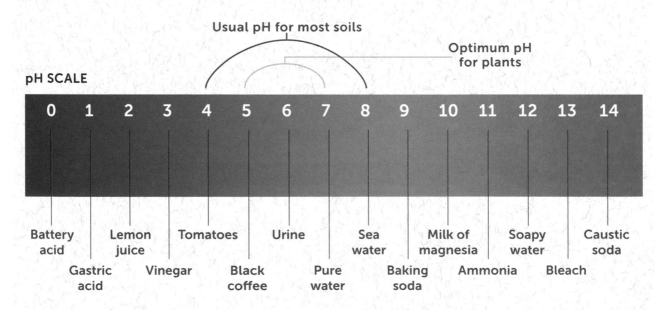

LIMING AGENTS TO RAISE PH

LIMING AGENT	AMOUNT EQUIVALENT TO 1 KG OF LIME	COMPONENTS
Lime	1 kilogram	Pure calcium carbonate
Magnesite	840 grams	Pure magnesium carbonate
Dolomite	920 grams	About two parts calcium to one part magnesium carbonate
Builder's lime	740 grams	Pure calcium hydroxide

USING LIME OR DOLOMITE TO RAISE PH

SOIL TEXTURE	FROM PH 4.5 TO 5.5 (PER SQUARE METRE)	FROM PH 5.5 TO 6.5 (PER SQUARE METRE)
Sandy and loamy sand	85 grams	110 grams
Sandy loam	130 grams	195 grams
Loam	195 grams	240 grams
Silty loam	280 grams	320 grams
Clay loam	320 grams	410 grams
Clay	360 grams	500 grams

Lowering soil pH

Acidifying soil is not as commonly necessary as liming. It is sometimes needed for acid-loving plants, where a high pH has been induced by overzealous liming or natural alkalinity (such as limestone-based soils).

The safest thing to use on your soil is a handful of iron sulphate per square metre every month until the pH is down to around 6.5. Use a hose or watering-can to wash off any iron sulphate that gets on the foliage of plants straight away, as it will burn. Agricultural sulphur (or 'flowers of sulphur') can be used if the pH is very high, as it is much stronger than iron sulphate – but only use one dose of half a handful per square metre. Its action is much slower than that of iron sulphate, and it is very insoluble so it must be dug in to the soil. Water your soil well afterwards to help it dissipate more quickly. Measure the soil pH three months later to check how much it has dropped – if you have

a heavy lime soil, you may find that you need to apply another dose of agricultural sulphur at this time.

ASSESSING SOIL SALINITY

As we mentioned earlier in this chapter, elements supplied as either organic or mineral fertilisers must break down into very simple forms known as salts before they can be absorbed by plant roots. If you are not careful when using fertilisers, it is quite easy to overfeed your plants; salts then build up in your soil until it becomes saline, and plants start to die. Salinity due to overfeeding of plants is a relatively common occurrence, thanks to the misguided belief that if some is good, then more is better.

To measure the salinity in the soil, we can make use of an interesting scientific phenomenon: pure water does not conduct electricity, but salty water does, and the higher the salt content, the higher the conductivity.

OPPOSITE When spreading lime over soil, note that one standard cupful equates to about 300 grams.

These days, there are inexpensive handheld electrical conductivity (EC) meters available that will measure the amount of soluble salt in water extracted from your soil. We highly recommend one if you have a commercial operation, especially with a hydroponic set-up.

Low conductivities equate to low total salt levels, which means that there is little nutrition in the soil. High conductivities mean that there are excessive salts in the soil. This may be due to the presence of common salt (sodium chloride), or the overenthusiastic application of fertilisers when poor plant growth is blamed on low soil fertility. Soil purchased from commercial centres commonly has too much compost, and is therefore quite saline.

In urban farms with good drainage and good-quality water, salinity is rarely a problem. However, the issue can arise when:

- poor-quality water such as bore water is used – we should always get the water tested in a new growing situation
- capillary or 'wick' watering is used – this is because we are operating in a 'closed system' where it is difficult or impossible to flush excess salts from the soil

- overfertilisation has occurred – it is always crucial to ensure that you are using fertilisers at an appropriate strength, whether they are mineral or organic in nature.

In summary, measuring the amount of salts in your soil is just as important as measuring the soil pH. A low-salinity reading is a sure indication that your plants are hungry and are almost certain to respond to an appropriate dose of fertiliser. On the other hand, if you have high salinity, then you need to take action in the form of heavy watering to wash the excess salts away.

ABOVE LEFT Commercial composts can be quite high in salts, so always ask for a nutrient analysis.

ABOVE Most vegetables, such as cabbages and parsnips, are salt sensitive and suffer if the salinity level is too high.

URBAN SOILS

As it turns out, cities are particularly conducive to plant life because of the incidental nutrients that are provided by simply being in an urban environment. The atmosphere is enriched with nitrogen, carbon and sulphur; soils are often enhanced with phosphorus and calcium; the pH levels are usually higher (the soils are less acid); and the important micronutrients zinc, copper and boron are available from a variety of sources. However, poor management choices and overzealous fertiliser use on urban farms can lead to soil chemistry imbalances. The Symptoms of Soil Chemistry Imbalances table on page 102 details some of the most common imbalances and their cures.

While nutrient deficiencies are usually the most frequently encountered problems with overworked urban soils, past practices can sometimes lead to nutrient excesses. The three elements most likely to accumulate to undesirable levels in urban soils are phosphorus, calcium and zinc.

♦ **Phosphorus** Because some organic fertilisers, such as poultry manure-based products, contain high levels of phosphorus, and because it adheres strongly to certain soil minerals (such as iron minerals) and does not leach (in other words, it cannot be washed out of the soil with either rainfall or irrigation), phosphorus often accumulates to exceptionally high levels in overused and urban soils. This is a problem, because phosphorus 'fixes' or reduces the solubility of – and therefore the availability to plants of – important micronutrients such as iron and manganese.

♦ **Calcium** Because there is so much concrete, lime and cement in urban environments, run-off from these surfaces contains large amounts of calcium; once it reaches the soil, this calcium does not leach easily and can sometimes accumulate to excessive levels. The other source of surplus calcium is urban farmers following well-meaning advice from gardening books and putting lime on legumes at planting. So, every year you apply lime to your garden, and eventually you end up with

inordinate amounts of calcium in the soil, which makes it alkaline.

♦ **Zinc** This essential micronutrient is, unfortunately, very commonly used in urban environments. It is present on galvanised objects (roofs and gutters), in car tyres (up to 2 per cent by weight) and in many metal items. Feedlot cow manure is often contaminated with zinc, as feedlotters have the mistaken view that very high levels of zinc are good for cattle. Thus, run-off from roads, roofs and many organic fertilisers has elevated zinc levels. After many years, this zinc accumulates in soil, largely because it does not leach quickly. High levels of zinc can be toxic to some plants.

Pollution in urban soils

Although the dangers of pollution in urban soils are perhaps not as great as some would have us believe, there are a few potentially harmful contaminants of which we need to be aware. First, it is important to understand the three principles that determine the toxicity of an element in an urban farming context:

1 It is harmful to mammals (that's you and me). Some metals (such as lead and mercury) are quite toxic, while others (such as zinc and copper) are of no real concern.
2 It is harmful when taken up by plants (not all toxic elements are taken up by plants; we can manipulate the situation if this occurs).
3 It is deposited on the outside of the edible portion (leaf or root) as dirt or dust and is dangerous when directly ingested.

Let's consider the most likely contaminants to cause problems for either people or plants.

♦ **Zinc** As discussed earlier, zinc is the 'heavy' metal element most likely to be elevated in urban soil. Since it is not toxic to mammals in any conceivable amount, it is of no concern to human health. It does impact on plants, however, because many species will absorb significant amounts, and it can poison them. While it is an essential element – or perhaps because it is an essential element – an excess of it will antagonise the uptake of other elements, such as copper, causing deficiencies of these elements. In some very old urban soils (for example, around historic houses), the zinc level is now so high that any seedlings planted there are severely injured – with symptoms including yellowing, stunting and deformity – or even killed.

♦ **Copper** Many of the objects we use in irrigation and urban water supply are made of copper or brass (an alloy of copper and zinc), so soils can easily become contaminated with copper. Old orchards where 'bluestone' (copper sulphate) was used as a fungicide can also show elevated levels. Copper, like zinc, is not toxic to humans in almost any conceivable amount, but it can cause toxicity in plants. The main symptom of copper toxicity is the bleaching of the old leaf tissue between the leaf veins.

♦ **Lead** This is the second most likely element to be elevated in urban soil, thanks to lead having been used in petrol, old paint, roof flashings and batteries. It is taken up by some plants, is present in dust and is poisonous to mammals. Lead is not very poisonous to plants, which

SYMPTOMS OF SOIL CHEMISTRY IMBALANCES

SYMPTOMS	LIKELY CAUSES	CURE
Plant is spindly, weak and yellowish; older leaves drop early	Usually nitrogen deficiency; less commonly sulphur deficiency	Apply chicken manure, high-nitrogen compost or nitrogen fertiliser
Youngest leaves are yellowish, especially during growth spurts	Usually iron and manganese deficiency; less commonly zinc and copper deficiency; sometimes toxic levels of zinc	Identify the deficiency, then correct with soil applications or foliar sprays of appropriate chelated elements
Margins of the leaves are burned	Salt burn; ammonia burn; fertiliser burn	Deeply water the plant to clean leaves and leach salts from soil
Yellowish margin to leaves, with leaf tips burned; worse in older leaves; poor fruit set	Potassium deficiency	Apply potassium-rich compost or sulphate of potash
Growing tips and leaf margins distort, yellow and then blacken	Calcium deficiency	Apply lime (if soil is acid), or gypsum if it is not

explains why very high levels – in excess of 1000 milligrams per kilogram (normal soils have around 10–30 milligrams per kilogram) – are needed to cause any problems for plants. However, it is the most common toxic element to cause problems for humans, especially children. Fortunately, poisoning does not usually result from eating the produce of urban farming, but from ingesting contaminated dust. Little children, for example, often put odd things in their mouth (such as soil), and this can be an issue if they play in inner-city backyards where the lead from old plumbing and paint has made its way into the soil. If you are on a main road, lead levels can be elevated in soils because of years of lead-contaminated vehicle exhausts. Lead has been removed from modern fuels, but it should be considered from a historical context.

🌢 **Arsenic** This can accumulate in urban soils affected by industrial pollution. Arsenic was used as a termite and insect killer in the old days, so it may still be encountered around old houses and stock dipping pens. We have seen seaweed products being sold for their soil health benefits, but they contain a very high proportion of arsenic at levels likely to cause toxicity in humans. Not all seaweed is high in arsenic, but some is, so it is highly

BONUS NUTRIENTS IN URBAN SOILS

Contrary to popular opinion, various discharges and incidental substances in urban environments can be quite beneficial to plants, as they offer extra nutrition. Oxides of nitrogen in the atmosphere are rapidly converted to valuable nitrate within both the plant and the soil, while sulphur dioxide from smelters and diesel emissions quickly becomes soil sulphates that are a source of sulphur for plant growth.

ABOVE LEFT Even today, soils located next to major roads may be contaminated with lead, thanks to decades of exposure to the exhausts of vehicles run on leaded petrol.

ABOVE Be very careful of toxic dust settling on the edible leaves of plants, such as parsley. Always wash your farm produce well.

desirable to see an analysis of any seaweed products you might use on your soil.

♠ **Cadmium** Toxicity is unknown in plants, and very rare in animals. When cadmium toxicity does occur, it is quite dangerous to humans as it accumulates in the bones over time. Cadmium appears in rock phosphate deposits, and the older forms of phosphorus fertiliser had restrictions placed on them regarding how much cadmium they could contain. Today most forms of phosphorus fertiliser are safe.

♠ **Nickel** The most common source of nickel is the metal industry, where it is used in alloys and for plating metals. While certain enzymes need nickel, an excessive amount of it interferes with the metabolism of other metals, such as manganese and zinc, reducing plant growth. In animals, nickel inhibits certain enzyme and hormone pathways, but fortunately it is not readily absorbed and is rapidly excreted, so toxicity is very rare.

♠ **Mercury** Toxicity in plants is almost unknown. When it occurs in mammals, the mercury does not usually come from plants grown in soil. Mercury problems are far more likely to arise from consuming contaminated seafood. Plants will take up mercury from soils, but less readily from well-aerated, iron-rich and lime-rich soils. Fortunately, the main cause of elevated mercury levels in soils and plants – the use of mercuric fungicides – has now been completely banned.

Golden rules to follow

Keep in mind that soils in urban areas are not always natural, and they may have been radically altered from their natural state. Research the history of the area if you can. If your site was once part of an industrial development, or is an old inner-city housing area, it pays to have your soil analysed in depth by professionals.

If your soil is significantly elevated in any of the elements toxic to humans (lead, cadmium, mercury, arsenic and nickel), take the following precautions:

- Always wash your hands after gardening; if the conditions are dry and dusty, wear a protective dust mask while working in the garden. Dust and dirt are a more likely source of contamination than eating the produce from your garden. Don't let children play in the dirt if it is high in lead.
- Always wash your produce to remove any potentially contaminated dust from it before you consume it.
- Lime your soil to increase the pH to above 6.5. Contaminant metals are more soluble in acid soils, so liming reduces their uptake by plants.
- Ensure that the soil has plenty of organic matter, as this 'chelates' or locks up the contaminant metals.

ABOVE In heavily built-up urban areas, it is strongly advised to have soil-contaminant testing done. For larger communal urban farms, testing for nutrients is also useful.

- Make sure there is plenty of phosphorus in the soil. The phosphates of these contaminant metals are insoluble, and this will also lock them up chemically.
- If your soil is moderately elevated in metallic contaminants, it may be best to avoid root crops such as potatoes. These are in direct contact with the soil, and the metals can accumulate in the edible part, particularly in the epidermis or 'skin' of the tuber. If you really want to grow them, then always peel your root crops. This will get rid of most of the contamination.
- If your soil is really elevated, not only consider not growing root vegetables, but also don't consume too many leaf vegetables, particularly silverbeet or spinach, which are known accumulators. Grow fruit-like vegetables such as tomatoes and eggplants, or fruit trees. The developing fruits are each protected by a structure similar to a placenta, which largely prevents toxic elements from getting into the fruits and future seeds. Fruits are perfectly healthy to eat even when grown in quite high contaminant levels.
- If your soil is very highly contaminated with the dangerous metals mercury, cadmium, arsenic and lead, consider soil replacement. These metals cannot be removed from soil, and replacement is the only option. This applies to zinc and copper, too, as they are toxic to plants.
- Using raised garden beds with a growing medium that you have created yourself is a sure-fire way to avoid any issues with contaminants. There are also some ingenious proprietary growing systems available to urban farmers that completely circumvent problems with pollution.

Contamination should not be a problem where soils and growing media are purchased from reputable commercial suppliers, but don't take this for granted – some manufacturers recycle soils from skip bins and construction sites, so always ask for an analysis. Alternatively, make your own growing medium from ingredients you know to be free of contaminants (see Constructing Beds and Plots, pages 106–31).

PROFESSIONAL SOIL TESTING

There are soil-testing laboratories in every state, and an internet search for soil-testing services should locate one that can give you the analysis you need. Be warned: it can be quite expensive, and should be considered only when all the simple and obvious problems such as pH, drainage and disease have been discounted, or if you suspect that your soil has substantial levels of elements that are poisonous to humans.

ABOVE Fruits are usually quite strongly protected from moderate levels of soil contaminants.

CONSTRUCTING BEDS AND PLOTS 6

PERFECT PLACES TO GROW YOUR PLANTS

Urban-farming plots will use anything from natural soil profiles to hydroponic culture in pipes and gutters without any soil whatsoever. Where natural soil is available, this is usually the lowest-cost alternative, but in rooftop or balcony areas this is obviously not an option. Saving space and protecting young plants are also important considerations, so this is where green walls and greenhouses come into play. Regardless of the size of your urban farm, there is always a way to create efficient and productive garden beds or plots that receive the perfect amount of sunlight and nutrients for plant growth.

USING NATURAL SOIL

Examine your soil profile to a depth of at least 500 millimetres. While the usual rooting depth of crops is seldom more than 300 millimetres, you need to know if there are clay layers or hard pans (for example, a rock seam) that might interfere with drainage. Make a note of the colours, textures and structures you encounter in each horizon as you dig down. A dark, loamy topsoil overlying a well-structured clay subsoil (bright red or orange in colour) with no signs of impeded drainage is ideal.

If you find very hard layers, you will have to think about an initial cultivation to loosen the soil to at least 200 millimetres. If your testing shows that the soil also needs some conditioners (lime, dolomite or iron sulphate to adjust the pH level, or gypsum to 'break' the clay) and initial fertilisers (to increase the level of phosphorus or potassium), add these to the surface first, and then work them in to depth. For big urban farms, it certainly pays to hire or borrow a cultivator (a tractor for large areas, or a walk-behind mechanical hoe for medium-sized areas). For smaller areas, forking is the best way to add conditioners and fertilisers to the soil (and it's good exercise!).

If you need to increase organic-matter levels, add some compost. Apply a 20–50-millimetre layer of either homemade or commercial

LEFT Plants are traditionally grown in the ground, but today there are many choices when it comes to planting places, from raised beds to soil-less hydroponic set-ups.

OPPOSITE Vertical gardens are often called green walls. They are becoming increasingly popular for urban farms with little horizontal space.

compost to the top of the soil – along with the other conditioners that may be required – and work the material into the soil to a depth of 200 millimetres. If you don't want to do any digging, or your soil doesn't need loosening up, then just leave the compost for the worms and other soil organisms to do their job. This will be much slower, but will eventually achieve the same aim.

Sand and clay

With extremely sandy soils, organic matter is certainly helpful – but adding some clay will also improve water- and nutrient-holding capacity. Using purchased bentonite clay or another clayey soil, apply it to a depth of about 10 millimetres and work it in to 200 millimetres. You have to work it in, as leaving it on the surface will cause crusting and water run-off.

If you have a light topsoil that is dominated by sand, and a heavy clay subsoil, then it is a good idea to turn over the soil to mix it up a

LEFT To ensure you have healthy crops, it is vitally important to use a suitable growing medium as the foundation for your garden bed.

bit so there is not such a contrast in texture between the two soil horizons. If there are indications of poor drainage (for example, white or poorly structured clay, or obvious soil wetness), then you will need to think about improving the drainage. See the Water and Drainage chapter (pages 212–27) for more information.

COMMERCIAL SOILS

There are soil yards in most urban centres that will supply soil for making gardens where needed. Often the manufacturers of soil also run composting systems using locally available garden or yard waste and other organic and solid wastes from industry.

Commercial soils vary greatly in quality. There are some good and reliable products, and others where the manufacturer has not done the proper product-development work to get the soil right. Some are downright toxic to plants. In our consulting and laboratory-analysis work, we see a few major problems that you need to be aware of when purchasing commercial soils.

♦ **Poor structure** Commercial soils have very little to no structure. This makes them potentially poorly drained and subject to low aeration. They will develop structure with time, but make sure subsoil drainage is excellent or the raised bed is at least 500 millimetres high, or the soils can tend to become waterlogged.

♦ **Too much compost** Organic-matter levels in commercial soils are often very high – in fact, higher than they need to be or should be. This is because good mineral soil is hard to get as an ingredient, so manufacturers tend to incorporate plenty of compost in their soils. We have seen 'soil' that is 95 per cent compost and so high in nutrients that it is actually saline and acutely toxic to plants. About 40 per cent compost by volume is as high as you would want to go, and 30 per cent is a more sensible limit if the compost is rich. A high level of organic matter combined with poor drainage capacity causes anaerobic conditions if the soil gets wet at depth. Ideally, do not use organic-rich soil any deeper than 250 millimetres. If your garden or raised beds are deeper than

this, use a sandy, well-drained, low-organic mix beneath the organic-rich soil. Ask the producer how much organic matter they have put into their mix. If it's any more than around 40 per cent, it is probably best avoided.

♦ **Too much manure** Many soil manufacturers think that if some is good, more is better – so their soils feature up to 20 per cent poultry manure or cow manure when 5–10 per cent would provide perfectly adequate fertility levels. I had a gardener once who lost everything except tomatoes and capsicums when they planted a vegetable garden in a commercial soil. (Tomatoes and capsicums are very tolerant of salt and ammonia, which is why they survived in a mix that was around 20 per cent manure.) Manufacturers that analyse their products in a laboratory and can provide test certificates, or those that have demonstration plots of their products at the yard, are more trustworthy, but do obtain a statement of how much manure is in the mix if you can. If it's any more than 10 per cent, then ask if you can have a sample and do a germination test.

♦ **Alkaline soil** Lime from cement and mortar is everywhere in urban areas, and it is also prevalent in marine deposits that are often mined as sand. Soils from building and construction areas are often screened and sold as commercial soils, and these are always high in lime and gypsum from plasterboard. Unfortunately, there is so much lime (5–10 per cent) in these soils, they cannot be acidified in an economic way. Iron-inefficient (acid-loving) plants cannot be grown in these alkaline soils, so it's a good idea to always do a pH test on commercial soils (see Testing the pH of Your Soil on page 95). You can also do a lime test. Place some of the soil in a diluted acid, such as one part hydrochloric acid (sold as swimming-pool acid) and five parts water. If it fizzes, then the soil is probably more trouble than it's worth. Note that strong acid can burn the skin and eyes, so always wear rubber gloves and eye protection when diluting acids. Vinegar is a weaker acid that will work in a pinch, but don't dilute it; look carefully after the soil has been added, because the fizz reaction is not so strong as with mineral acid.

ABOVE Rooftop gardening demands a premium growing medium, especially given the large investment of time and money that is necessary to create and maintain the garden beds.

DISCOVER NO-DIG GARDENS

LEFT No-dig gardens can be set up anywhere you like – just ensure that the plants growing in the bed have access to enough full sunlight.

Where a site has no useful soil, there is an insufficient depth of soil or the plot is on a constructed surface, such as a concrete slab or roof, it will be necessary to construct a soil profile. A very simple and effective constructed soil is a system called the 'no-dig garden', developed by Australian gardener Esther Deans in the 1970s.

In a no-dig garden, an edge – which is usually made of timber – is constructed, and then a thick blanket of newspaper is laid down on the existing soil to suppress weeds. The newspaper is covered with alternating layers of manure, organic fertiliser, straw and compost. Little holes are made in the growing-medium 'sandwich', into which are placed handfuls of compost followed by the seeds or seedlings. As the name suggests, there is no need to dig the garden bed – effectively, earthworms do the digging for you. Over time, the soil beneath is enriched and the organic matter is incorporated. Straw and compost are added regularly to top up the level as the 'soil' breaks down.

No-dig gardens are useful for placing over existing soils that are compacted or otherwise infertile. In addition, they can be used over a constructed surface such as a concrete slab if the garden bed is 300–500 millimetres in depth.

MAKING RAISED BEDS

Creating raised beds is a great way to control the fertility and drainage capacity of your growing medium, and you can make sure that the beds are located in places where they will receive optimum sunlight levels. If you are making raised beds on soil (rather than sowing plants directly into the ground), ideally they will be at least 300 millimetres deep.

When raised beds are placed not on soil but on rooftops, concrete slabs, compacted fill or some other impermeable material, then they need to be at least 500 millimetres deep. If the beds are any deeper than this, then adequate drainage can become a major problem – there is always a 'wet' zone in deep beds following rain or irrigation. To solve this issue, place at least 200 millimetres of a low-organic and freely draining sandy medium in the bottom of the bed – a coarse layer will help keep plant roots happy.

Where raised beds are 300 millimetres or shallower – such as container plantings – using soil as your growing medium is not a great idea. There are three reasons soil cannot be utilised in these situations:

1 Soil becomes waterlogged very easily in shallow containers and pots. These types of raised beds require a growing medium with more porosity than soil and which includes coarse particulate matter such as pine bark, ash and perlite. Look at any modern potting mix, and you will see how open it is compared to soil.

2 Shallow beds need to retain some – but not all – water. Soil-less growing media such as peat moss are ideal because of the suitable water-holding ability of these natural materials.

3 Soil can become compacted and heavy in shallow raised beds. However, containers often need to be lightweight, especially when they are located on rooftops or must be moved – so a lighter growing medium is preferable.

Creating raised beds is a great way to control the fertility and drainage capacity of your growing medium.

OPPOSITE, RIGHT
One big advantage of raised beds is that you do not have to bend down as far to cultivate the bed or harvest your crops.

ABOVE Raised beds can be made from a variety of materials, such as corrugated iron or stone, but timber creates a solid, cost-effective and aesthetic option.

OPPOSITE Plants will thrive in a raised bed if the growing medium is well drained. If the bed is on soil, it is also a good idea to ensure that it is no shallower than 300 millimetres.

For best results, you must utilise a very open and porous medium such as potting mix. One that incorporates ash, sand and compost works well and does not lose its structure. If you use a pure organic potting mix, remember that it will lose volume with time as the coarse particles decay. The bed will need regular topping up with potting mix as this shrinkage occurs.

Soil-less growing media

When it comes to soil-less growing media, there are many different choices. The Soil-less Media Options table on page 116 lists the properties of some of the most common materials used to make growing media that are highly porous yet hold water well.

Clever concoctions

For a lightweight growing medium that has a longevity of up to five years – making it useful for containers located on balconies and rooftops – a good mix of components would be:

- a premium-grade commercial potting mix (20 per cent by volume)
- vermicompost or garden compost (20 per cent by volume)
- sand (20 per cent by volume)
- perlite (coarse grade) or horticultural ash (40 per cent by volume).

Such a mix would usually not need any lime or other conditioning agent, as the compost

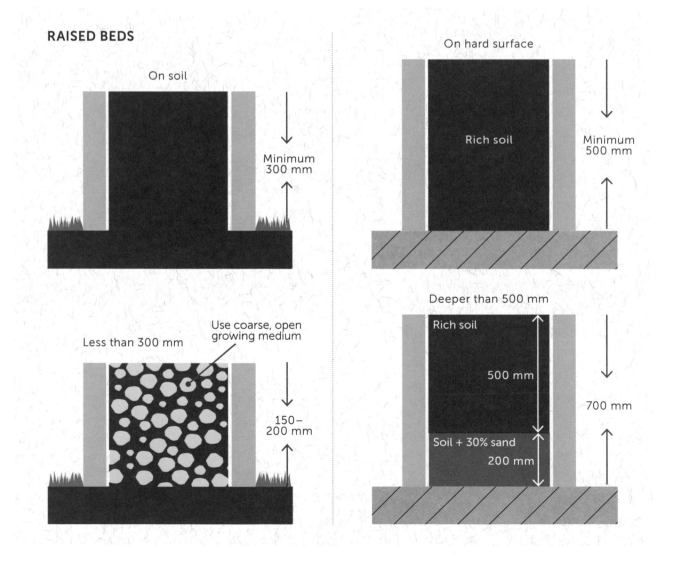

RAISED BEDS

On soil

Minimum 300 mm

Less than 300 mm

Use coarse, open growing medium

150–200 mm

On hard surface

Rich soil

Minimum 500 mm

Deeper than 500 mm

Rich soil

500 mm

Soil + 30% sand

200 mm

700 mm

SOIL-LESS MEDIA OPTIONS

MATERIAL	DESCRIPTION	BENEFITS AND ISSUES
Composted pine-bark fines	Usually the less than 12-mm fraction of composted plantation pine	Lightweight, high water-holding capacity, medium cost
Composted coarse pine bark	Usually the 12–20-mm fraction of composted plantation pine	Lightweight, very high porosity, poor water-holding capacity, medium cost
Composted sawdust	Composted sawdust from timber sawmills	Lightweight, high water-holding capacity, high nitrogen drawdown, medium cost
Coarse sand	A sand predominantly in the 0.5–2-mm size range	Heavyweight, poor water-holding capacity, good aeration and root anchorage, high longevity (years), coarse and abrasive, low cost
Boiler ash, washed and screened, or power station bottom ash	Coarse fused mineral material from high-temperature combustion of coal	Lightweight, reasonable water-holding capacity, high longevity (years), coarse and abrasive, low cost
Perlite	Fused aerated silica balls	Very lightweight, very high water-holding capacity, high longevity (several years), high cost
Pumice and scoria	Aerated volcanic extrusion	Variously lightweight, high water-holding capacity, high longevity (many years), not readily available, high cost
Diatomaceous earth	Fossilised siliceous skeletons of diatoms laid down in almost pure beds	Very lightweight, excellent water-holding capacity and longevity, high cost
Composted garden-waste fines	Council collection yard or garden waste that is chipped, composted and screened into compost fines and mulch fractions	Good nutrient content, high water-holding capacity, readily available, poor aeration, low cost
Coconut coir	The pith surrounding the shell of the coconut, milled into various-sized fractions (usually around 2 mm)	Very lightweight, excellent water-holding capacity, reasonable longevity (two years), high cost
Peat moss	Preserved remains of plants growing in saturated environments	Very low density, high water-holding capacity, high cost
Vermiculite	Expanded mica clay	High cation and water-holding capacity, high cost
Plastic foams	Expanded balls of either polystyrene (Styrofoam) or phenol formaldehydes	Very lightweight, Styrofoam is inert but formaldehyde foams hold water, low cost if recycled
Zeolites	Hard aluminosilicate clays	Good cation and water-holding capacity, high cost
'Soil'*	Usually comprises mined alluvium from river terraces	Provides mass and water-holding capacity, poor aeration, low cost

*Note: The 'soil' we obtain commercially is quarried soil-like material and not actually real topsoil, so it is still technically a soil-less medium.

provides a balance of all the required nutrients. However, because they just don't have the acid-buffering capacity of natural soils, artificial mixes such as the one detailed on page 114 can quickly change their pH level. A pH check should be performed at least once a year, and a lime/dolomite mix applied if the pH measures 5.5 or less. Otherwise, there is no reason why artificial mixes should not last many years and maintain good porosity.

There is an almost infinite array of potting mixes that you can create as soil substitutes. One that is widely used in the United States is equal parts peat moss, good-quality compost and vermiculite. This is a relatively expensive option, but it will certainly give excellent results. By studying the Soil-less Media Options table on the opposite page, we can work out which materials will perform the specific functions we require of growing media, such as water holding, nutrient storage, aeration and being lightweight. If we have a ready supply of ingredients (preferably free ones), such as compost, we can then experiment and create our own 'home brews'. This not only saves us money, but also allows for recycling of household organic materials. When designing artificial soils for constructed gardens, remember the golden rule: the shallower the bed, the more open and porous the mix must be.

LOOKING AT THE FUTURE OF SMALL-SPACE GROWING

As a species, humans have always been incredibly inventive and agile when our survival depends on it. Hence, we predict the emergence of all sorts of flexible and adaptable technologies for growing and fertilising plants in smaller and smaller spaces. A recent innovation that is available for purchase is an Australian-made growing system called Composta, which enables us to utilise any extremely small space (such as on rooftops or balconies) for growing food in the urban farm.

An excellent solution for inner-city urban farmers, Composta comprises a large bowl of potting mix with a cylindrical worm farm embedded in the centre. The cylinder has holes at its base that remain covered with potting mix at all times – this means that the worms can move easily between the worm farm and the potting mix, distributing nutrients and beneficial microbes (which they produce whenever they feed) as they go. The bowl has a single large hole that not only drains the unit, but also allows you to collect the liquid that leaves the system. This drainage liquid is still rich in nutrients and can be used to fertilise other plants on your urban farm.

FAR LEFT Perlite is a soil-less media option that offers a lightweight way of improving drainage in growing media as an alternative to coarse sand.

BELOW LEFT A clever idea for an apartment balcony, Composta is a worm farm that transforms kitchen scraps into useful fertiliser for plants growing in it.

NEXT PAGES, LEFT Containers of any size can be used on the urban farm, as long as you're mindful of the drainage capacity and fertility of the growing medium you place in them.

NEXT PAGES, RIGHT It's handy to grow herbs in pots or a raised bed close to the kitchen, so you can access them quickly and easily when cooking.

CASE STUDY: RAISED BEDS

Helene's Garden at Berowra

Helene moved from inner-city Sydney because the gardens there were not big enough to cater for her aspiration of growing all her own vegetables and fruits, and owning chickens that would supply her with eggs. Her father was an agronomist from Russia, and this initially sparked her interest in food-plant growing when she was young.

Because the soil is so thin and poor on the sandstone ridges around Sydney, she decided to go with raised beds, including water tank-type planters, timber-edged beds, old wine barrels cut in half and borders against the house. The 'soil' in her planters originally comprised purchased potting mix, but it is now entirely made up of her own compost. She has three large compost heaps that were constructed from landscape sleepers by her WWOOFer (Willing Workers on Organic Farms) friends. She still hosts WWOOFers from Europe, Japan and Australia to this day.

Helene is now pretty much self-sufficient in vegetables; the only thing she buys is lettuce. She has stone fruit, mango and persimmon trees and passionfruit vines for fruit production, but is thinking of pulling out the stone fruit trees due to a persistent fruit fly problem as well as the lack of 'chill factor' in the suburbs these days, which results in poor fruiting. To deal with pests, Helene uses the herb tansy to repel flies and leaf-eating insects, traps to catch fruit flies, and occasionally a little pyrethrum spray. She physically nets the mangoes to prevent damage from fruit flies and possums, believing that such large fruits are worth the effort.

After noticing pale leaves on her plants, we tested her soil and leaf tissue and worked out that she had an inadequate level of manganese in her garden. Sandstone soils are notoriously low in manganese, so we recommended she use some manganese sulphate to correct the deficiency.

The raised beds help prevent damage from the chooks that roam at will during the day. She has four Buff Orpingtons, one Black Orpington and one ISA Brown that provide all the eggs she and her WWOOFer visitors need. She often has extra eggs and vegetables that she gives away to friends or takes to the local market.

CLOCKWISE, FROM OPPOSITE TOP
Corrugated iron beds are a cost-effective alternative to timber; half wine barrels and railway sleepers are more traditional ways of creating raised beds; this ISA Brown hen helps keeps the weeds down between Helene's beds; sweet potato is a great crop to grow in raised beds, if it is given room to move; Helene learned farming skills from her father; virtually every space in the garden is devoted to food production; fruit trees are grown in sunny corners of the garden.

GROWING IN BAGS OR BOXES

A system being adopted more and more in the commercial production of vegetables and cut flowers is where plants are grown in a 'semi-hydroponic' way; this is particularly suited to trellis crops such as cucumber. Seedlings are planted in 25-litre bags of potting mix that have the top cut open and holes pierced in the bottom. Some people use Styrofoam boxes filled with potting mix. Seedlings grow and develop on trellises, and are nourished by liquid feeds that are virtually identical to hydroponic feeds. Controlled-release fertilisers can also be used as a base in the growing medium.

The nutrient solution does not need to be recycled continuously, and it can be alternated with irrigation water. The good water-holding capacity of the potting mix means that plants don't die if the pumps fail, unlike with hydroponic crops. Bags can be re-used for up to five crop cycles before the structure of the potting mix collapses; hygiene and weed problems are much easier to control than when planting in natural soil.

Hydroponics uses a recirculating ... solution designed to provide all the nourishment that the plants need.

HYDROPONICS

Essentially the science of growing plants without soil, hydroponics uses a recirculating nutrient solution designed to provide all the nourishment that the plants need. Conventionally it utilises refined soluble mineral fertilisers, as their composition is known and the balance of essential nutrients can be precisely calculated to suit plant needs. It is possible to make organic nutrient solutions, but several problems must be overcome.

- Organic sources of nutrients, such as manure, blood and bone, fishmeal, and hoof and horn, are not soluble, so they have to be 'steeped' in water for some time, usually a week or so. Essentially, this means they decompose anaerobically – which can lead to odour issues.
- Blockages can occur if any undissolved organic matter is not filtered out.
- Organic materials have a variable composition, and some, such as wood ash as a source of potassium, are not easy to obtain. Often this means supplementing or 'topping up' your solution with purchased synthetics.

That being said, it is not really difficult to grow plants hydroponically and organically at the same time. If we look at Angus' worm 'wee' on pages 196–7, for example, this is very close to an ideal hydroponic feed. By steeping it with just a little poultry manure to boost the nitrogen content, an excellent balance of nutrients

ABOVE The dark hue of the mustard greens plants sits in striking contrast to the white PVC pipes used in hydroponic production.

LEFT This 'grow bag' utilises perlite as the growing medium to create a lightweight system ideal for rooftops and courtyards.

would result. Another terrific hydroponic feed is a nutrient solution created from quality, balanced compost. The advantage of compost and vermicast (compost made by worms) is that the nutrients have already been largely solubilised for hydroponic feeding.

Solution management

There are two methods of solution delivery used in hydroponic systems: run-to-waste and recycling. In run-to-waste, as the name suggests, the solution is passed through the system once only, with sufficient time for the plants to (hopefully) take up most of the nutrients. This method is very wasteful and causes significant water-pollution events if regulations are lax. Even with the best-balanced feed, the plants will take up what they need and leave significant quantities of nutrients in the remaining solution.

More common – and much less wasteful – is recycling, whereby the solution is passed through the hydroponic system many times, with a top-up of fertiliser at regular intervals to maintain the strength of the solution. Ultimately, however, even when using this method the solution becomes imbalanced and accumulates undesirable salts such as sodium, so it eventually needs to be 'dumped' and made afresh.

Hydroponic systems should always be managed so that the waste solutions and their nutrients are beneficially re-used, for example on neighbouring pasture, gardens or even tree crops. The solutions should never be discharged into dams, rivers or streams, where they will foul the water and kill aquatic life. This is one of the principal problems in countries where regulations are insufficient to prevent such irresponsible behaviour.

'Soil' for hydroponics

In practice, hydroponics uses some kind of mechanism to support the plant. This ranges from thin film – essentially a gutter that the hydroponic solution runs along; roots grow in the continuously wet bottom of the gutter – to artificial media such as Rockwool®, which is spun silica fibre. One of the most successful systems I have seen was roses for cut flowers growing in 20-litre drums brimming with 10-millimetre blue metal or rock aggregate, through which a hydroponic solution was cycled. With the high porosity and access to air, the root systems were fabulous showers of white roots disappearing into the bluish stones – a perfect combination of aeration, water and available nutrients.

Regardless of the type of 'soil' used, the fundamental requirement of hydroponic systems is to provide sufficient aeration to the root zone. Even short periods of stagnation and less-than-perfect aeration results in fungal-disease invasion and eventually root death. Mushy roots that are dark or black are the first indication of damping off and other root diseases.

AQUAPONICS

When raising fish is integrated with urban farming, it is known as aquaponics. This system is being used increasingly across the world, but one of the big problems with fish farming is the large amount of nutrient-polluted water that fish produce as waste. This wastewater is an ideal nutrient solution for crop growing, as one of the main reasons fish farmers have to change the water is the accumulation of nitrogen waste (urea and uric acid), which is poisonous to fish. It might be poisonous to the fish, but plants love it!

In one system we have seen, the polluted water is carried into aerated ponds that have floating Styrofoam trays planted with lettuce and other seedlings. The farmers find that little if any additional fertiliser is needed, as the polluted water full of fish excretions is sufficient to grow plants to a saleable stage. Lettuce and other fast-turnover leaf crops with a high-nitrogen requirement are their main crops.

There is no reason why the polluted water from a fish-farming set-up could not simply be used as irrigation water either in a hydroponic system – where the wastewater is run through conventional gutters – or in troughs, where the plants are grown in conventional soil or an artificial medium. Fish-farming itself is quite a skilled activity and requires plenty of knowledge and experience. Re-use of the water from fish farming would likely be far less demanding than producing the wastewater in the first place.

CASE STUDY: THE DUTCH SOLUTION

A formula for a nutrient solution that has long been used by Dutch growers is known as the 'Netherlands Standard Composition', and is shown in the table below. There are many other variations, and the internet is full of recipes, both mineral and organic.

NETHERLANDS STANDARD COMPOSITION

FERTILISER SALT	GRAMS PER 1000 LITRES	GRAMS PER 200 LITRES
Dipotassium phosphate (K_2HPO_4)	136	27.2
Calcium nitrate ($CaNO_3$)	1062	212.4
Magnesium sulphate ($MgSO_4.7H_2O$)	492	98.4
Potassium nitrate (KNO_3)	293	58.6
Potassium sulphate (K_2SO_4)	252	50.4
Potassium hydroxide (KOH)	22.4	4.5
Chelated trace element mixture (Fe, Mn, Zn, Cu, B, Mo)	6	1.2

A standard 1000-litre container used by the food industry is ideal for making this solution, and it can be obtained second-hand quite cheaply. Another convenient vessel is a 200-litre olive drum or food-grade drum.

To make 1000 litres of solution, dissolve the dipotassium phosphate separately in about 50 litres of water, and then dissolve the other fertiliser salts all together in about 900 litres of water. When fully dissolved, slowly pour the dipotassium phosphate solution into the 900 litres of fertiliser solution while vigorously stirring the mixture. This is to prevent precipitation of calcium phosphate. To make 200 litres, simply scale down the amounts as shown in the table.

A variation on this occurs when concentrated solutions are made up. An 'A' tank holds the dissolved dipotassium phosphate, while a 'B' tank contains the rest of the nutrients. Each of these solutions is then diluted to its correct strength before the two are carefully mixed together, to avoid the calcium phosphate precipitation problem. Such systems are the most common in large commercial production.

GREEN WALLS

In the very confined spaces of inner-city environments, sometimes walls are the only spaces available – located away from traffic and pedestrians – with the right aspect and levels of sunlight to grow plants. While the original concept for green walls was to provide an insulating and evaporative cooling system for buildings, there is no reason they could not be used for growing food.

Commercial green-wall systems can be quite costly, but with a little ingenuity they can be made by anyone with average construction skills and some common tools. In principle they use a rack system like shelves, some kind of container to hold the growing medium and some kind of irrigation/liquid-feeding system. For more detailed information on how to construct a green wall, see the step-by-step instructions within the Vertical Food Garden section on pages 128–9.

Capitalise on your green wall

Generally, green-wall systems are best for herbs and smaller plants such as chives, garnish-type crops and perennial forms of leaf crops, such as small-leaf forms of lettuce and rocket. However, smaller fruiting vegetables such as capsicums, cherry tomatoes, cape gooseberries and chillies can be planted in larger bottles.

Always have more bottles or pots on hand than are immediately needed to fill the wall, as some will be rotated to the propagating area to be replanted – and you don't want to see gaps. Most green walls can be watered by hand, but it is best to install an irrigation system for taller green walls. This can either involve drippers to each bottle/pot, or semicircular sprayers projecting out from the wall at intervals, with the sprayers directed backwards towards the plants. An inexpensive irrigation timer saves a lot of work, and it can be adjusted according to the seasonal conditions.

ABOVE LEFT Many green-wall systems are based on wide plastic containers like these, which can hold a lot of different plants.

ABOVE Corrugated iron gutters make for an innovative vertical strawberry garden – painting them red is very eye-catching!

OPPOSITE, LEFT Ideally, green-waste compost should form no more than 10 per cent of the growing media for edible green walls.

Growing media for green walls

Using a growing medium comprising more than about 20–30 per cent organic components is problematic for green walls, because as the components decay over time they lose volume and porosity, and therefore plant roots can't get enough air for respiration. This has caused several expensive disasters in the early days of green-wall installations. It's not an issue in nursery production, where turnover time is short, but it causes plenty of trouble for permanent installations.

For several large green-wall projects in Sydney and Melbourne, Simon used a mix very similar to the one in the table below.

PRODUCT	PERCENTAGE BY VOLUME
Horticultural ash	40 per cent
Perlite	20 per cent
Composted pine bark	10 per cent
Sand	10 per cent
Coconut coir	10 per cent
Green-waste compost	10 per cent

A humorous yet highly workable example of a green wall was the 'Salad Bar', which was created by Turf Design Studio in 2004 for the Year of the Built Environment Future Gardens exhibition. It was a 128-module system that provided 65 square metres of garden surface but occupied only 25 square metres of floor space. A quirky and amusing play on outdoor living, it is best described by the designers themselves:

> The Salad Bar provides a modular vertical-growing structure with a smaller footprint to the generic garden … integrating a 'bar' within the vegetated wall provides a playful vision of how self-sufficiency can be incorporated into modern urban living.

The bartender can pick garnishes and make a salad without leaving the bar! The system stores and uses rainwater for irrigation. Each growing module can be removed and replanted, or it can be placed in another area (such as a greenhouse) for recovery.

The mix led to excellent root development and terrific growth rates when the plants were fed using coated controlled-release fertiliser (but organic fertilisers would work just as well). The coarse ash may cause root vegetables to become deformed, but it would be a suitable addition to growing media for all other vegetables and fruits. If you replaced the horticultural ash with brick dust or fine-crushed terracotta, which is available in some places, this might overcome the problem.

Vertical Food Garden

Australia is home to some of the world's most innovative horticulturists, and we would rate Mark Paul – founder of The Greenwall Company (www.greenwall.com.au) – as one of our finest. He has specialised in green walls and green roofs for over 25 years, and his design for a vertical food garden using recycled bottles provides a practical way of growing edible plants in the smallest of spaces. This design has been used in a variety of community garden projects, and has also been utilised as a wonderful educational tool in school gardens across Australia and overseas.

Mark perfected his vertical food garden concept at his nursery in northern Sydney, where he experiments with all manner of green walls, most of which are designed as low-maintenance permanent installations. His extensive experience with vertical gardening has taught him that edible plants need a much higher level of care than ornamental plants, which can cope with the variable moisture levels that most green walls experience. Mark's long-term green walls feature plants such as succulents and bromeliads, some of which can provide an edible yield; however, this is not usually substantial enough to offer anything more than novelty value.

The popularity of growing your own food and urban farming led Mark to develop solutions to the problems of the high-maintenance requirements of edible green walls. He stresses that most edible crop plants are either too large for vertical gardens (for example, sweet corn), or demand higher levels of water and nutrients than are practical to supply in vertical installations.

Mark's greenhouse has provided him with an environment that mimics the balcony and verandah situations that are typical for urban farmers in areas of high population density. He recommends installing a drip-irrigation system and using either controlled-release fertilisers or liquid feeding to maintain the high level of nutrition that crop plants need. Mark suggests that perennial herbs (such as mint and thyme) are more suitable for long-term plantings, and notes that fast-growing annual crops (such as lettuce) require nutritional input every day or two to reach their full potential.

Edible green-wall gardens require a considerably higher investment in time and inputs than ornamental gardens. However, in confined spaces where horizontal space is limited, the judicious use of the sort of concepts that Mark has developed can provide a viable solution.

MAKE YOUR OWN

This very simple system devised by Mark Paul is cheap, effective and very strong. Unlike commercial systems, which usually have fixed positions suitable for amenity plantings, Mark's design works well with food-producing plants that vary greatly in size. It is made using the following materials and method.

Materials

- Galvanised wire mesh, 1200 by 1800 mm, 2.5-mm wire thickness
- 8 x 23-mm screw hooks
- Electric or cordless drill and appropriate drill bits
- Masonry plugs if screwing into brick, stone or concrete
- 90 x 1.25- or 2-L PET bottles, washed and without caps
- Porous fabric squares cut from a material such as kitchen bench wipes
- 2.5-mm thick galvanised wire
- Metal-cutting shears or aviation snips
- Pliers

Method

- Line up the mesh on the wall so that the long axis is horizontal, and mark the positions of the eight screw hooks – there should be four along the top, and four along the bottom.
- Fix the eight hooks to the wall by drilling (for a wooden wall) or using a masonry bit and plugs (for a brick, stone or concrete wall).
- Hang the mesh on the wall using the hooks. The mesh should end up hanging just a couple of centimetres off the wall.
- Cut the bottom off each PET bottle at an angle so that the bottle ends up being about 200 millimetres in length on the long side. Then make a 3-millimetre hole in the long side.
- Turn one bottle upside down, plug up the hole in the neck of the bottle with fabric squares, and fill the bottle with growing medium to the top of the short side.
- Make a small S hook with the galvanised wire, and use this to suspend the bottle in whatever position you want. Repeat the process for the remaining bottles. A 1200- by 1800-millimetre piece of mesh should hold around 90 bottles.

You can make as many of these units as you like, joining them together to create larger green walls. In addition, you can use small plastic pots instead of bottles. The little pots will lean forwards a little, which looks very appealing once they are filled with lush plants. This simple system has the advantage of allowing you to move plants around at will, depending on their size, so you can close up the spacing between smaller plants or open up the spacing between larger plants – consequently, you can maintain the overall green appearance of the wall very easily. You can also change pot sizes as required, provided that weight does not become an issue for the larger pots.

CLOCKWISE, FROM OPPOSITE Marli Paul attaches containers to wire mesh using cable ties; this recycled PET bottle has various holes so that it can be hung on the wire mesh, and for drainage and aeration; porous material is used to prevent the potting mix from falling out of the drainage hole; a lightweight, freely draining, 50:50 blend of perlite and coconut coir is an ideal potting mix for this green-wall system; plant your choice of seedling herbs or salad greens in the PET bottle, and hang the bottle on the wire mesh.

PROTECTED ENVIRONMENTS

Greenhouses, glasshouses and poly-tunnels are used to extend the growing season of warm-season crops, hence they are most beneficial for gardens located in cool climates. They are often used for the growing of tomatoes and cucumbers in the 'off-season', or the winter months. Market prices are better in the off-season, which justifies the added cost (if you plan to sell your produce), or you can use the structures to ensure you have vegetables on the table year-round (if you are harvesting for your own use).

The most common form utilised these days is the relatively low-cost poly-tunnel. A semicircular metal structure is placed over natural soil (which has been hilled up to improve drainage) or a raised bed, and then covered with a horticultural-grade plastic that has been manufactured to better withstand ultraviolet radiation from the sun. Small kits can be purchased fairly cheaply, and there are also systems available that are made from partly rigid plastic agricultural pipe bent into a series of semicircles, like ribs. The pipes are then joined together with wire to form a self-supporting structure, before being covered with plastic film. This is an affordable and very effective approach.

Pros and cons

'Protected environment' houses, as greenhouses, glasshouses and poly-tunnels are often called these days, have some advantages in climate and pest control. They are great for propagating plants, because the success rate for growing cuttings and delicate seedlings is improved by the increased heat and humidity, as well as your ability to exclude snails and other pests.

However, there are a number of problems of which you should be aware. The first is that daytime temperatures can rise too high and

ABOVE
Greenhouses or conservatories are best constructed beside eastern- or northern-facing walls in Australia.

'cook' your plants. It is essential that these houses are ventilated at both the top and bottom of the structure to promote airflow. If necessary, open the vents during the day to cool the structure, and close them at night to conserve heat. This also helps to reduce humidity when it is too high. If humidity rises too much, plants can't transpire water and hence can't photosynthesise. If you have water dripping down the inside walls of the structure, it is too humid and you will have to allow in some fresh air.

Another problem is the build-up of salts in the soil or growing medium. Because there is no natural rainfall leaching the salts away, and you only provide enough water for your crop's needs, salts and other nutrients can accumulate – sometimes to harmful levels. Make sure drainage is suitable, and give the plants a heavy watering to remove excess salts and nutrients every month, especially during the warmer months.

PHYSICAL SUPPORTS

Whether it is grown in the ground or in a raised bed, a plant needs to be held upright by something, and the job is usually done by the soil or growing medium. If the plant cannot support itself, it will fall over – and rotting of produce will become a problem. In the urban environment, we often want plants to grow upwards rather than outwards due to space and light issues. We can provide plants with all kinds of ingenious methods of physical support, such as stakes, trellises and wires.

ABOVE LEFT A small-scale 'greenhouse' constructed from protective wire mesh is known as a cloche.

ABOVE Plastic mesh supports for plants are an ideal option for urban farms, as they are cheap, lightweight and re-usable.

'Protected environment' houses ... have some advantages in climate and pest control.

PROPAGATING AND CULTIVATING PLANTS

7

FROM REPRODUCING PLANTS TO HARVESTING CROPS

The garden beds in your urban farm are ready, but what sort of crops will you plant in them? You can purchase all kinds of plants from local nurseries and garden centres, but propagating your own plants from seed or cuttings, for example, is a fairly simple and very satisfying process. Later, when your plants are flourishing, it's time to think about important maintenance issues, such as pollination and pruning, as well as harvesting the delicious products of your labour. In this chapter, we will reveal a wealth of handy suggestions and techniques that will help you on your cultivation journey.

THE ART OF PROPAGATION

Learning how to propagate plants is one of the most basic and vital skills we can teach you. The good news is that you can accomplish most of the propagating you need to do with very simple facilities, and often right where the plant will grow to maturity.

The first principle you need to master is when to use sexual (seed) or asexual (vegetative) propagation techniques. Seed is produced by a sexual process that requires both a male and a female parent; this leads to genetic variability in the progeny (see the seed-saving section on page 139 for more information about this subject). Most agricultural crops propagated from seed are annuals that complete their cropping cycle within a year. Farming has largely been built on sowing the seeds of our major food plants – cereal crops, such as wheat and barley; vegetables, such as pumpkins, melons, beans and peas; and leafy crops, such as lettuce – directly into the soil in the position in which they will grow.

Asexual (vegetative) propagation allows us to make exact copies (clones) of a single parent plant by taking cuttings or by using techniques such as division, layering, budding and grafting. An obvious advantage of asexual propagation is that we can reproduce precisely

LEFT Many fruiting crops, such as this pumpkin, produce numerous viable seeds that, when planted, become the next generation.

OPPOSITE Peas are best sown in situ, as they put down roots very quickly from their large seeds.

an outstanding individual plant. The vast majority of crops that are propagated in this way are long-lived perennial plants, such as fruit or nut trees, but there are also many soft-wooded perennial food plants that we propagate vegetatively, such as potatoes, garlic and sweet potatoes.

Tips for success

The source of your propagation material (propagule) is extremely important, as it determines the genetic potential of your crop. That potential is then realised when you provide an ideal growing environment for the crop (see The Environment for Urban Farming chapter on pages 26–37 for more information). Heirloom varieties of various fruits and vegetables are rising in popularity for urban farms, as they have important genetic characteristics that have disappeared from varieties bred for industrial-scale agriculture and horticulture.

When propagating your own plants, it is essential that you start with seed or vegetative material that is free of pest and disease issues, as many problems can arise from using infected propagation material. A good example of this is utilising potatoes purchased for food as a source of propagation material. Even though the newly sprouted tubers seem to produce healthy-looking shoots, the chances are high that they will be infected with one or more viral diseases that will significantly reduce the yield. The answer is to source virus-free seed potatoes from a reputable source, rather than use potatoes bought from a supermarket. Research the various issues that can affect a crop you want to propagate, so you can adopt strategies to ensure you minimise the risk of propagating a pest or disease along with the plant.

Let's look at how to propagate plants using the various methods that can be easily applied on the urban farm.

PROPAGATION FROM SEED

For the vast majority of plants that you may wish to grow from seed in your garden, all that is required to get them established is an area of prepared soil. Clear away any existing plants, and then use a mattock or hoe to break up the topsoil. Finish the tilling process with a garden fork and/or a stiff rake to create a very smooth seedbed. Soil conditioners, amendments and solid fertilisers (see the Fertilisers chapter on pages 150–75) can be added at this point.

Once you have prepared your seedbed, dig a furrow; the depth should be about double the diameter of the seed you will be planting. Sow enough of the seeds so that you will have extra plants if some of the seedlings are lost to pests and diseases. If too many seedlings survive, they can always be thinned out later. Fine seeds can be mixed with a spreader, such as fine sand, to ensure a more even distribution.

It's important to remember that the larger the seed, the more successful direct sowing will be. The large seeds of plants such as beans and peas are easier to handle than the fine seeds of plants such as parsley and broccoli, and there is a greater risk of the delicate seedlings of fine-seeded plants being eaten or otherwise damaged before they can grow large enough to be self-sufficient. If you have trouble establishing fine-seeded species, they will generally have a much better chance of survival if they are grown in containers in a protected environment before being planted into the ground.

Growing seeds in containers

Propagating seeds in pots or punnets allows you to control the growing conditions as well

BELOW, LEFT TO RIGHT It is vital to prepare the seedbed well for good soil-to-seed contact. Sow the seeds at a depth that is twice their diameter, and cover the seeds with soil.

as to protect small, vulnerable plants from predation and weed competition. This can greatly increase your success rate, particularly with very fine seeds, although larger seeds will also benefit from being grown in containers. For the urban farmer, commercially available seed-raising mix is a good investment, because it is specially formulated to accommodate the more difficult-to-raise seed types, and it is free of weeds, pests and diseases (although I have found over the years that a wide range of plant species will grow just as happily in general-purpose potting mix). Follow the same seed-sowing procedure as in the previous section on direct sowing.

Seeds are very forgiving and will generally germinate perfectly well if the containers in which they are growing are left in a sheltered spot in the garden and are kept moist but not wet; this is achieved by watering them every few days in the absence of rain. A foolproof way of watering fine-seeded species is to stand the containers in a tray of water; the liquid moves up to the roots by capillary (wicking) action. This avoids the need for overhead watering, which can damage delicate new growth.

Once the seedlings are big enough to handle, they can be transplanted either straight into their final growing position in the urban farm or into larger, individual containers such as plastic propagation tubes or (preferably) biodegradable pots. Seed germination times vary enormously from species to species, and it is worth doing a little research on what to expect. Most common food crops, for instance, have been bred for centuries, and their seeds have been selected for rapid and uniform germination. On the other hand, species that have not been widely cultivated – such as Australian bush-food plants – still have

ABOVE LEFT Fine seeds are best sown in a seed-raising mix, and then transplanted when the seedling is strong enough.

ABOVE Big seeds, such as those from zucchini, can also be successfully sown in pots. The resultant seedlings can then be planted in their final place in the garden.

dormancy mechanisms that prevent all the seeds from germinating at once, a characteristic that ensures survival of a species by keeping some seeds in reserve in the soil.

Self-sown seeds

Many of the species we grow for food are annuals that are propagated from seed. These plants grow rapidly and, depending on the weather conditions, will sometimes progress quickly to the flowering stage (known as 'bolting') and subsequently a seeding stage. A classic example of this is the herb coriander – it often runs to seed within weeks of being established, and it will readily produce viable seeds. We can easily save these seeds for future plantings, but often they are dispersed by birds or the wind before we have the chance or the inclination to collect them. If a seed falls onto a bare bit of earth in the garden, it will often germinate and grow in situ. There are three options for dealing with the resultant seedling:

1 Leave the plant in place, and let it grow.
2 Transplant it to another position in the garden, where it may be better suited.
3 Consider it a weed, and pull it out (as the definition of a weed is 'any plant that is growing out of place').

♠ **Seed collection** For plants that shed their seeds as soon as they are ripe (such as beans and peas), tie an old stocking over the seed pods, and then remove it once the seed pods have opened. For fruits such as pumpkins and melons, simply scoop out the seeds and wash them under running water to remove any remaining flesh, then dry them in a cool, moisture-free place.

♠ **Seed storage** Regardless of the type of seeds you have, ensure that they are thoroughly dry by laying them on paper towelling (to absorb any excess moisture), then expose them to sunlight and moving air. To guarantee the longest possible life for your seeds, place them in an airtight container and store them in the coolest part of your fridge (not in the freezer).

PROPAGATION FROM CUTTINGS

This process refers to taking a part of a plant and using it to generate a whole new plant. While leaf or root cuttings can be used to propagate some plant species (see Angus' website, www.gardeningwithangus.com.au, for more information on these uncommon forms of cuttings), the most important type of cuttings used to breed edible and medicinal plants is stem cuttings.

ABOVE, LEFT TO RIGHT Leaf cuttings work well for edible succulents, but you can try them for any large-leafed crop. Cut off the midrib from the leaf, slice the leaf halves into smaller pieces if they're too big, and insert each leaf section – long cut side down – into a propagating medium.

It is possible to take cuttings from either woody plants (such as shrubs and trees) or soft-wooded (herbaceous) plants. Cuttings from herbaceous plants (such as sweet potato and many herbs) generally root much more easily than those from woody plants. However, the advantage of using cuttings from woody plants is that they are much tougher and will not dry out as easily as soft-wooded cuttings, and they can generally be placed under a shady tree and left to their own devices (however, we still need to water them every few days). A bit of research in books or on the internet will tell you the best type of wood and what time of year to take cuttings for the species in question.

Step-by-step guide to taking cuttings

Shoot tips that are not in flower make the best cuttings. The length is generally not critical, but the cutting should have several nodes (the points where the leaves join the stem). If you have enough material, we recommend making your cutting as long as possible – this ensures that there is plenty of stored energy in the cutting. Always make the cut a couple of millimetres under a node, as this is usually the most active site for new root formation. Remove the leaves from the bottom third of the stem by simply running your finger and

PLANT BREEDING ON A LOCAL SCALE

For thousands of years, farmers have been selecting and reselecting parent plants and saving seeds from them to create their own varieties (called 'land races' by plant breeders). Modern plant breeding for 'factory farming' has taken a different direction, because we are rearing plants that are designed for the needs of the grower and retailer, rather than those of the consumer. So, instead of breeding for the best crop nutrition or flavour, they breed plants that look perfect and are easy to transport, allowing them to survive the dreaded modern 'supply chain'. Tomatoes are the perfect example of how fruits grown originally for taste and nutrition are now selected for their ability to bounce off the wall.

Selecting and saving your own seeds is a very rewarding pastime that enables you to create varieties that are well adapted to your particular growing environment and that offer nutritious and tasty produce. You can use heritage species or modern plant varieties as the basis for your very own breeding program.

BELOW, LEFT TO RIGHT Root cuttings work very well for perennial plants, such as horseradish. Wash the soil off the roots, and slice them into sections with a slanted cut at the bottom. Push the slanted end into a propagating medium, so the top of the cutting is level with the surface.

thumb down that particular part of the stem. Easy-to-root cuttings, such as those taken from sweet potato and tomato plants, can be planted straight into their final growing position, while species that take longer to root (using cuttings from woody material) are usually planted in containers so that the growing environment can be controlled. This will generally result in much better success rates.

There are plant hormones that can be used to stimulate the growth of strong and healthy roots. These are commercially available as gels or powders – simply dip the bottom of the cutting in the hormone just before planting. The hormones have various brand names, and there are differing strengths; the weakest are usually used for soft-wooded cuttings, while the strongest are reserved for semi-hardwood or hardwood cuttings from woody plants. Scraping a sliver of bark from the bottom couple of centimetres of the cutting before applying the hormone treatment generally improves strike rates, as this exposes and stimulates cell growth in the tissue that will form the new roots.

♠ How do I look after my cuttings?

Those with lots of soft, moisture-filled leaves need to be kept fairly humid or they will dry out and die. For a small number of cuttings in a pot, you can create a mini greenhouse. Take a rigid plastic bottle, and cut the bottom off. Then simply place the bottle over the cuttings with the lid on, and position your pot in a shady spot in the garden. Other cost-effective options include planting your cuttings in recycled cherry-tomato containers or small portable trays (with a plastic lid) that are specifically designed for propagation.

♠ When are my cuttings ready?

After a week or two, take the lid off the bottle (if you needed to protect the cuttings); after a few more weeks (or sometimes months), when you see roots emerging from the base of the pot, the bottle itself can be removed. It will take a few days before the plants have become fully 'hardened off', so keep them in a shady spot; ensure that the plants are well watered if the weather is warm. Soft-wooded cuttings should take a few weeks to strike roots, while woody cuttings will generally take a few months and will therefore require a little more patience.

♠ What do I do with my cuttings?

Once they have 'hardened off' for a few days, they are ready to transplant. They can be either put into individual pots or planted straight into their final growing position.

ABOVE, LEFT TO RIGHT Soft-wooded cuttings benefit from being treated with plant hormones. Cut off a section of the plant below a node, remove the leaves from the bottom of the stem, and then dip the cut tissue into the hormone treatment before planting the cutting.

PROPAGATION BY LAYERING

A handy method for vegetatively propagating species that are hard to strike from cuttings is layering. This is like taking a cutting, except that it is left attached to the mother plant, which continues to nourish it until it has developed its own root system. This method has no special requirements for greenhouses or other environmental controls. Another advantage is that much larger plants can be produced than is possible by cuttings – your layered section can have 30–50 centimetres of growth above the area where the roots are induced to form. By the time it is ready to go into the ground, the new plant will be quite substantial in size.

For most plants, it is best to start the layers off in late autumn or winter, before the plant starts its surge of growth and new root production in spring. There are a couple of particularly useful layering techniques that are successful for a wide variety of plants: simple layering and aerial layering.

Simple layering

This method is most suitable when plants, such as strawberries or raspberries, have branches or shoots that are close to the ground. A long stem is bent down to ground level; its neck is buried, and its tip is left sticking up out of the soil. The stem can be tied to a small stake with an old piece of stocking or similar flexible material to ensure that it stays under the soil. Once it is sufficiently well rooted, the stem can then be removed from the mother plant and potted up, or even planted straight back into the garden.

Another layering option is to follow the same procedure, but bury the stem in a pot filled with coarse potting mix (a 50/50 blend of general-purpose potting mix and either coarse river sand or perlite). This second option is very handy, as it eliminates the possibility of root damage when the layer is eventually removed from the mother plant.

To encourage root formation, make a cut in the part of the stem that is to be buried; this also makes it easier to bend the tip of the stem up. It is also a good idea to mix a generous amount of coconut coir into the soil that is

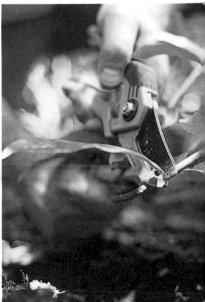

For most plants, it is best to start the layers off in late autumn or winter, before the plant starts its surge of growth and new root production in spring.

ABOVE, LEFT TO RIGHT To layer a plant, pick a suitable stem and remove the leaves. Dig a shallow hole, and then bury a few centimetres of the stem in the soil – you can hold the stem in place with bent wire.

used to backfill around the cut stem. Ensure that the soil does not ever dry out excessively during the root-formation process.

Aerial layering

This method is suitable for fruit trees, such as apples and quinces. Choose a stem on the plant that is up to 50 centimetres in length and up to a finger size in thickness. Select a straight section of the stem, where you would like the new root system to form, and remove any leaves and shoots for about 10 centimetres along the stem. Then use a sharp knife to make a nick in the stem a few millimetres under the bark and about 2–3 centimetres long. This creates a flap of bark and stimulates the stem tissues where new roots will form.

Coat the cut area with a rooting-hormone preparation, which is available from most garden centres. Take some moist sphagnum moss or coconut coir and pack it into the cut to hold the flap open, as this will encourage root formation. Double over a generous length of aluminium foil, place a couple of large handfuls of the moist growing medium onto it, and then mould the foil around the cut area. It is also a good idea to enclose the foil 'bubble' in a layer of heavy plastic that is tied off at both ends, as this prevents the growing medium from drying out in warm weather. The moisture contained within should be sufficient to allow you not to have to unwrap your aerial layer during the rooting process.

♦ **After-care for layered plants** One of the key indicators that a layer is ready to remove from the mother plant is shoot growth on the new plant. Success should come in a matter of weeks for easy-to-root species, but for more difficult plants it may take a number of months for a viable new root system to form. Carefully inspect the growing medium for new roots before cutting the 'umbilical cord' to the mother plant. To ensure success, it is a good idea to pot your layer, place it in a sheltered position and wait until roots emerge from the drainage holes before planting the layer into the garden in its final position.

Not only does the process of division rejuvenate the original plant ... it also gives you a swag of new plants.

PROPAGATION BY DIVISION

One of the easiest of all propagation methods is the division of perennial plants. This is particularly suitable for plants that have a clumping habit, such as lemongrass, and those that form an underground stem (rhizome), such as banana, ginger and turmeric. Not only does the process of division rejuvenate the original plant and make it flower better, it also gives you a swag of new plants. It is a very simple process that is usually best undertaken in autumn; however, it can be done at most other times of the year.

Gently dig up the plant with a spade or garden fork. Split the clump up by simply pulling it apart with your bare hands; you can also use garden forks or an old serrated-edged bread knife for harder-to-break-apart types. Try to split sections off in such a way that you do not damage any healthy new shoots, although this is sometimes unavoidable and will not do any permanent harm. Err on the generous side when splitting up the clump – the larger the piece, the better the chance it has of survival. Leave at least three full-sized shoots and as many fresh white roots as possible on each piece to maximise your chances of success.

SPECIALISED PROPAGATION METHODS

There are many specialised techniques for propagation that are beyond the scope of the average urban farmer due to the expertise and/or facilities required to perform them. These methods include:

- grafting, where two different plants are joined together
- budding, which is used for many fruit and nut trees
- plant-tissue culture, which is used to produce clonal, disease-free plants.

It is certainly possible to use any or all of these techniques if you are working on a commercial scale, and there is abundant information on them in Angus' book *Let's Propagate!* as well as on his website; also try the Australian and foreign websites of the various branches of the International Plant Propagators' Society (IPPS).

BELOW, LEFT TO RIGHT To divide a plant, dig up the root 'crown', and wash it to remove as much soil as possible. Carefully separate the clump into 'plantlets' that have plenty of healthy roots. These smaller plants can be potted up or planted directly into the ground.

ABOVE, LEFT TO RIGHT Bulb propagation is very easy. Divide the bulb into separate bulblets, and plant these at the right depth (about as deep as the bulblet is wide). Cover the bulblets with soil or compost.

OPPOSITE Grafted and woody plants are best placed in the ground at the same depth as they were in their pot, so the soil reaches no higher than the junction between the roots and the stem tissue.

Remove any obviously dead sections as well as any withered leaves and roots and old flower stems before replanting. Finally, use a sharp pair of secateurs to cut the top third of the remaining healthy leaves to reduce the demand for water as the new plant re-establishes a root system. Many species can be planted straight back into the garden with good results; however, to be on the safe side, it is better to first plant your newly divided clumps into pots in a freely draining potting mix, and then place them in a shady spot until new growth starts.

PROPAGATION FROM BULBS AND TUBERS

Crops such as garlic, onion and their relatives can be propagated from bulblets formed at the base of the parent bulb; in the case of garlic, it can also be propagated from tiny bulblets known as bulbils that form spontaneously on the flower heads at the end of the flowering season. These bulblets are planted in the same way as seeds, and they will take a year or two to grow to maturity.

Plants that grow from tubers, such as potato and Jerusalem artichoke, are handled in the same way you would a bulb – the small tubers are planted directly into their final position in the garden. A handy tip for propagating plants that grow from vegetative structures such as tubers is that the tender new shoots can often be used as a source of soft tip cuttings or simple layers to further multiply your stock, should you need to do this.

PLANTING

We covered seed sowing earlier in this chapter; however, we also have some helpful tips for transplanting established seedlings and cuttings that will improve your success rates. First and foremost, we recommend 'deep' planting soft-wooded plants such as tomatoes and potatoes. In other words, place these plants in the ground below the level at which they were planted in their pot. By burying the stem deeper than it was in the pot (particularly if the plants are a bit floppy anyway), you will stabilise them in the soil. Over time, new roots will form along the buried stem, which will stimulate increased water and nutrient uptake, resulting in better overall plant performance.

For long-term woody plants, such as fruit trees, we recommend planting at the same depth as the trees were in their pots. These trees are often grafted, and deep planting may cause failure of the graft union.

Whether you use the 'deep' planting method or the normal technique, your plant will benefit greatly from appropriate soil preparation before planting. Dig a hole that is at least three times the volume of the root ball, and mix in some compost with the soil you have dug out of the hole (this will be used as backfill around the plant's roots). After planting and backfilling, it is worth creating a small well around the base of your plant to allow water to collect and then soak in directly around the root system.

POLLINATION

Where we are growing and harvesting fruits, pollination is a vital process that needs to be understood and considered. Our definition of fruit in this case is the seed-bearing part of the plant, so it includes vegetables such as tomatoes and pumpkins. In many situations, pollination happens spontaneously without our intervention; however, if we understand the process, then we can ensure that a pollination process occurs that maximises our desired result, whether that is a harvest of food or the collection of seeds for the next crop.

Many important crops – such as beans and tomatoes – self-pollinate, and they will not need any assistance from pollinators such as bees. Other crops – such as cereals – are wind pollinated (the clue here is that the flowers are inconspicuous, as they don't need to attract pollinators). However, for most crops grown on urban farms, pollination is an essential process.

What is pollination?

Pollination occurs when pollen from the male parts of a flower (anthers) makes its way onto the female part (stigma). If the pollen is genetically compatible with the stigma, it germinates and grows a tube that transports the genetic material down into the ovary, where fertilisation of the ovule (which grows into a seed) takes place. Once fertilised, the seed develops and the fruit 'sets' and begins to grow. As the seed develops to maturity, the fruit reaches full size and usually changes colour to indicate that it is ready for harvest.

Whether you use the 'deep' planting method or the normal technique, your plant will benefit greatly from appropriate soil preparation before planting.

There are two reasons why pollination is vital for the crops from which we harvest fruits:

1 The pollination process is often essential for fruit development. Indeed, for many crops, if pollination does not occur, the flowers will drop off without any fruit set at all. There are exceptions, however, as some crops can revert to self-pollination (in other words, they are pollinated by their own flowers) if cross-pollination does not occur. It is worth researching each crop to see whether it needs cross-pollination for the best possible fruit set, as some fruit and nut trees will need other varieties planted nearby for good pollination. In another interesting example, pumpkins and their relatives have separate male and female flowers. It is sometimes necessary to transfer pollen by hand from male to female flowers if insect pollinators are not present in sufficient numbers.

2 If we want to collect seeds for subsequent crops, then it is particularly important to understand the pollination process. When we collect seeds for propagation, we can be positive about the female parent because that is the plant from which we are gathering the seeds. However, unless we have hand pollinated the flower and ensured there was no chance of pollination from another source, we cannot be sure of the male parent. In turn, this means that we cannot be sure that the progeny from those seeds will be 'true to type' with the parent plant. In many cases, the progeny will be perfectly acceptable for your purposes. However, there may be the odd case where the progeny is not as good as the parents, particularly if you have started with F1 hybrid seeds that have been specially bred by commercial seed companies. The answer, if you want to collect your own seeds, is to research your sources and find varieties that have been produced by open pollination (where the seeds will breed true). Open-pollinated varieties can be sourced from entities such as Seed Savers (www.seedsavers.net), a not-for-profit organisation dedicated to maintaining the genetic diversity of food plants.

Ensuring pollination occurs

Bees and other insect pollinators are attracted by colourful flowers – the showier the better. Therefore, growing a selection of plants with brightly hued blooms that appear at the same time as those of your crops is a good strategy. Long-term perennial herbs such as rosemary, lavender, bergamot, mint and thyme are the perfect complement to edible crops with less spectacular flowers, and they can be used as border plants around cropping areas.

It is not just exotic bees that are important as pollinators on the urban farm. Many other insects play a significant role, so having a garden that includes a variety of ornamental plants, both native and exotic, is extremely desirable. Australian bees are increasingly being kept in urban areas so they can be used as pollinators, and looking after these insects is a fascinating pastime to boot!

OPPOSITE Hover flies look like bees, and they feed on nectar and pollen. As they move from flower to flower, they help to pollinate plants.

ABOVE Bees see colours, so planting bright flowers will attract them to your orchards and vegetable plots.

PRUNING

Management of plant growth through pruning is a particularly useful tool whenever you are farming in small urban spaces. We normally think of pruning in association with woody plants such as fruit trees, but a little judicious pruning of herbaceous edible plants can also greatly increase yield and make plants easier to manage. It is important to observe very good hygiene when pruning, because fungal, bacterial and particularly viral plant diseases are readily transmitted from one cut surface to another.

Here are some examples of simple pruning techniques for commonly grown crops (as it is not an exhaustive list, it is useful to research the specific pruning needs of each plant on your urban farm).

◆ **Espalier** This is a technique whereby fruit trees and vines are trained to grow in a single plane, such as flattened on a trellis or wall, by pruning unnecessary branches and carefully tying others to the vertical structure. It is a useful technique for urban farms, where space may be limited, as an espaliered plant does not take up much ground area. Keeping the trees flattened makes it much easier to maintain them and to reach the fruits for harvesting, while a wall can be used to create a warming microclimate in frosty regions.

◆ **Removing tomato laterals** When growing tomatoes on a support, such as a stake, it is advisable to thin out the number of shoots that are allowed to grow and fruit. By pinching out the small lateral shoots that develop from the nodes along the stem, we can stop the plant becoming too dense with foliage, something that tends to encourage fungal and bacterial diseases of the foliage and fruits.

◆ **Maintenance pruning** Regular annual pruning of fruit trees and vines keeps edible woody plants, such as citrus trees and grape vines, within a manageable framework in urban environments. Different groups of fruiting plants have their own particular growth patterns, and it is important to

BY THE LIGHT OF THE SILVERY MOON

'Moon planting' – an odd technique that involves planting according to the moon's phases – lacks any evidence base. Our experiments have shown that plants are completely insensitive to the moon and its phases. They are, however, sensitive to day length (increasing or decreasing) and temperature, which is why we divide plants roughly into two types: cool season (plant in late summer to winter) and warm season (plant in late winter to summer). If you plant corn seeds in autumn, they won't germinate – not because of the phase of the moon, but simply because they need soil to be at least 20°C to germinate. Plant cabbage in mid-summer, and it will bolt straight to seed – as its genes are hardwired to equate the long day length with the notion 'seed fast before the summer heat kills you'. Our advice? Completely ignore any nonsense about moon phases. At best, it is an entertaining waste of time; at worst, it can lead to plant death.

research pruning techniques on a case-by-case basis. It is beyond our scope to go into that level of detail here; however, the information is readily available in horticultural literature.

HARVESTING YOUR PRODUCE

Picking fruits and vegetables that you have grown is one of life's greatest pleasures. With an understanding of the physiology of plant development and fruit ripening, we can harvest our crops in such a way as to maximise both the yield and the flavour of our food. Some crops, such as avocados and tomatoes, can be harvested before they have fully matured, and the ripening process can be finished indoors to protect your precious crop from predation by pests (particularly large animals, such as birds and possums).

Regular and timely harvesting of your crops every few days (or every day for some types of crops) will not only minimise any losses to pests, but also encourage your plants to produce more fruits or foliage. Generally speaking, leaving crops unharvested will cause plants to run to seed and to finish their growing cycle, so we can prolong their life (and total yield) by harvesting as often as possible.

Health and safety issues

Washing your fruits and vegetables properly after they have been harvested is a routine with which most of us are familiar. There are also two other dangers to look out for:

1 **Chemicals** – while we recommend avoiding the use of toxic chemicals wherever possible on the urban farm to control both pests and diseases (see our safer solutions described in the Pest and Disease Management section, pages 230–6), sometimes they are an absolute last resort if your crop is being devastated. If the use of a toxic biocide becomes unavoidable, be aware that washing your produce will only remove surface residues of applied chemicals. Many chemicals are also absorbed by the plant. The clue to this is if a chemical is labelled as 'systemic', in which case it is transported within the sap of the plant – and you will be eating whatever residues are left in the

OPPOSITE Espalier pruning saves a lot of space and allows light to enter the canopy – it also looks appealing!

LEFT Remove most lateral shoots on tomato plants to encourage larger fruits and better air circulation.

plant. It is ALWAYS critical to observe the withholding periods that are given on the labels of biocides.

2 **Microbial contaminants** – there are some dangerous microbes living in soil, manure and water that we need to be aware of when growing and harvesting food on urban farms. In most cases these microbes do not build up to a point where they are dangerous, but sometimes they do – so it is ALWAYS important to wash or process your produce thoroughly before it gets to your table. This is particularly vital for root crops and plants that may be affected by rain splash of soil, such as lettuce.

RIPENING TRICK

Ethylene is a naturally occurring gas that regulates various growth responses across a wide range of plant species. Among these fascinating processes, a particularly vital one is that ethylene is generally the key trigger for fruit ripening. Placing unripe fruits – such as tomatoes and avocados – in an airtight container with ripe fruits (particularly bananas), hastens the ripening process. You will soon have perfectly edible fruits, and avoid the devastation of discovering pest-damaged fruits in the garden.

FERTILISERS   8

THE IMPORTANCE OF ENRICHING YOUR SOIL

Why do we need to 'improve' or 'fertilise' soils to use them for horticulture? In most parts of the world, soils in their natural state do not have sufficient nutrients to grow the types of plants we want to cultivate in urban farms. It is usually high-yielding vegetable and fruit crops we want to grow, and all of these – with very few exceptions – need exceptionally fertile soils to produce the quality and quantity of produce we require.

Even where natural soils are fertile enough to support essentially zero-input farming, they start to decline in fertility as nutrients are exported in crop produce. With the halt in the normal system of organic-matter cycling, these soils soon exhaust their organic matter, and consequently their physical soil fertility is reduced. No soils can run on zero-input farming forever. In this sense, farming is a bit like mining for plant nutrients.

The classic example of zero-input farming is the traditional slash-and-burn farming practised by most traditional tribal groups in rainforest areas all over the world. They cut down and burn the vegetation from a patch of mature rainforest, and the ash returns the minerals from the vegetation to the soil. In the first couple of years, yields are worth the effort of farming the plot, but after three to five years the plot is abandoned and the process starts again. The abandoned plot takes a minimum of 20 years to recover, as nutrients slowly dissolve from the weathering of rock and bioaccumulate in the soil again.

This is a reasonably stable system when there is low population pressure. However, as the population increases, the period before returning to previously slashed and burned plots diminishes, so the soil has not had time to fully recover. Rainforest areas all over the world bear the ruins of early civilisations that collapsed thanks to the loss of soil fertility.

It follows that if we want agriculture in urban areas to be truly sustainable, we have

OPPOSITE Thick organic mulch both protects and eventually improves the soil in this street-side raised bed.

to not only improve soil fertility to support the crops we want to grow, but also replace those nutrients that are lost in the export of produce. The weathering of rock and the subsequent process of bioaccumulation is simply too slow to maintain soil nutrients at the levels we need to support the productivity of an urban farm.

A HISTORY OF FERTILISER

While there is clear evidence that the ancient Romans widely used the ash and slag from steelmaking (as a source of lime) to boost their soils, it was only in the first half of the twentieth century that industrial-scale manufacture of fertilisers became a reality. So, what did we do before that?

For most of the long history of adding nutrients to soil, organic fertilisers and improvers were the only options. Agriculture

and horticulture traditionally relied on the recycling of nutrients from everyday materials, such as manure and urine. Indeed, human faeces and urine were mainstays of plant nutrition in some places. While there are definitely health and hygiene considerations in using such materials, it makes sense that the nutrients being removed from the soil via the crops are returned in pretty much the same balance via the manure and urine that animals, including humans, excrete. As late as the 1940s, my grandfather in Yorkshire took the 'night soil' can to his allotment down the lane, where he grew beautiful potatoes (and brussels sprouts) that caused no apparent health problems for his wife and four daughters when they ate them. This makes me think that we sometimes exaggerate health risks.

Exploration and knowledge

By the beginning of the nineteenth century, the importance of bone in agriculture was well established. The blood and bone-rendering industry forged ahead, at first using the bones of soldiers killed during Napoleon's wars of conquest, but later relying on the efficient re-use of all abattoir wastes.

Exploration of the oceans during the nineteenth century revealed a raft of new fertilisers. There was worldwide industrial-scale mining of 'guano', the fossilised droppings of seabirds, and extensive quarrying of the rock phosphate reserves of Morocco and many islands of the Pacific. So important was rock phosphate to the feeding of the burgeoning populations of Europe, that most of the world's high-grade reserves are now depleted, including those on Christmas Island and Nauru. Long used to make gunpowder, Chile saltpetre (sodium nitrate) was present in such large quantities in the Chilean desert that it was mined and bagged as fertiliser.

In the late nineteenth century, with the advancement in knowledge about chemistry and the elements that make up living things, agricultural science made great strides. We started to understand that it was deficiencies of certain chemical elements that held back agriculture and plant growth. The new science of chemistry explained that the success of blood and bone as a fertiliser was due to the phosphorus and calcium in the bones, and that guano was rich in nitrogen and phosphorus, essential for plant growth.

ORGANIC OR CHEMICAL?

In a scientific sense, everything we can see and touch is made from chemicals. The word 'chemical' usually has negative connotations, but for horticultural purposes it's the same as saying 'mineral'. Scientifically, the word 'organic' means anything that is or was once living and made of carbon. Unfortunately, 'organic' has been so heavily entrenched as meaning 'natural' – with its implications of wholesomeness and purity – that it is almost impossible to knock it off this lofty pedestal. To be clear, this is how we will use various terms when discussing fertilisers in this chapter:

- **organic** – derived from once-living things (for example, compost, urines, manures, guano and vermicast)
- **mineral** – not organic, but essentially 'natural' materials dug up and used as fertiliser (for example, rock phosphate, lime, kieserite and gypsum)
- **synthetic** – made during an industrial process, either deliberately or as a by-product (for example, highly refined urea, potassium nitrate and other purified materials used in hydroponics).

In terms of plant nutrition, you just need to remember one thing: plants only take up nutrients in mineral form. All organic nutrients have to decompose or break down into their mineral constituents before plants can take them up, usually via the roots. This breakdown is mediated by the living organisms either in soil or in the compost heap. One of the most important reasons for composting is to promote the rapid breakdown of the organic molecules and to solubilise the minerals so they are readily available to plants.

Organic fertilisers and composts

There is a very broad range of products in this category, and, unfortunately, they differ greatly in their nutrient content and balance, and hence the purpose for which they are used. Some are so low in nutrients that they actually consume nitrogen, while others are so high that they work as fertilisers but are not really a good source of

TERRA PRETA SOILS

These are palaeological urban soils that show greatly increased levels of black carbon ash (charcoal) in them. Ancient peoples made them by burning forests and adding the ash to their garden soils. Many benefits are extolled by true believers in its modern reincarnation, known as biochar, and it is said to have permanently solved the problem of soil fertility. Keep in mind that every society which produced terra preta soils is now extinct. Not only was this process not a permanent solution to the problem of growing high-yielding crops on poor soils in essentially urban environments, it was so environmentally destructive that the people practising it were exterminated by the environmental havoc they wrought.

TYPES OF ORGANIC FERTILISERS

ORGANIC PRODUCT (PERCENTAGE OF ORGANIC MATTER)	COMMENTS	USUAL APPLICATION PER SQUARE METRE
Sawdust, pine bark, peat, straw (very high, 80–95 per cent)	A good way to introduce bulk organic matter to improve soil, but will generally require the addition of other fertilisers to compensate for extremely low nutrient levels; it can cause nitrogen drawdown; source of organic matter only, not nutrients	10–20 litres
Commercial composted green waste (moderately high, 45–70 per cent)	A good way to introduce bulk organic matter to improve soil, but may require the addition of other fertilisers to compensate for low nutrient levels; about 1 per cent nitrogen; some fertiliser value	5–20 litres
Composts containing food waste (moderately high, 45–70 per cent)	A good way to introduce bulk organic matter to improve soil, and will generally provide enough nutrients for crops with moderate nutritional requirements; moderately high nutrient levels; moderate fertiliser value	5–10 litres
Domestic compost and worm castings (moderately high, 45–70 per cent)	A good way to introduce bulk organic matter to improve soil, and will generally provide enough nutrients for crops with moderate nutritional requirements; moderately high to high nutrient levels; moderate fertiliser value	5–10 litres
Composted manures and mushroom compost (moderately high, 35–50 per cent)	A good way to introduce bulk organic matter to improve soil, and will generally provide enough nutrients for crops with moderate nutritional requirements; moderately high to high nutrient levels; moderate fertiliser value	2–10 litres
Raw manures (low to moderately high, 25–70 per cent)	A good way to introduce bulk organic matter to improve soil, and will generally provide enough nutrients for crops with moderate nutritional requirements; moderately high to high nutrient levels; moderate to high fertiliser value	2–5 litres
Pelletised fortified manures (low to moderate, 25–50 per cent)	A concentrated source of nutrition that will also introduce small amounts of organic matter for soil improvement; high to very high fertiliser value	100–300 grams
Blood and bone, rendered animal by-products, fishmeal (low, < 20 per cent)	A concentrated source of nutrition that will also introduce small amounts of organic matter for soil improvement; high to very high fertiliser value	100–300 grams

Note: A standard household bucket holds 10 litres. A standard 250-millilitre cupful of organic fertiliser weighs about 100 grams.

FAR LEFT Fortified organic-based fertilisers add a good balance of nurients to the soil, so they have a high fertiliser value.

LEFT Woodchips make excellent mulch, but they cause nitrogen drawdown. Soils topped with this mulch need extra nitrogen added to them.

organic matter. The Types of Organic Fertilisers table on the opposite page outlines the various organic fertilisers and their usage.

This table gives some important clues as to what to use in each situation. For example, if you want to improve organic matter without adding much in the way of nutrients, you would not use pelletised poultry manure – as this is really only applied to the soil for its nutrient value. You would use green- or garden-waste compost instead. You could even use sawdust, as long as you compensate for the nitrogen drawdown by adding some blood and bone or mineral nitrogen.

Nitrogen drawdown occurs when microbes consume the available nitrogen in the soil as they break down high-carbon materials (for example, woody items such as bark or woodchips, or fibrous components such as straw). This often leads to plants becoming deficient in nitrogen, and their foliage begins to turn yellow. It is commonly seen when straw, woodchips or bark are used as mulches, and insufficient supplementary nitrogen is supplied.

Manures as fertiliser

We do not recommend utilising raw animal manures for any soil used to grow salad greens or vegetables that are eaten raw, because of the possibility of salmonella poisoning. However, they may be suitable for other urban farm plots.

One of the most fascinating things about manures is that the nutrient balance can vary dramatically between the different types. This is related to the particular diet of the animal whose manure you are using. Here are a few generalised observations on such materials.

♦ **Feedlot cattle manure** Because it is very easy and economical to collect manure from feedlots, this is what tends to be available for purchase at garden centres. Feedlot animals are often fed diets that are high in mineral salt, protein and sometimes zinc. Manure products from feedlots are consequently usually high in nitrogen and salt, and have zinc levels that can be toxic to plants. Obviously, it is better if you can source manure from free-range animals if at all possible.

LEFT Large amounts of green waste are often commercially composted to make an excellent organic fertiliser that can improve the physical fertility of soil.

♠ **Poultry manures** Chickens and other commercial poultry are fed a diet that is very high in protein (for meat production) as well as phosphorus and calcium (for bone and egg production). Consequently, their manure tends to have excessive amounts of phosphorus and calcium, and to be deficient in potassium. For this reason, extra potassium is often used to supplement pelletised poultry manures.

♠ **Manure from naturally fed animals**
The manure from farm or zoo animals fed on a diet resembling that of animals in the wild will be generally better balanced than feedlot manure. We find that manure from pasture-fed animals has the best balance of all, although it can sometimes cause weed problems – especially if the animals in question have been kept in a weedy pasture and consumed its seeds.

MANUFACTURED FERTILISERS

As seen on page 90, the common soil ions can be mixed and matched to make just about any mineral fertiliser you like. Actually, many of them are simply dug up as minerals, ground down and put in a bag. Unprocessed mineral fertilisers include things such as lime (calcium carbonate), dolomite (calcium magnesium carbonate), kieserite (magnesium sulphate), gypsum (calcium sulphate) and glaserite (potassium, sodium sulphate).

Some minerals are dug up and then refined by dissolving them in liquid and precipitating them by drying. Sulphate of potash and Epsom salts (magnesium sulphate) are made this way.

One mineral fertiliser that seems to receive unwarranted bad press is superphosphate, which is rock phosphate that has been dissolved in sulphuric acid (a waste product from the metal-smelting industry). Rock phosphate is insoluble, so it is generally unavailable to plants; dissolving it in acid changes it to a soluble form that plants can take up. For many years superphosphate has been the mainstay for broadacre farming, but for intense urban farming it is inefficient and unnecessary. It is worth mentioning that there are soil microbes which help make phosphates more available to plant roots, so applying compost to your soil will help this process.

The most synthetic of all manufactured fertilisers are the nitrogen fertilisers: urea, ammonium salts (for example, ammonium sulphate) and nitrates (for example, potassium nitrate and ammonium nitrate). These are made in a similar manner to the way bacteria 'fix' nitrogen from the atmosphere. Called the Haber process, it was invented by German chemist Fritz Haber before the First World War (where it was used to make nitrogen-based explosives). Basically, it's a way of extracting the abundant nitrogen in the atmosphere to make ammonia gas, which is then combined with carbon dioxide to produce urea, the simplest naturally occurring organic molecule. Urea is also a waste product found in the urine of all animals.

Pros and cons

We support the use of manufactured fertilisers if there is a sound reason to introduce them, and in some situations, where only a single element is missing (for example, potassium), there is really little alternative. Some organic certifying bodies will now accept minerals that have been purified from natural deposits by simple processes such as precipitation, but they will not certify manufactured products such as superphosphate and urea.

This doesn't make much sense scientifically, as the plant doesn't care where the nutrient ion comes from. However, we can see a couple of good scientific reasons why you might object to the use of manufactured fertilisers:

1 They don't represent a balanced diet – it's a bit like feeding kids sugar and vitamin tablets, instead of fruit and vegies. Hence, using a fertiliser that just supplies nitrogen, such as urea, will tend to encourage soft, leafy growth but will not give as good a yield for fruiting plants or nutritionally dense food.

2 They consume large quantities of fossil fuels during their production and distribution, which is detrimental to the environment as a whole. If the same nutrients can be supplied from locally recycled wastes, then we avoid creating pollution. This same argument, however, could be levelled at compost made commercially from green waste that is picked up by trucks, transported to centralised facilities, chipped, turned and watered for 12 weeks, screened, loaded back into trucks

Choose a practical composting system that suits your lifestyle and space, and you can readily generate virtually all the fertiliser you need for free.

and transported to retail outlets – all using pollution-causing diesel engines and electricity. Nevertheless, the essential message remains the same: we should maximise our own recycling and the utilisation of suitable local wastes.

The bottom line is that the various organics we generate in our households every day (particularly kitchen scraps) usually contain the right balance of nutrients that need to go back into the soil to grow all of our own food. Choose a practical composting system that suits your lifestyle and space, and you can readily generate virtually all the fertiliser you need for free. Having said that, we have no problem with using a mineral fertiliser to correct a specific nutrient deficiency when required, as long as it is part of a holistic soil-management program that involves regular applications of organic matter to keep a good balance of overall soil fertility.

ABOVE Domestic compost is likely to be richer in nutrients than commercial compost because it has less wood and more leaf and vegetable matter.

FAR LEFT Wood mulches often cause nitrogen drawdown, so plants growing in that soil need a simple fertiliser to fix the imbalance.

LEFT Yellowing of foliage and early leaf drop are both signs of nitrogen deficiency. Urea fertiliser will quickly address this issue.

COMPOSITION OF FERTILISERS

There are two different types of fertilisers: simple (those that contain only one fertiliser salt) and complete (those that incorporate a deliberate or natural mixture of one or more mineral fertilisers). There are no organic fertilisers in the simple category, as all composts and organic-based fertilisers are complete – they contain most, and sometimes all, the essential plant elements.

Simple vs complete

Simple fertilisers have one fertiliser salt only. However, they may contain one plant nutrient (for example, urea has only nitrogen) or two (for example, sulphate of potash has both potassium and sulphur). Simple fertilisers are useful when a single nutrient deficiency occurs. A common example is when a woody mulch or carbon-rich compost is used, and it causes nitrogen deficiency with obvious yellowing of plants. An application of urea fertiliser to supply some extra nitrogen is all that is needed.

Another example is adding sulphate of potash to blood and bone (which is a more or less complete organic fertiliser but is quite low in potassium). By adding 20 per cent by weight sulphate of potash to the blood and bone, a well-balanced and complete fertiliser results. Another common deficiency, that of iron and manganese in alkaline soil, can be solved by spraying plants with a simple solution of iron or manganese sulphate (about 1 gram in a litre of water).

A fertiliser that contains more than two elements is known as a 'compound' or complete fertiliser. All organic fertilisers (including domestic composts and worm castings) are complete fertilisers. Composts that are really low in plant nutrients are not used for their fertiliser value but for the organic matter they contribute to the soil.

Properties of complete organic fertilisers are discussed in the Types of Organic Fertilisers table on page 156. You will appreciate that not all of them are as well balanced as we need them to be. The more sophisticated packaged organic fertilisers will usually provide information on the nutrient contents in the product. Bulk manures and composts rarely do so, and you are left guessing. Use the table as a rough guide to what might be in these products.

COMPARING FERTILISERS

By law, manufactured mineral or synthetic fertilisers must have a nutrient analysis on the package in which they are sold. This is not the case with all organic products, as an analysis is only mandatory for those claiming to have fertiliser value, such as pelletised, fortified manures. Look on the back of any fertiliser package, and you will see a label that shows the nitrogen (N), phosphorus (P) and potassium (K) content (and sometimes other nutrients), given as a percentage.

FERTILISER LABEL	
Nitrogen (N)	4.2%
Phosphorus (P)	5.4%
Potassium (K)	0.7%
Sulphur (S)	9.6%
Calcium (Ca)	10.5%
Magnesium (Mg)	1.02%
Boron (B)	0.1%
Manganese (Mn)	0.08%
Copper (Cu)	0.04%
Zinc (Zn)	0.02%
Iron (Fe)	0.01%
Molybdenum (Mo)	0.03%

The purpose of the label is twofold:

1 Just like a label on packaged food in the supermarket, it allows you to compare the ingredients and value of one product with another. This is important for both professional farmers and gardeners, so they can get the best value for money.
2 It allows you to calculate how much of the product to use, so you don't over-apply it. This is vital for the productivity of plants in the urban farm and also to prevent pollution caused by the run-off of nutrients.

LEFT Before using a mineral fertiliser, check the nutrient analysis – does it have the correct ratio of elements you need for your garden bed?

ORGANIC, MINERAL – OR BOTH?

We should strive to supply nutrients in a sustainable, cost-effective way that also provides plants with the right balance of nutrients for strong growth and a high crop yield. Our first preference is to use recycled organic fertilisers, as these can not only supply a plant's nutritional needs, but also add valuable humus and possibly beneficial microbes to the soil at the same time. However, organic forms of fertiliser, such as compost and manures, are sometimes not well balanced and need to be corrected. This is where a dual approach comes in handy, where you take advantage of the best of both organic and mineral worlds. For example, blood and bone and poultry-based manures are notoriously low in potassium and other essential elements for fruit and leaf production in fruit and vegetable crops. By adding 20 per cent by weight of sulphate of potash to the blood and bone or manure, a fertiliser that is beautifully balanced for plant growth results.

FERTILISER VALUE FOR MONEY

PRODUCT	COST OF FERTILISER
Controlled-release, plastic-coated, mineral NPK	$43.70
Pre-prepared liquid feed, mineral NPK	$42.50
Pre-prepared liquid feed, organic plus mineral NPK	$27.80
Solid soluble liquid feed	$26.50
Fortified blood and bone (organic plus mineral additives)	$17.10
Pelletised poultry manure with mineral additives	$16.80
Pelletised poultry manure, standard	$16.00
Commercial green-waste 'soil improver'	$13.10
Complete mineral NPK plant food	$5.50
Synthetic urea	$2.20

Controlled-release fertiliser

Fortified blood and bone

Pelletised poultry manure, standard

Keep in mind, however, that efficiency of use, convenience and labour saving should also be considered when assessing the value for money of the various fertiliser products.

Working out the value

With a bit of simple maths, you can compare the value for money of various fertilisers. The Fertiliser Value for Money table on the opposite page reveals the cost of assorted fertiliser types that we purchased from a local retail outlet. We simply worked out how many dollars per kilogram the product is, and then divided by the percentage of total fertiliser content.

As you can see, the highly manufactured, coated, controlled-release fertilisers are very expensive. Next worst in value is pre-prepared liquids (liquid concentrates that are diluted for use). Even the soluble forms of powdered fertiliser that you simply dissolve in water are comparatively expensive. The solid value-added pelletised poultry manure products represent much better value. They rank with commercial compost made from green garden waste, which we normally think of as a soil improver rather than a fertiliser. Far and away the fertilisers with the lowest cost are ordinary solid complete plant foods made from a mixture of mineral and synthetic fertilisers.

Keep in mind, however, that efficiency of use, convenience and labour saving should also be considered when assessing the value for money of the various fertiliser products. Controlled-release fertiliser is really made for use in pots, where adding solid soluble fertiliser would cause burning, and liquid feeding would need to be done at least twice a week. Thus, using a controlled-release product saves an enormous amount of labour for commercial nurseries, and this may also be a big incentive for the time-poor urban farmer. Having said that, various organic fertilisers – such as blood and bone or manure – also release their nutrients slowly and can play the same role as a controlled-release fertiliser at a much lower cost, albeit with less precision on the nutrient content.

The lesson to learn from this comparison exercise is that the price you pay for nutrients varies dramatically from product to product. We need to work out whether an expensive fertiliser has significant advantages (such as a controlled release rate, or adding humus as well as nutrients) that may justify the price

tag. The bottom line, as always, is that there are abundant sources of nutrients available to you for free if you can devote the time and energy to recycling them.

BEWARE OF 'SNAKE OILS'

There are many products on the market that make all sorts of claims about their ability to boost the growth of plants. Many, if not most, carefully avoid the label 'fertiliser', as that would bring them under the relevant fertiliser laws and force them to state the analysis of the product. Most use alternative wording and do not print the product's composition.

Seaweed is widely touted as a marvellous tonic for plants, but there is very little evidence

ABOVE There are numerous pre-packaged fertilisers available to buy – but collecting your own garden waste and kitchen scraps to make compost is the cheapest way to obtain fertiliser.

to back up this claim – especially when it is used in small amounts. If applied at high rates, in the same way that you would use garden compost with significant amounts of nutrients and organic matter added, then you may have some success. Liquid seaweeds, in our experience, are usually recommended at rates that do not demonstrate any significant benefit to plant growth and represent poor value for money. Unless you live near the sea where seaweed is free, and you use it at high rates as mulch or in composted form, save your money and spend it on fertilisers and soil conditioners that have a far more quantifiable benefit to plants and soil. Most of the claims made in regard to seaweed are entirely unproven, and some seaweeds – for example, seagrass – contain toxic levels of boron and should never be used.

Various seaweed products have plant hormones, such as auxins, that stimulate the formation of roots in plants. If your plants are healthy and growing normally, we see no benefit from applying seaweed products – and this could actually upset the fine balance of naturally occurring hormones in mature plants. The only time such hormones might be beneficial is when rooting cuttings or when transplanting, because the auxins found in seaweed products can improve propagation strike rates and assist with root recovery following the inevitable damage caused by transplanting.

FIGURING OUT FERTILISER NEEDS

There is no escaping the fact that growing food crops results in the removal of substantial quantities of nutrients from the soil. Our job as urban farmers is to make sure that there are enough nutrients for our plants from start to finish to ensure that our crops reach their full genetic potential.

We always approach the subject of feeding soil from two directions: 'getting it right' and 'keeping it right'. The former often means taking a low-fertility soil and rapidly bringing it up to the correct level and balance of fertility for the intended crop. It can also mean rebalancing a soil that has been abused or mistreated or is simply out of balance because it has too much

of one thing, such as poultry manure. Before we start to understand how to get the best out of fertilisers, we need to distinguish between soil conditioners (also known as ameliorants) and fertilisers.

♦ **Soil conditioners (ameliorants)** These are things we add, often once only (or at least only rarely), to correct basic soil properties like acid or alkaline pH, low calcium, poor soil structure, low organic-matter levels or grossly deficient nutrient levels. Some ameliorants have a fertiliser value as well, for example gypsum (calcium sulphate) – it contains the important minerals calcium and sulphur, but we usually add gypsum to the soil because of its ability to improve the soil's physical properties (calcium binds clay particles together).

We do not use ameliorants regularly, as they will end up unbalancing the soil in the other direction. For example, Simon once had a rose-growing client who was told he had acid soil, so he applied lime to his garden every year for about 15 years – he ended up with an alkaline soil and severe iron deficiency in his roses! 'Flying blind,' Simon calls it. Never use conditioners without first testing whether or not they are needed. Regular testing of soil pH and gypsum requirements is vital so you know when to use soil conditioners.

ABOVE LEFT
Liquid fertilisers are usually sold as concentrates, so they must be diluted before they are applied to plants.

ABOVE Check the pH of your soil at least every two years, and use a soil conditioner to adjust the acidity or alkalinity if necessary.

♦ **Fertilisers** On the other hand, fertilisers are things we apply to our garden on a regular basis to improve growth and maintain soil nutrient levels (they replace nutrients lost by the removal of produce and through the leaching process). There is usually an emphasis on nitrogen and potassium, the two elements that are lost in the largest amounts. Relatively smaller amounts of phosphorus as well as the other macronutrients and micronutrients are usually also required.

Note that there can be a fine line between a conditioner and a fertiliser. For example, if a soil is so alkaline that we are seeing iron deficiency in plants, we use iron sulphate both for its ability to neutralise the alkalinity and for the fact that it adds iron to the soil.

GETTING IT RIGHT

Using soil conditioners is all about getting the pH and calcium levels right. In many unimproved soils, however, other nutrients may also be required to allow high-quality produce to be grown. Phosphorus and potassium may be so grossly deficient that, in order to bring a soil up to a general level of fertility consistent with the needs of intensive farming, we might need to add more of these nutrients than we would to simply maintain a soil. For example, the natural soils of an area may be known to be deficient in phosphorus (a common reality in Australian soils), and a one-off application of up to 50 grams of phosphorus per square metre may be required for good crop growth where the maintenance level would be 5 grams per square metre.

The same applies to organic matter. Initially, we might need to add a high proportion of organic matter because it improves soil structure and texture, water- and nutrient-holding capacity and root penetration. Then we only need to use a fraction of that amount of organic matter every crop cycle.

ABOVE Using a pre-prepared liquid feed is one of the most expensive fertiliser options, but it is very convenient for pots on rooftops and balconies.

Because you can't 'see' the nutrient content within a soil, other than via observations of plant growth, soil structure and organic-matter levels, you often need to test your soil to work out how to get it balanced in the first place. However, there are a few rules of thumb that can be used.

- Many – if not most – natural soils are too dense and heavy for horticulture.
- Dense soil is partly due to low levels of organic matter. The ideal organic-matter content is 5–10 per cent by weight, whereas most natural soils have less than 3 per cent organic matter (unless you are on some very special soils, which usually show dark colours and good structure). Otherwise, you will need compost and/or manures to quickly improve organic matter.
- Many low-fertility natural soils will also be acid and low in calcium – these need lime. As previously discussed, pH testing for acidity or alkalinity is a simple process (see Testing the pH of Your Soil on page 95).
- Most natural soils in Australia, as well as in many other parts of the world, will be too low in phosphorus for intense use in urban farming.
- Soils with a low clay content (sands and sandy loams) will often be low in potassium.

Using mineral fertilisers to get it right

There are many different soil conditioners available. The Common Mineral-based Soil Conditioners table below reveals the mineral-based additives that are most frequently used to improve a new soil.

COMMON MINERAL-BASED SOIL CONDITIONERS

SOIL CONDITIONER	EFFECT	INDICATIVE RATE
Lime	Neutralises pH and adds calcium	50–500 g/m²
Gypsum	Adds calcium as a 'clay breaker' to improve structure	100–1000 g/m²
Superphosphate	Rapidly builds phosphorus levels to those needed for horticulture in deficient soils	20–100 g/m²
Sulphate of potash	Rapidly builds potassium levels to those needed for horticulture in deficient soils	20–100 g/m²
Composted organic matter*	Raises organic-matter level of topsoil to around 5–10 per cent; in larger-scale orchards, it is more cost effective to do this by growing green manure in the winter months	20–50 litres/m²

Note: All organic matter contains mineral nutrients, so it can be thought of in one respect as a low-nutrient source of mineral fertiliser.

Using organics to get it right

Interestingly, there is one rather specialised product that will do most of this job for you, and that is mushroom compost. It contains organic matter, lime, phosphorus and gypsum, and is almost a 'one-hit wonder' for improving acid, low-phosphorus soils. A high level of nitrogen gives it fertiliser value, but its potassium is not so high. Apply 10–50 litres (1 to 5 bucketfuls) per square metre, as well as 50 grams per square metre of sulphate of potash – and stand back!

Here's a warning, though: don't keep using mushroom compost year after year, as its very low levels of magnesium and potassium – and its excess of calcium – make it imbalanced as a fertiliser. A prominent rose grower learned this the hard way after applying mushroom compost to his extensive display of roses for years. Initially the mushroom compost was ideal for correcting gross problems in the natural soil of the rose garden, which is why the grower was so enthusiastic about it. However, the soil eventually became highly alkaline, it had far too much calcium and phosphorus, and it was deficient in potassium and magnesium. Simon got him onto a corrective fertiliser/ameliorant program, and he then instigated a long-term sustainable program using lucerne hay (a well-balanced product) as mulch; lucerne hay gradually breaks down to both feed and condition the soil with superb results, as it is naturally well balanced.

An alternative to mushroom compost for virgin soils is commercial chicken litter or manure (10–50 litres per square metre, supplemented with 50 grams per square metre of sulphate of potash and lime if required). Depending on the diet of the chickens, their litter usually has no liming value but it does contain calcium – so you don't need gypsum, but still need some lime if the soil is acid. You can use a whole range of other organic products as well. The Sources of Organic Fertiliser table on the opposite page lists the most common organic sources of fertiliser and their nutritional properties.

Rather than simply using mineral fertilisers or organics to improve an acid, low-fertility soil in its natural state, you could use a combination

BELOW Using a nutrient-rich blend of organic and mineral fertilisers is an excellent way to help leafy crops obtain rapid early growth.

SOURCES OF ORGANIC FERTILISER

ORGANIC NUTRIENT SOURCE	PRINCIPAL ELEMENTS	LOW OR MISSING ELEMENTS
Chicken and turkey litter and manures	High nitrogen, phosphorus, calcium, trace elements	Potassium and magnesium; usually acidifying because of the nitrogen
Duck litter and manure	High nitrogen, phosphorus, calcium, magnesium, trace elements	Potassium
Feedlot cow manure	Moderate nitrogen, phosphorus, potassium, salt, zinc, copper; sometimes very high zinc	Calcium and magnesium
Sheep manure	All elements in moderate amounts and good balance; can be high in salt	—
Horse manure	All elements in moderate amounts and good balance; high nitrogen	—
Mixed commercial or domestic green-waste compost	All elements in low to moderate amounts and good balance	Can be low in nitrogen if very woody
Mixed kitchen-scrap compost (vegetables only)	Elements in moderate to high amounts depending on inputs; usually good balance	—
Mixed kitchen-scrap compost (including meat scraps)	All elements in good balance; high nitrogen	—
Lucerne hay and compost	All elements in excellent balance; high nitrogen	—
Blood and bone, fishmeal	Very high nitrogen, phosphorus and calcium if bone is included	Magnesium and potassium
Mushroom compost	High nitrogen, phosphorus, calcium, sulphur, zinc; very high in lime and gypsum (mushrooms love lime!)	Potassium and magnesium

Soil amendments need to be dug in to the soil.

Compost should be added as a pre-plant fertiliser.

of the two. Here are two different mixtures that will achieve an excellent result.

Alternative 1:

Poultry litter or manure (10 litres per square metre)

Domestic kitchen compost or commercial green-waste compost (10 litres per square metre)

Sulphate of potash (50 grams per square metre)

Garden lime (200 grams per square metre)

Alternative 2:

Cow manure (10 litres per square metre)

Domestic kitchen compost (10 litres per square metre)

Sulphate of potash (100 grams per square metre)

Garden lime (100 grams per square metre)

Gypsum (100 grams per square metre)

If you compare these mixtures with the Common Mineral-based Soil Conditioners table (page 167) as well as the Sources of Organic Fertiliser table (page 169), you will see that they are adding:

- potassium from the sulphate of potash
- nitrogen and phosphorus from the manures and mushroom compost
- calcium from the poultry litter and lime
- potassium and many other nutrients from the domestic and commercial green-waste compost.

KEEPING IT RIGHT

This is really about fertilising and maintaining soil-nutrient levels to protect against the vast losses caused by the removal of produce and the leaching of nutrients during rainfall and irrigation. Ideally, we would feed plants with fertilisers that exactly parallel the ratios of elements found in their tissues. Disregarding the elements that plants obtain from the atmosphere, the Element Levels in Plants table (see page 68) in The Needs of Plants chapter shows the approximate concentration of each element in most plant leaves.

All plants need a balanced diet of essential nutrients, and there are various strategies that can be employed to ensure you are optimising the growth of your crops as well as keeping your soil or growing medium in good shape for future crops. The strategy you choose for your particular circumstance will depend on a variety of factors.

ABOVE LEFT Liquid feeding is a useful fertiliser strategy, but always shake organic liquid feeds well as they can have heavy residues.

ABOVE Quality commercial composts add many important nutrients to fertiliser mixes, particularly potassium.

♦ **Availability and cost of fertilisers**
There may be a ready source of locally available recycled or free material, such as worm castings and liquid or stable manure. If you can utilise the nutrients that you generate from kitchen scraps each day, then it lessens your dependence on purchasing expensive packaged products.

♦ **Your growing system** Growing in soil lends itself to using a solid fertiliser worked in prior to planting and supplemented by liquid feeding as necessary, whereas a hydroponic growing system will need to have a fairly precise and constant liquid-feeding program. Never use solid soluble fertilisers in potting mix, as they will burn plants. You must utilise slow-release or liquid feeds.

♦ **The nutrient-storage capacity of your soil or growing medium** Fertile soils rich in clay and/or organic matter will have a higher capacity for nutrient storage than sandy soils or hydroponic media, meaning you don't have to feed so often. Fertile soils will release nutrients to the plant on demand. A pre-plant fertiliser will often be sufficient, but look at the plants and decide if they need extra liquid or side dressings.

♦ **The amount of material being harvested**
Heavy-yielding plants, such as potatoes, will lead to the removal of significant quantities of nutrients every time you harvest. These nutrients will need to be replenished in the same quantities before the next crop is planted. Leguminous crops, such as beans, will tend to need less nitrogen because they fix their own nitrogenous fertilisers from the air around them, but they still need all the other nutrients.

There are generally two types of fertilisers used during a plant's growing cycle: a pre-plant fertiliser, which is added to the soil or growing medium before the crop is planted and helps early growth, and a side dressing, which keeps the nutrient levels up towards harvest time.

Pre-plant fertiliser
These can be mineral, organic or a mixture of both, and they usually provide a broadly balanced spectrum of all the essential nutrients. If you

HINTS FOR OPTIMISING YOUR FEEDING STRATEGIES

Green-manure crops are plants that are dug into the soil prior to the sowing of a crop. The idea is to turn in the green-manure plants while they are still at a very succulent stage of growth – at the latest when they have started to flower – as it is at this point they have the maximum nutrient content, which will quickly break down and be released back into the soil. The most common choice for a green-manure crop is some type of legume, such as beans and peas – whatever you can get hold of at a reasonable price (or you may save seeds specifically from previous crops). Members of this plant group all have the ability to convert atmospheric nitrogen into fertiliser, courtesy of a bacterium called *Rhizobium* that forms nodules on the plant's roots. In return for the nitrogen that the bacterium passes on to the plant, it receives sugars from the plant's photosynthetic activities – a true symbiotic relationship where both parties benefit.

Liquid feeding may be the sole means of delivering nutrients in systems such as hydroponics, however, in other systems it can be a very handy tool for supplementing the nutrients that you have previously added as solid fertilisers. The liquid (leachate) from a worm farm, or a liquid manure (prepared by placing manure into a porous bag and soaking it in a bucket of water for several hours), is a handy homemade liquid feed that is generally a well-balanced fertiliser, and can be used as a general boost for most crops on your urban farm.

Foliar feeding is a particularly useful form of liquid feeding in winter, when the soil is cold and it is more difficult for plant roots to take up nutrients from the soil. Liquid fertiliser is applied to the leaves, rather than the soil. It is important to ensure that your liquid feed is not too strong, as this could cause a salinity problem that might burn the foliage. It is also advisable not to foliar feed in the heat of the day.

Specific liquid fertilisers can be used to correct particular nutrient deficiencies that may show up on either a seasonal basis (for example, iron deficiencies through winter) or as a result of a lack of nutrients in the growing medium. Nutrient toxicities can sometimes also be addressed through liquid feeds – for instance, an application of dissolved iron sulphate can help to reduce the availability of excessive levels of phosphorus in soils.

know that your soil or growing medium has a particular deficiency, solid forms of a specific fertiliser (for example, potassium to encourage better fruiting) can be added. Pre-plant fertilisers are best dug into the garden bed as a whole; they can also be placed close to where the new plant will be located and dug in around the planting hole, or dug in along the planting row. Some ideal pre-plant fertilisers are:

- mixed yard waste or garden compost with 20 per cent (by weight) blood and bone added
- blood and bone with 20 per cent (by weight) sulphate of potash added
- poultry manure with 10 per cent (by weight) sulphate of potash added
- a 'complete' plant food with an NPK ratio around 10:3:8.

The perfect pre-plant fertiliser releases its nutrients slowly, so the nutrients are not all instantly soluble and prone to leaching during rainfall or irrigation. For this reason, organics such as blood and bone and the richer composts or pelletised manure products are ideal. Coated controlled-release products are also excellent because they are very restrained in their release, but they are the most expensive fertilisers weight for weight. They do, however, largely avoid the need to fertilise later in the progress of the crop.

Application rates vary, but the Application for Vegetable Production and Application for

LEFT Beds for seeds and small seedlings should have pre-plant fertilisers well worked in to the soil using a rake or shovel.

Orchard and Tree Production tables (see below and opposite) are useful guides to how much to apply per square metre for vegies and crop trees.

When using very rich poultry manures containing a lot of ammonium nitrogen (the smell of ammonia is often very obvious), it pays to either wait a week before planting or ensure the manures are not put into direct contact with the seed or seedling. Ammonium in high concentrations can be toxic to plants, but the soil will absorb it and metabolise it into the non-harmful nitrate form of nitrogen.

APPLICATION FOR VEGETABLE PRODUCTION	
FERTILISER TYPE	APPLICATION RATE (PER SQUARE METRE)
Garden compost	5–10 litres (half to one bucketful)
Animal manures and worm castings	2–5 litres
Fortified pelletised manures	0.3–0.5 litres
Compound mineral fertilisers	50–100 grams (2–4 tablespoons)
Coated controlled-release fertilisers	100–200 grams

With trees, avoid putting the fertiliser close to the trunk, as there are few feeder roots here to take advantage of it. For trees in a row, place the fertiliser along the drip line of the foliage canopy, where the greatest concentration of feeder roots is likely to be found, and treat the entire row, not just the soil under the canopy.

Side dressing

This refers to putting fertiliser (either solid or liquid) alongside the crop to give the crop a mid-season boost of nutrition. The need for side dressing depends on the reliability of your initial pre-plant fertiliser (for example, how slowly it releases nutrients) and, of course, how fertile your soil is. If you are using sufficient amounts of either nutritious compost or coated synthetic fertiliser, you may not need to apply side dressing at all.

If plants are growing well – with dark green, glossy leaves and plenty of setting fruits – then the need for side dressing is reduced. However, if plants look spindly and pale, don't hope they'll get better – start side dressing straight away.

Any side dressing should comprise soluble and readily available forms of nutrients and should not contain high ammonium nitrogen levels. Raw poultry manures, for example, carry a risk of ammonia toxicity. Likewise, fertilisers such as urea must be utilised very carefully as they can cause root and leaf burn if they are overused. Apply only well-rotted composts and manures as side dressing. The nutrients will be in partial-soluble form, and the ammonium nitrogen will have dissipated.

> The need for side dressing depends on the reliability of your initial pre-plant fertiliser ... and, of course, how fertile your soil is.

Soluble fertilisers and liquid feeds are ideal for side dressing. Some people rely totally on a side dressing of liquid feed and don't use a pre-plant fertiliser at all. Compost 'tea', wormcast 'tea' and purchased soluble liquid feeds all make excellent side dressing.

To apply a side dressing, use about half the amount utilised as pre-plant fertiliser. For greatest efficiency, place the fertiliser close to (but not touching) the plant stem, where the root system is most likely to be concentrated, and water well to ensure that the soluble nutrients are carried into the soil. Fortnightly to monthly applications are usually required when side dressing with composts. With mineral fertilisers, monthly applications are adequate. Because they are not very strong, liquid feeds need to be used between twice a week and once a fortnight, depending on how much pre-plant fertiliser you have used. If you didn't apply a pre-plant fertiliser, then use liquid feeds twice a week for best results.

NEXT PAGES
When planting tree crops, such as papaya, it pays to put in the hard work and condition (ameliorate) the soil properly before planting, as this is very difficult to do later on.

APPLICATION FOR ORCHARD AND TREE PRODUCTION

FERTILISER TYPE	APPLICATION RATE ON ROW OR UNDER THE CANOPY (PER SQUARE METRE)
Garden compost	5–10 litres (half to one bucketful)
Animal manures	2–5 litres
Fortified pelletised manures	0.3–0.5 litres
Compound mineral fertilisers	50–100 grams (2–4 tablespoons)

COMPOSTING AND MULCHING 9

RECYCLE YOUR ORGANIC MATERIAL

As we saw earlier in the Soils and Soil Fertility chapter (pages 72–105), natural soil systems are replenished and improved via the cycling of nutrients and organic matter from the all-important litter layer on the soil surface. In an urban farm's soil system, this litter cycling does not occur, and both soil fertility and organic-matter levels will decline with time if nutrients are not replaced.

You can run farming systems entirely on synthetic fertilisers, but even in such systems it is usual for organic matter – and hence soil structure and physical fertility – to decline with time. Broadacre farmers rotate crops, working some of those crops back into the soil as 'green manure' to build up the soil's organic matter; while this can be done in intensive urban-farm situations, land area is usually limited so crop rotation is not feasible. This is where composting comes into play – transforming organic matter into a substance that is suitable for fertilising the soil. There are many benefits to composting:

- It returns the farm's nutrients back to the soil, reducing the need for outside fertiliser inputs.
- It maintains and improves the soil's organic matter by adding humus, which is a soil conditioner. Humus works like a sponge, soaking up water and nutrients, and then later releasing them back to the plants. It also acts as a glue between soil particles to improve soil structure.
- It transforms the nutrients in organic waste from complex biochemicals, such as proteins, to simple soluble forms that can be taken up by plants.
- It sanitises waste, killing weed seeds and soil-borne diseases.
- It maintains a healthy soil fauna and flora.
- It suppresses plant disease.

Given the enormity of these benefits for creating a sustainable farming system, composting of organic wastes – in our view –

LEFT The natural cycle whereby leaf litter returns nutrients to the soil is mimicked on the urban farm by the regular addition of compost to garden beds.

should be a substantial part of any urban farm. There are two main types of composts – hot (thermal) composts, which heat up enough to kill weeds and disease organisms, and cold (non-thermophilic) composts, which are ideal for weed-free kitchen scraps – and a multitude of composting techniques. It is important to choose a system that is appropriate for your particular urban-farm operation.

GETTING STARTED

The process of transforming fresh organic matter into useful, clean, weed-free humus and available plant nutrients takes time. All composting should be aerobic – that is, enough air should be maintained in the pile so that it does not rot and develop a foul smell. Anaerobic conditions result in toxic by-products that can cause damage to crops.

The most important decision is to select a system that suits the size of your urban farm, the amount and types of organic matter that are available to you, and the amount of time you can put into composting. For example, don't buy a 100-litre compost bin if you have a small balcony, and don't use 'cold' composting methods if you have a lot of weeds, dog manure or meat scraps to add to the pile.

A compost heap goes through various stages of decomposition, and it is critical to understand when the compost is fit for your specific purposes. Composts can be used as soil conditioners, fertilisers or mulches (or combinations thereof). Those that are to be used as soil conditioners and/or fertilisers for seeds and seedlings need to be fully 'mature' (well rotted), while mulches that will, by definition, just sit on the soil surface and act as an insulating blanket do not need to be fully broken down; in fact, mulches should contain a lot of coarse fibrous matter, not fine and earthy humus that will germinate any weed seeds that may blow in.

'Mature' vs 'immature'

The major difference between a 'mature' compost and an 'immature' compost is that a 'mature' one will be suitable for very sensitive seedlings and seed germination, whereas an 'immature' compost will not. If an 'immature' compost is dug into a soil, it is likely to contain ammonium nitrogen that is potentially toxic to sensitive seedlings. If it is low in nitrogen, various composting microbes will decompose it further; in doing so they will be competing with plant roots for the available nutrients and oxygen in the soil. By the time composts are 'mature', ammonium nitrogen is no longer present and the potential for nitrogen drawdown is reduced. 'Immature' compost can be used, but only on established robust crops and as a pre-plant fertiliser at least two weeks before seeding or transplanting.

'Mature' and 'immature' composts both contribute plenty of humus to the soil, but 'immature' compost takes longer. Humus is a kind of biochemical end point in the breakdown of organic matter. It is a very complex substance that is made up of numerous individual organic substances and is therefore very difficult to quantify. Each batch of humus isolated from compost will likely be slightly different in chemical composition and nutrient content, depending on what went into the compost in

LEFT A dark colour and a somewhat spongy texture are evidence that a soil has a good level of organic matter.

BELOW Compost bins and worm farms come in a variety of shapes and sizes – choose the system that is most appropriate for your urban farm.

the first place. However, the overall properties of humus are what make it an essential substance for urban farmers.

Humus creates excellent soil structure by holding soil particles together to form aggregates, or peds. Particles of clay, silt and sand all benefit from this capacity. If your soil has lots of crumb-sized peds, then water can drain around the peds – this leads to good soil aeration. The peds themselves absorb and store some water, which is used for plant growth; thus humus improves a soil's water- and nutrient-holding ability.

LEFT A large system with bays for holding the various ingredients for compost as well as the actual compost heap is ideal for big farming plots.

IGNORE EXTRAVAGANT MARKETING CLAIMS

Despite what you may hear or read to the contrary, there is no proof whatsoever that it is beneficial to add any particular strain of microbes to your compost. The various types of organisms that are responsible for composting are a normal part of the environment, and they will colonise your compost in a variety and form determined by what you put into the compost. So please don't waste any of your money on so-called compost 'activators', because you actually get them for free with everything you put into your heap.

If you are genuinely worried about the number of organisms living in your compost, place a handful of a previous compost batch, some worm castings (if you have a worm farm) or even soil into your new mix, and your compost is sure to get all the beneficial microbes it could ever possibly need.

MAKING A BALANCED COMPOST

Like us, composting microbes and worms need a balanced diet to operate at peak efficiency. They also require the right mix of water and air. If compost gets too wet, for example, the composting process shuts down and the worms all try to escape from the heap because there isn't enough air to breathe.

The nutrient value of your finished compost will vary depending on inputs. As with plant growth, the first and most important element is always nitrogen. It stands to reason that if we use organic matter that is high in nitrogen, then the compost will also be high in nitrogen. If we use woody (high-carbon) waste that has a poor nitrogen level, then the compost will be low in nitrogen and could, in fact, consume nitrogen when applied to soil (a process known as nitrogen drawdown). The same principle applies to the other essential nutrients for plant growth: the nutrient value that goes into the compost will reflect what comes out in the 'mature' compost.

In practice, even if we get the mix wrong, nature will always guide the compost towards a natural balance of nutrients. This is easy to demonstrate. If we put too much nutrient-rich manure in compost, it will stink of ammonia. This is the excess nitrogen that the microbes can't use being driven off as gas, or 'volatilised'.

On the other hand, if we put high-carbon compost on the garden, the decomposing microbes will rob the soil of nitrogen so they can continue to break down the woody material in the compost, eventually causing a nitrogen deficiency in our plants. This is nature readjusting the nutrient balance. It is also why it is impossible to make 'mature' and stable compost that has any more than 1.5–2 per cent nitrogen in it. If you compost pure manure, which has 3–3.5 per cent nitrogen, it will actually decline in fertiliser value as ammonium is removed as a gas.

Getting the mix right

Loss of ammonium nitrogen is a waste of precious fertiliser nitrogen, while hungry carbon-rich compost will actually rob your plants of nitrogen. To avoid these two major problems, we have to be careful when we choose the raw ingredients that we include in the compost.

We also want to prevent bad smells from permeating urban environments, so it is very important to avoid adding any material with excessive nitrogen to your compost. Too much water or too much wet vegetable matter leads to poorly aerated (anaerobic) compost, which also produces foul odours – and you risk becoming alienated from your neighbours!

The best, fastest and easiest compost to create and manage – without odour and offence – has the right balance of carbon, nitrogen and other nutrients necessary for your particular urban farm. The Compostable Materials table on page 182 shows you what can be added to compost, and the nutrient value of each material.

Your job in composting is to find the right blend of the ingredients listed in the Compostable Materials table to optimise the moisture content and nutrient levels (especially nitrogen) for the composting organisms or worms. Any material that has once been living is capable of being composted, but some materials are much easier than others.

LEFT Compost should be open and porous so that it admits air, and it should look moist but not wet.

CARBON VS NITROGEN

Effective composting is largely a balancing act. We need to consider the carbon to nitrogen ratio of the materials to be composted if we are to make compost that supplies sufficient nitrogen for plant growth. The woody parts of plants are rich in cellulose and lignin, which makes them very high in carbon but low in nitrogen. Wood has a carbon to nitrogen ratio between 100:1 and 500:1; dead leaves are between 40:1 and 80:1. At the other end of the scale, vegetable and fruit scraps have a carbon to nitrogen ratio between 15:1 and 20:1, coffee grounds are 20:1 and manure is between 5:1 and 25:1. Ideally, when a compost pile is mixed together, it will average out to have a carbon to nitrogen ratio between 20:1 and 30:1.

The mix should look damp but not shiny with wetness, and it should only just moisten the hands when you touch it. For composting, if it glistens in the sun and you can squeeze any water out of it, the compost is definitely too wet. For worm farms, you should be able to squeeze just a few drops of water out of it to indicate the moisture content is about right. If the compost looks wet and smells rotten, then it is anaerobic. If it smells of ammonia, then you have too much nitrogen and not enough carbon in the mix.

COMPOSTABLE MATERIALS

ORGANIC WASTE	MOISTURE CONTENT	NITROGEN CONTENT	NUTRIENT CONTENT
Paper and cardboard	Very low	Very low	Very low; high carbon to nitrogen ratio
Sawdust, woodchips, tree bark, straw	Low	Very low	Very low; high carbon to nitrogen ratio; indigestible
Dead leaves (including sclerophyllous leaves, such as those from eucalypts), sticks, stems	Low	Low	Very low to low in all nutrients; digestible carbon
Mixed chipped garden waste	Low to moderate	Moderate	Moderate and well-balanced in all major nutrients; reasonably digestible, except the woody matter
Fresh green-leaf matter (for example, lawn clippings or leafy prunings)	Moderate	About right, moderate	Moderate and well-balanced in all major nutrients; highly digestible
Fleshy vegetable-type leaf matter	High	High	High in all major and minor plant nutrients
Fruit and tuber wastes (for example, tomato, potato and carrot)	Very high	High	Tubers very high in digestible carbon; fruits very high in nitrogen and potassium; highly digestible carbon
Herbivorous manure (for example, from horses, cows, rabbits or sheep)	Low to high	High	Concentrated nitrogen and other major and minor nutrients; feedlot manures can be poorly balanced and have excessive levels of trace elements; high fertiliser value
Carnivorous manure (for example, from poultry, pigs, dogs or cats)	Often high	Very high	Very high in nitrogen, phosphorus and calcium; high fertiliser value
Meat and bone scraps	High	Highest of any organic fertiliser	Very high in nitrogen, phosphorus and calcium; very high fertiliser value

Useful compost blends

There are an infinite number of combinations of organic wastes. However, the following 'recipes' usually work well (all proportions by volume).

A typical urban-farm compost
- 4 parts dry leaves, stems and/or twigs
- 2 parts grass clippings and fresh weeds
- 1 part vegetable and fruit scraps
- 1 part poultry manure

This mix has the right moisture content, is open and porous enough to let in air, and has enough nitrogen and nutrient-rich component. It is also likely to be digestible enough for the composting organisms that are found naturally in the heap to heat it up if conditions are right.

A typical worm-farm compost
- 4 parts vegetable and fruit scraps
- 2 parts shredded paper and straw

This is ideal for 'worm bin' systems, as it is a little richer and wetter than the typical urban-farm compost. If you can get stable manure, a suitable brew for vermicomposting might be:
- 4 parts stable horse manure
- 2 parts rich vegetable and fruit scraps
- 1 part grass clippings

A typical hot-composting brew
- 4 parts shredded garden waste
- 1 part grass clippings and fresh weeds
- 1 part vegetable and fruit scraps
- ½ part animal manure

Based on shredded plant material and prunings, this recipe is likely to be a hot (thermal) compost and will sterilise the compost quite well.

ABOVE, LEFT TO RIGHT Alternating layers of rich food scraps and straw or shredded paper is ideal for creating a worm-farm compost. Add a little water if the mix is too dry.

TYPES OF COMPOSTS

There are two main types of composts:

1 **Hot** (thermal) composts.
2 **Cold** (non-thermophilic) composts (worm composts, or vermicomposts, also fall into this category).

Each has its pros and cons, but they are both designed to achieve the same aim – to increase the fertility of the soil. The most important thing is to select one that suits the scale of your garden or farming enterprise and the types of organic products available to you.

If, for example, you have a balcony set-up and only have access to your own kitchen scraps and maybe some lawn clippings, it will be difficult to get sufficient mass to ensure hot composting. Make do with cold composting, or use a small worm farm. Since you won't have much of a weed problem, hot composting – which kills weeds – is not necessary anyway.

Hot (thermal) composts

Most of us have experienced the heat build-up in a pile of grass clippings from a recently mown lawn. Within hours, that heap of grass clippings can turn into a hot, steaming pile. What we are seeing in this situation is the energy generated by the explosive growth of groups of microorganisms called mesophiles (those that grow at moderately high temperatures) and thermophiles (those that grow at high to very high temperatures).

Hot composting is a method where we construct a heap that favours the development of both mesophilic and thermophilic microbes. It has the advantage that the high temperatures generated within the heap act to pasteurise the finished compost, and this process kills the vast majority of weeds (both vegetative structures, such as runners and bulbs, as well as seeds), pests and plant pathogens. However, it should be noted that hard-coated seeds (such as those from many legumes) often survive the pasteurisation process.

ABOVE LEFT This compost bay has no floor, so it has been invaded by living plant roots. This has caused the compost to lose nutrients and water.

ABOVE Sturdy and easy to use, a proprietary compost 'screw' is ideal for turning over small amounts of compost.

A successful hot-compost heap goes through several phases. The first one is monopolised by thermophilic microbes, which bring the temperature up to levels where pasteurisation occurs (50–70°C); this eliminates most of the harmful organisms that may be present. The second phase involves the dominance of mesophilic microbes, which complete the breakdown of organic materials, and proceeds at temperatures of up to 35°C. The third and final phase involves the maturation of the pile, and it begins as the nutrient supply starts to dwindle. Non-thermal organisms start to take over, as the temperature drops to more moderate levels. At this stage, many different microbes – such as actinomycetes (a group of fungus-like microbes) – start to appear that are associated with disease suppressiveness. These types of organisms are thought to be the best ones for stopping plant pathogens, such as root-rotting fungi.

In order to achieve a temperature that is high enough to kill weed seeds (50–60°C) with small volumes of compost, it is necessary to contain the compost in some kind of vessel, such as proprietary plastic bins or homemade structures (for example, bays made of bricks). In a commercial composting facility, a large yet simple windrow is quite sufficient to maintain heat; in fact, these compost rows often have the problem of excessive heat. In cold climates or where you have a real weed problem and need reliable heat, an insulated vessel can be used.

A means of occasionally turning the compost pile is also important. Either utilise a compost tumbler, which you can rotate with ease, or make a bay with three sides and a concrete or brick floor, so you can access the compost and turn it with a shovel or pitchfork.

Cold (non-thermophilic) composts

People often become concerned when their compost does not heat up. It does not need to be hot to produce good compost. Natural decay processes will eliminate most plant diseases (compost is not the natural home of diseases that directly parasitise plants), and if you don't put a lot of weeds in the compost, then this should not be a real issue, either.

Cold-compost bins are available in all sorts of shapes and sizes, with most looking something like a Dalek from *Doctor Who*. They are a great option for many households, especially if they produce a moderate amount of organic matter from the kitchen and yard. If you take a little care as to what material goes in, they will produce a balanced compost that doubles as both fertiliser and soil conditioner.

Trench composting is one of the simplest and easiest methods of cold composting, as it involves burying organic materials in soil that you want to enrich. Earthworms and various other macroorganisms, such as soldier fly larvae, will often breed in large numbers while this food is available. And, of course, microbes such as bacteria and fungi will arrive en masse to complete the composting task. It is not hot composting, however; it is best considered a type of vermicomposting. If the organic materials are buried deep enough, this will prevent the germination of any weed seeds.

In most natural soil profiles, there is an organic ('O') soil horizon above the mineral soil. The 'O' horizon is composed of leaf litter, bark, animal manure and so on, and it acts as a mini compost layer that is constantly adding small amounts of humus to the mineral soil in the 'A' horizon below. Trench composting is, in some respects, like creating a very thick 'O' horizon in your soil. Provided you are using a good balance of nutrient-rich materials with carbon-rich ingredients, your soil will obtain the maximum benefit – as any nutrients that are leached out of the compost will be deposited in the soil below for the subsequent crop.

Dig a trench or hole that is between 300 and 500 millimetres deep, and place all of your kitchen scraps in it. You can add meat, dog

manure and oily waste – just about anything. Cover the organic material with the soil, wait four weeks for it to rot down, and then plant over the top of it. The plant roots will soon be colonising the nutrient-rich zone of decayed waste and humus.

In wet conditions or in heavy clay subsoils, conditions in your trench compost can become anaerobic. This does not stop the decay of the organic material or create bad odours, since the material is buried deeply, but it will prevent roots from colonising the decaying waste. Add a mixture of coarse particles, such as chopped straw, to ensure better aeration. Also, depending on the size of the trench, a covering such as a sheet of corrugated iron will help stop large vermin digging up the trench while initial decay occurs.

ABOVE, LEFT TO RIGHT Trench composting is easy and labour saving. After covering the organic material and allowing it to rot down for about four weeks, you can plant straight over the top of the trench.

OPPOSITE Worm farms can be used to generate worm 'wee', which is a perfect liquid feed for your crops.

WORMS AND VERMICOMPOSTING

Worm farming is a very fast and efficient way of processing high-nutrient organic materials, such as kitchen scraps, that are regularly generated in urban areas around the world. Feedstock can be added to a worm farm on a daily basis if necessary, in contrast to 'hot' composting systems that start with a large 'batch' or volume of material, which usually cannot be added to once the composting process has commenced.

The worm population found within a vermicomposting system will ebb and flow in accordance with the amount of food available to it. If feed levels are gradually increased over a period of weeks, the population is able to expand reasonably rapidly.

Above-ground worm farming is also the perfect way to generate substantial quantities of liquid organic fertiliser, which can be used to liquid feed the urban farm in a sustainable way. The digestion process in the worm's gut produces vermicast, which includes a lot of soluble nutrients and beneficial organic matter. The nutrients can be leached out, or the

CASE STUDY: TOM'S COMPOST

The Mature Semi-thermal Compost table shows the make-up of mature compost from a 'semi-thermal' system producing only slight warming. The producer (Simon's dad, Tom) has two plastic bins with lids but no bottoms, so both bins connect to the soil. One is actively composting a feedstock comprising dry and fresh leaves, mixed kitchen scraps, eggshells and lawn clippings, while the other contains more mature material that is colonised by worms, so it's part worm compost as well. Tom doesn't turn the mature material, as the healthy earthworm population does that job for him.

MATURE SEMI-THERMAL COMPOST

PLANT NUTRIENT ELEMENT	TOM'S COMPOST
Nitrogen	2.28 per cent
Phosphorus	0.31 per cent
Potassium	1.61 per cent
Calcium	2.58 per cent
Magnesium	0.32 per cent
Sulphur	0.25 per cent
Iron	1580 mg/kg
Manganese	88 mg/kg
Zinc	245 mg/kg
Copper	45 mg/kg
Boron	30 mg/kg

The compost is very well balanced, although it has a relatively high level of calcium thanks to the eggshells. The NPK ratio is just about perfect. Zinc levels are higher than normal because Tom's yard has been contaminated with zinc, which has probably found its way into the lawn clippings. This is not a problem, as zinc is not harmful to the health of humans or the worms – and his fig and mandarin trees don't seem to mind it either!

vermicast can be used to make a 'tea'. Depending on the feedstock, a worm farm will usually produce a fertiliser that contains all the essential nutrients for plant growth in the right balance to replace those removed when we harvest our various food crops.

In addition, as food moves through the gut of an earthworm, a complex range of beneficial microbes is added to it. Consequently, it has been claimed that if you use fresh worm liquid on your garden, it has the added benefit of acting as a probiotic for your soil as well. Whether the microbes in fresh worm liquid are any better than the vast microflora produced in conventional composting systems is open to debate until more research has been done on the subject. We prefer to think that the positive results obtained from using vermicast and worm-liquid preparations are due to the soluble nutrients and soluble organic compounds found within them as much as to the beneficial microbes that they add to soil.

Advantages of worm farming

One of the great benefits of the organic and liquid fertilisers produced from a worm farm is that the nutrient balance tends to be well matched to the needs of the food crops in the urban farm (assuming you're feeding your worms the full range of food scraps from your kitchen). Essentially, you are returning the appropriate balance of nutrients back into your soil because you are feeding your worms scraps from the fruits and vegetables that were (mostly) grown in that soil to begin with, thus recycling the nutrients.

In larger, more commercially oriented urban farms, worm farming can be used to recycle the trimmings from the harvesting sheds, but in order to replace all the nutrients

LEFT Successful vermicompost uses a mixture of fine as well as open and coarse particles to keep the mass well aerated.

OPPOSITE This clever proprietary worm farm is a hanging fabric bag with an opening at the bottom from which liquid and solids are collected.

lost during the process of harvesting, it will usually be necessary to obtain additional organic feedstock from the farm and elsewhere. This could be manures, vegetable scraps from markets and retail outlets, and high-carbon sources such as wastepaper and sawdust, provided they are not contaminated.

There are two distinct types of worm farms – above-ground and in-ground – but above-ground systems usually best serve urban farms. Above-ground worm farms are ideal where you want to extract high-quality liquid organic fertiliser for everyday use on the urban farm. In addition, the system will also generate significant quantities of solid fertiliser in the form of worm castings, but this occurs less regularly than the production of liquid fertiliser.

Depending on the feedstock, a worm farm will usually produce a fertiliser that contains all the essential nutrients for plant growth in the right balance.

WORM FARM

WORMS DO NOT LIKE LIGHT
wet blanket cover and replace
r adding kitchen scraps

WORM MENU
ve to eat soft kitchen scraps
O onions or citrus (too acidic)

- THANK YOU -

Above-ground systems are also better suited to larger commercial enterprises, where a constant and significant demand for fertiliser occurs. Again, these worm farms will usually require the addition of off-farm wastes to make up volume requirements.

Operating worm farms

There are many different factors that must be dealt with when running a worm farm, including the amount of air and water in the farm, the ammonia and nitrogen levels, and achieving the correct temperature for optimum results.

◆ **Balance of air and water** In our opinion, this factor is arguably the most important consideration for worm farms, as worms are particularly sensitive to drying out so they need a constantly moist environment, but also one that provides plenty of oxygen so they can breathe. There needs to be a range of particle sizes within the body of your worm farm; the larger ones hold the air for worm respiration,

and the smaller ones hold the moisture that worms need to keep their skin damp.

If you have very wet vegetable scraps, add them to the worm farm along with dry material such as shredded paper, sawdust or dryish grass clippings – this will help reduce the moisture content and provide aeration. Too much moisture in the form of waterlogging will drive the worms out of the worm farm; if such conditions develop, regularly add coarse organic materials, such as chopped straw or shredded cardboard, to the worm farm to provide the large particle size that creates extra air spaces.

Unpleasant odours emanating from your worm farm are always a sign of waterlogged, anaerobic conditions developing, which in turn leads to the production of gases such as methane and hydrogen sulphide (rotten-egg gas) that are toxic to worms. You will also often find pockets of the worm farm harbouring white maggot-like creatures that are displacing the worms – these are soldier fly larvae, and they thrive in very wet conditions. A good worm farm provides a refuge

ABOVE LEFT Fresh food scraps are regularly added to the surface of this vertical above-ground worm farm.

ABOVE Pouring water over worm farms is necessary, especially for small systems that can dry out quickly. Any excess water can be collected as nutrient-rich leachate.

for worms to escape toxic conditions, such as a chamber or ledge above the composting mass, out of the sun and exposed to fresh air.

♦ **Ammonia and nitrogen** The first product of decaying protein is ammonia, which is also the form of nitrogen excreted by birds. So, having too much meat and manure from carnivores (including poultry) in your worm farm will risk the generation of ammonia gas – which is toxic to worms. High-carbon products such as straw, paper and sawdust will absorb ammonia – so if you smell this gas coming from your worm farm, adding these products will help.

Some people say that you shouldn't put meat in worm farms. However, provided you don't add too much – and you also include some dryish high-carbon material to absorb the ammonia – this should not be a problem.

♦ **Temperature level** Like humans, worms prefer to operate in moderate temperatures of 20–30°C. Worms generate their own heat, as do the composting microbes that unavoidably share the substrate with your worms. In summer, the worm farm can get too hot – when exposed to the sun at this time of year, the dark surface of a worm farm can quickly get up to 50°C by midday. To avoid this, insulate your chamber from the sun. You can also add water to the worm farm, increase the ventilation or make a smaller mass so that heat can't accumulate. Again, always provide a refuge so that worms can escape the heat if necessary.

Cold slows the whole vermicomposting process, so insulation also helps here. Styrofoam (expanded polystyrene) is an excellent and readily available insulator. With windrow worm farming, it is always best to have a plastic cover on hand to preserve heat in winter, to exclude heat in summer and to prevent too much rain from waterlogging the windrows during the year.

TYPES OF WORM FARMS

Regardless of the size of your urban farm, there is a worm farm to suit your needs. Above-ground systems are the most popular, as they allow you to spread the nutrient-rich compost wherever you like around the garden, but in-ground systems are low-maintenance options that many people find very useful.

On-ground windrows

The simplest method of worm farming for larger enterprises is creating a windrow, where a long, tent-shaped pile is progressively built on a clean, weed-free surface of soil or something porous, such as polyethylene weed mat or shade cloth. The pile should not be so high that it starts thermally composting – making it 300–500 millimetres high and twice as wide usually works. One of the advantages of a well-constructed windrow, however, is that worms can move around to find a temperature that suits them.

As the vermicompost matures, worms will naturally head towards any new food waste that is added to the pile, but when harvesting the mature material it is often necessary to move worms to the vermicompost in progress. This can be done by scooping some or all of the worm castings from the windrow, and piling the material on a tarpaulin or plastic sheet that is in the sun. The worms don't like light, so they will head down into the dark, cool, moist castings below. The top layer of castings can then be removed and used as fertiliser, and the rest of the castings with the worms can be returned to the windrow.

Windrows are the most common system used by commercial worm farms, as they have the lowest capital and running costs. Such enterprises usually make money from both sales of vermicast (and worm liquid) and from selling the worms themselves as fish bait or as part of worm-farm kits.

Like humans, worms prefer to operate in moderate temperatures of 20–30°C.

Commercial above-ground worm farms

There are many different worm farms available commercially, and each one has pros and cons. Stackable worm farms comprise a series of trays that allow the worms to migrate upwards; as they exhaust the food supply in the lower trays, they move up to reach the fresh food in the higher trays. After a few months, the bottom tray can be emptied of its castings, and any remnant worms are sorted out and put back into the system. The now-empty bottom tray can be rotated in the system to become the new top tray. In our experience with such systems, however, we find that gaps develop because the contents of the trays diminish in volume as the worms feed; this makes it almost impossible for the worms to migrate from a lower tray to the one above.

Invented in New Zealand, hungry bin (www.hungrybin.co.nz) is a worm farm that looks and functions like a giant vermicomposting funnel. It claims to be able to compost up to 2 kilograms of organic material per day; the material is simply placed into the top of the funnel, where the bulk of the worm population lives and feeds. As the material is broken down, it works its way down the funnel, along with any liquid that is produced by the worms. This liquid flows out of the mesh bottom and can be captured; there is a trapdoor to allow the harvesting of the worm castings, which are fully mature and ready to use by the time they reach the bottom of the funnel.

Another interesting above-ground worm farm is the Worm Habitat, manufactured in Queensland by a company called Worms Downunder (www.wormsdownunder.com.au). These units are made from modified wheelie bins, which are the standard rubbish bins given to ratepayers by many Australian councils. The wheelie bin has a mesh base that allows liquid to drain into a chamber below, which can be tapped off. Openings have been added to the side of the wheelie bin to allow the removal of castings from the lower part of the bin as they move down from the active feeding layer at the top of the bin. In addition, this worm farm has three special features:

1 The unit has wheels, so it is easily moveable.
2 It can be retrofitted to wheelie bins of various sizes, depending on the amount of waste you are likely to generate.
3 It is a continuous-flow system that does not require you to move and empty heavy trays of worm castings.

Homemade above-ground worm farms

For a more cost-effective worm farm, why not create your own? Using an old bathtub is one of the best options in our experience, but other large containers will also work. Mount your bathtub worm farm so that it is easy to drain the liquid fertiliser it produces. Food is continually added to the top of the system until the bathtub is full, a process that will generally take a year or more. You can extract castings by digging down into the bathtub, and a very useful strategy is to dig out one end at a time. Carefully sort the castings from the worms, which are returned to the bathtub. As you fill the empty side with food, the worms will migrate from the other side into the food – this makes it easier to then harvest the castings from the remaining half.

Smaller-scale above-ground worm farms can be created from second-hand containers such as polystyrene boxes. Worms are not particularly houseproud, as long as you keep bringing them food and regulating temperature and moisture conditions. You can either create a drainage hole at one end of the box to collect the liquid from your worm farm, or you can make multiple holes in the bottom of the box – as you would for a plant pot – and sit the worm farm under a lemon tree or the like, where the liquid fertiliser can drain into the soil and feed the plants around it.

It is also very feasible to build your own large-scale above-ground worm farm. Timber planks, rainwater tanks, water troughs and a variety of other large farm vessels can all be adapted to worm farming, and it is well worth consulting some of the excellent books available on the subject (see the Bibliography on page 252).

Collecting liquid fertiliser

Regardless of the type of above-ground worm farm you choose, the greatest benefit will be your ability to easily harvest the liquid fertiliser from it, in contrast to the in-ground worm farm that we will talk about next. All worm farms generate a certain amount of liquid, and the quantity depends on the moisture content of the feedstock as well as the amount of moisture that might find its way into the worm farm from rainfall or by deliberate application. If you are pouring additional water through the system to generate liquid fertiliser, it is important to ensure there is good drainage and high porosity, and to supply a refuge for the worms.

Generally, if no extra moisture is added to the system, a relatively small amount of very concentrated liquid is produced that is about

LEFT, TOP TO BOTTOM You can deliberately add an excessive amount of water to your worm farm to create an excellent all-purpose liquid feed. Simply collect the concentrated leachate from the drainage pipe, dilute it with water, and then use it on your plants.

the consistency of strong black coffee – this liquid is usually too high in nutrients to be used undiluted in the garden. Add water until it is about the consistency of weak tea (in other words, you are able to see through it), and you can be sure that the liquid will not burn your plants. This is especially vital for seedlings and new transplants.

Large-scale above-ground worm farms represent a viable and sustainable option for generating high-quality liquid organic fertiliser on urban farms of a more commercial scale, including peri-urban farms located on the

edge of cities such as market gardens and cut-flower farms. If you are generating liquid fertiliser from an industrial-scale above-ground worm farm, then a more scientific approach to ensuring the optimum nutrient levels is worthwhile.

A particularly effective system utilises a bench system for the worm beds. Above it is mounted a micro sprinkler system, which sprays water over the beds to the point where it leaches through and drains into a holding tank. The worm leachate is aerated in this tank using an oxygenating device designed for aquariums; it is then pumped back to the worm beds and recirculated until it has attained sufficient nutrient concentration to be optimal for liquid feeding plants. An electrical conductivity meter is used to monitor the concentration of nutrient salts in the worm leachate, and a filter is utilised to ensure that organic-matter particles do not clog up the irrigation system. The solid worm castings are also harvested every year or so and applied directly to the soil (after the worms have been separated and returned to the worm farm) when the worm beds are renovated to ensure efficient operation.

In-ground worm farms

These units involve either trench composting (which is part composting, part worm farming) or some sort of structure, such as a large-diameter PVC drainpipe, which is partially buried in the soil and has slots or holes in the below-ground portion to allow the worms to move in and out of the surrounding soil. A section of the pipe is above ground level and should ideally have an aerated lid to allow the system to breathe. To add food to the top of the system for the worms to feed on, simply remove the above-ground lid.

Although an in-ground worm farm is usually a small-scale system, it still has several advantages:

- It is very low maintenance. Simply dig it in once, and add food scraps for 3–6 months before moving it to the next spot.
- The nutrients produced by the worms go straight into the soil to feed the surrounding plants up to a metre away.
- The worms can move away from unfavourable extremes of temperature or moisture (in other words, they self-regulate).

The only major disadvantage we have found with in-ground worm farms is that they do not allow you to distribute fertiliser around the garden. However, this issue can be overcome to some extent by regularly moving your in-ground worm farm to a different position in the garden. When you move the unit, it is desirable to lift the castings out and separate the worms from the castings – at least enough to 'seed' the next spot with some worms.

An in-ground worm farm starts fertilising your plants as soon as the worms get to work. The liquid from the unit carries nutrients and beneficial microbes into the soil, while the worms cultivate and aerate the soil whenever they travel out of the unit and tunnel beneath the soil surface. Indeed, a network of in-ground worm farms will save you the trouble of having to dig your soil to prepare it for future crops.

QUALITY OF VERMICAST AND WORM 'WEE'

We have said previously that the quality of compost you get out of worm-farm systems, in terms of its fertiliser value at least, will be dependent on what you put in. In Melbourne, the city council has encouraged the use of the worm-bin vermicomposting system in various institutions, including restaurants and blocks of flats. This has given us the opportunity to use laboratory analysis to compare the nutritional value of restaurant vermicast (vermicompost) with that of Angus' household vermicompost. The restaurant feedstock contained mixed vegetables and eggshells but no added water, while Angus' household feedstock featured mixed whole kitchen scraps, including eggshells and bones, with extra water added (so he can extract soluble nutrients as worm 'wee' compost). The results of the comparison are shown in the Nutritional Value of Various Worm Composts table on page 196.

The council-sponsored systems do not permit the use of meat scraps, but Angus does, which is one reason why Angus' worm compost has much higher phosphorus, iron and possibly zinc and copper levels. The restaurant worm compost – with its very high fruit and vegetable content – has high potassium levels, whereas Angus' is

An in-ground worm farm starts fertilising your plants as soon as the worms get to work.

leached to generate liquid feed, so much of the soluble potassium content has been removed and is now in the liquid feed.

Angus' compost is very mature, as it is taken from the lowest shelf of his layered system. This also explains why the insoluble nutrients phosphorus, calcium, iron, zinc and copper become so concentrated. As the compost gets older, the carbon content drops and the insoluble mineral matter increases in proportion. The restaurant worm compost, on the other hand, is fresher and hence shows a higher nitrogen content but a lower iron level.

ABOVE A small in-ground worm farm is a very simple and labour-saving system for the recycling of kitchen scraps.

Angus' worm 'wee'

Angus likes worm farming and often raves about the response he gets from using a 'juice' or 'wee' that he makes from his worm farm. All he does is pour the water from a full watering-can through the worm farm every time he needs some liquid feed. The excess water drains out, and the worms don't get too wet. He sent a sample of both the 'wee' and the solid worm compost to Simon's lab. The nutrients in the 'wee' are given in the Nutritional Value of Angus' Worm 'Wee' table on the opposite page.

The results are remarkable. Look at the 'ideal' levels for the different nutrients in a middle-of-the-road liquid or hydroponic feed compared with Angus' worm 'wee'. The 'wee' represents a very close approximation to the perfect liquid feed, as the ratios of the major and minor plant nutrients are all close to ideal for the average plant. This is not really surprising, since Angus uses all his kitchen scraps – which represent a cross-section of plants he grows on his urban farm – in the compost. He also adds some meat, bones and eggshells. Notice how high the potassium level is – this is higher than necessary for most plants, but perfect for fruit and flowering crops that need plenty of potassium.

The levels of nitrogen, calcium, phosphorus and iron are much higher in Angus' household vermicompost than in the worm 'wee', while the potassium level is much lower. This is not so surprising if you remember that the first four elements are not very soluble. Potassium, being very soluble, is quickly leached away into the 'wee', leaving the other elements behind. The very high calcium and phosphorus is no doubt the result of adding bones and eggshells to the mixture.

Nitrogen is a bit more complicated, as it forms very soluble minerals (nitrate and ammonium) but also remains as an integral part of the organic-matter matrix (seen as proteins and other insoluble living

NUTRITIONAL VALUE OF VARIOUS WORM COMPOSTS

ELEMENT	RESTAURANT*	ANGUS' HOUSEHOLD*
Nitrogen	2.62 per cent	2.24 per cent
Potassium	1.36 per cent	0.58 per cent
Calcium	6.21 per cent	5.57 per cent
Phosphorus	0.32 per cent	1.32 per cent
Magnesium	0.68 per cent	0.52 per cent
Sulphur	0.31 per cent	0.44 per cent
Iron	5235 mg/kg	18,900 mg/kg
Manganese	238 mg/kg	290 mg/kg
Zinc	70 mg/kg	268 mg/kg
Copper	49 mg/kg	127 mg/kg
Boron	19.7 mg/kg	45.2 mg/kg

Note: We usually measure macronutrients as a percentage by dry weight. Micronutrients are present in much lower amounts, however, so we express these as milligrams per kilogram, which is a more sensitive unit of measurement.

components). As it 'mineralises' during the process of decomposition, it releases slowly into the soluble nitrate (NO_3) and ammonium (NH_4) that we see in the liquid component.

The result: a perfect fertiliser combination. Use the solids as a pre-plant fertiliser for the beds before planting the seedlings or sowing the seeds. When they start to grow, use the liquid 'wee' maybe twice a week – depending on how the plants look – as a well-balanced and readily available feed to encourage rapid and healthy growth.

The only problem with worm farming the Angus way is that, depending on the size of your garden, you are more than likely going to run out of sufficient 'wee' and castings. You are left with trying to source alternative forms of organic waste for your worms to eat. However, this may not be an issue – friends and neighbours usually welcome the chance to join in this environmentally friendly (and productive) exercise.

LEFT A highly concentrated dark-coloured worm juice or compost tea needs to be diluted in a watering-can before use.

NUTRITIONAL VALUE OF ANGUS' WORM 'WEE'

ELEMENT	WORM 'WEE' (MG/L)	'IDEAL' LIQUID FEED (MG/L)
Nitrogen	200	150–250
Potassium	410	200–300
Calcium	89	50–100
Phosphorus	39	30–60
Magnesium	23	20–50
Sulphur	50	30–60
Iron	4.6	2–5
Manganese	0.24	0.2–1
Zinc	0.28	0.3–0.8
Boron	0.1	0.05–0.1
Sodium	59	< 100
Chloride	89	< 100

The important thing to know about Angus' vermicomposting method is that he uses a cross-section of normal plant material. Do what you can to source natural plant material that worms like. Vegetable waste from the local greengrocer, spoiled lucerne hay and animal manures from pasture-fed horses or poultry are all perfect for the process.

Unfortunately, other kinds of easily available organic material are not so well balanced. Many of the commercially available animal manures are from stall-fed chickens, cows and ducks. The diets of such animals and birds are very high in protein (nitrogen), calcium and phosphorus for rapid bone and egg growth. Some manures, such as those from feedlot cows, have extremely high zinc levels. This is because farmers feed these cattle a diet with excessive amounts of zinc, in the mistaken belief that it aids growth rates. The zinc level in the manure can actually make it dangerous to use on the garden for any length of time (see page 101 in the Soils and Soil Fertility Chapter). None of the commercially available animal manures are very good sources of potassium, one of the most important elements for vegetable and fruit production.

Because additional water is not poured through the worm farm ... the salinity of the restaurant's worm juice is ... concentrated.

Melbourne Council worm juice

The Melbourne Council worm farms produce a different kind of liquid extract. They have a lot of moist vegetable and fruit waste, which actually results in excess water slowly but continuously dripping out of the bottom without the need to add any extra water. This liquid exudate is collected and bottled for use as a fertiliser, just like Angus' worm 'wee'. We analysed the liquid from the Melbourne restaurant worm farm mentioned earlier in this chapter, and the results are shown in the Nutritional Value of Restaurant Worm Juice table on the opposite page.

These results tell a very interesting story. The liquid that slowly drips out of the worm beds in the restaurant worm farm as the various vegetable components decay is highly condensed. Because additional water is not poured through the worm farm, unlike in Angus' system, the salinity of the restaurant's worm juice is much more concentrated. In fact, it is far too concentrated to be put straight onto many plants. The electrical conductivity (EC), a measure of the salt content of liquid, is 12.6 for the restaurant's worm juice, but only 1.9 for Angus' worm 'wee'. Liquid feeds for plants should be between 1.5 and 3 EC units, so a 1 to 5 dilution of the restaurant's worm juice (in other words, 2 litres of this worm juice into a 10-litre bucket) would be about right and bring it very close to the concentration of Angus' worm 'wee'.

In the worm juice, potassium is the outstanding component and needs to be diluted. Sodium is also quite high, maybe due to the use of salt in the restaurant. Both sodium and potassium are, of course, very soluble, so they obviously become highly concentrated in worm farms that are not flushed out with extra water.

The worm juice is not very well balanced, so diluting it may make the potassium level acceptable but the other nutrients will then be too low. This is not a great concern, as both the liquid and the castings are applied to urban plots in the city, with the one offsetting the other. Using both together provides the perfect balance of nutrients.

LEFT This large-scale set-up for dealing with organic restaurant waste in Melbourne produces highly concentrated worm juice and solid compost.

NUTRITIONAL VALUE OF RESTAURANT WORM JUICE

ELEMENT	RESTAURANT (MG/L)	ANGUS' WORM 'WEE' (MG/L)
Nitrogen	395	200
Potassium	3900	410
Calcium	125	89
Phosphorus	68	39
Magnesium	148	23
Sulphur	223	50
Iron	10	4.6
Manganese	0.9	0.24
Zinc	0.48	0.28
Copper	0.55	0.30
Boron	0.44	0.1
Sodium	788	59
Organic carbon	2700	—

BOKASHI COMPOSTING

Developed in Japan, this radically different form of composting may be of interest to the urban farmer because it can be done in very confined spaces and it generates significant quantities of liquid fertiliser that is rich in nutrients and beneficial microbes. It is perfectly feasible to set up this system in a home unit or high-rise flat, because it uses a bucket with a snap-on airtight lid that excludes vermin, vinegar flies and other insects, unlike most other composting systems.

However, there is a distinct downside to this system – compared to the other composting methods that we have looked at, it is relatively complicated. It requires a regular input every few days of the particular microbes required to make the system work efficiently. Nevertheless, in our opinion, the benefit of producing a rich liquid organic fertiliser in confined spaces makes this system well worth investigating.

The Bokashi system is rather unique among urban composting structures in that it is based on fermentation of the ingredients, usually kitchen scraps. A particular group of beneficial microorganisms that thrive with little or no oxygen is used. Normally, anaerobic microbes produce a negative result; however, these ones have been carefully selected to produce a positive result. The microbes can be either cultured at home or purchased from a commercial enterprise, and they are added to the mix every time a deposit of organic material is made into the system.

Unlike other composting methods, the Bokashi system does not produce mature compost. The microbes break down the internal contents of the composted material until there is just a shell left behind, in the process creating a liquid brimming with a large proportion of the nutrients from the raw ingredients, as well as a range of organisms that are beneficial to soil biology. Any material remaining in the system can be buried in soil, placed in a compost heap or added to a regular worm farm to complete the breakdown process.

The Bokashi system, in our experience, works best for high-nutrient organic material, such as kitchen scraps. However, there is no reason it could not be used for other organic material, such as wastepaper or animal manure. It is certainly worth considering using this system if you are in a confined space that does not have room for alternative composting systems.

UTILISING 'WASTE' ORGANIC MATERIAL

We mentioned earlier that compost is used in several ways on the urban farm, for example as mulch, soil conditioner or fertiliser. So let us explore these ideas further.

♠ **Compost as mulch** If you have a lot of woody materials (such as sticks, twigs, bark or woodchips), it will take a lot of extra nutrients to break down these materials into fully mature compost that will not draw extra nutrients from the soil when it is mixed in. However, compost that is partially broken down and still full of coarse, woody materials

TO PEE OR NOT TO PEE

An obvious source of nitrogen and other nutrients is animal urine. Most of us have a diet that is particularly rich in all sorts of goodies that plants and other organisms can use to fuel growth. The tragedy of modern society is that we have not focused more on ways to capture and use this nutrient stream in a sustainable way.

One time-honoured method of utilising the nutrients in urine is to add the liquid to composts, where the breakdown process destroys or denatures any health issues that may arise. We realise that it may not always be feasible to urinate on your compost heap in heavily populated urban environments; however, we can both attest to the great benefits of adding urine to compost if you can somehow make it happen!

The Bokashi system is ... based on fermentation of the ingredients, usually kitchen scraps.

can still be readily used as mulch. In this case, it is spread over the top of the soil to act as an insulating blanket that keeps moisture in the soil, eliminates temperature extremes and suppresses weed growth. It is better for mulch to be coarse and open, as this allows it to admit rainfall or irrigation water but also provide excellent insulation.

● **Compost as soil conditioner** If you have compost that is 'mature' (in other words, it has fully broken down), then it is ready to be dug into the soil. Some composts in this category may have lower nutrient value, as the nutrients have all been used up during the composting process, while others may have quite a lot of nutrients. It all depends on the feedstock, with high-carbon materials having a lower nutrient value. If there is very little in the way of extra nutrients in the compost, then it should be considered as a soil conditioner and used to boost the soil's physical fertility. It can help with the water- and nutrient-holding capacity of the soil, as well as improve soil structure (which in turn improves drainage and aeration within the soil).

● **Compost as fertiliser** If the raw materials for your compost are high in nutrients (such as animal manures or kitchen scraps), then the 'mature' compost will not only act as a soil conditioner, but it will also be a source of plant nutrients. The nutritional value of compost diminishes over time, as nutrients can be lost via escaping gases (such as ammonia), by leaching (as water passes through the pile) or if the pile is exposed to rainfall for long periods. Understanding these processes can help you to minimise the losses – for instance, you can collect the nutrients that are being leached out and use them as a liquid fertiliser.

Solid compost is best dug in to the soil to some extent, because that's where the roots are. However, even if it is applied to the surface, it will be carried down slowly by rainfall and worm activity – so it's not useless. For poor soils with low levels of organic matter, results will certainly be much faster if the compost is dug in prior to planting.

● **Compost 'tea' for liquid feeding**
Well-matured compost has a lot of elements in highly soluble form that are easily extracted by steeping the compost (like making 'tea') or by leaching them out into an instantly available liquid feed. These liquid feeds can be applied strategically at the times they are most needed, for example to boost the growth of young seedlings, or to obtain a very dramatic and rapid response from plants that are starting to fruit. Ensure that your leachate or 'tea' is not so dark that you can't see through it – as this indicates that it is too strong to put straight onto plants. If the solution is too concentrated, add water until you can see through it – and you can be assured that you will not cause any fertiliser burn on your plants. This is particularly important for soft young seedlings, but it also applies to more mature plants.

ABOVE An on-ground cold-composting bin allows worms to enter from the surrounding soil. The flap at the bottom gives the urban farmer easy access to the matured compost.

CASE STUDY: INNER-CITY FARMING

FareShare and 3000acres

FareShare (www.fareshare.net.au) has extended itself far beyond the usual community-garden concept. As well as growing highly productive kitchen gardens on vacant parcels of disused city land, such as areas near train tracks and airports, the charity also sources food that might otherwise be wasted in supermarkets and restaurants to cook and distribute over a million meals a year to those in need around Melbourne.

3000acres (www.3000acres.org) is a not-for-profit organisation that seeks to influence 'the cultural and regulatory environment to make it easier to grow food'. Their goal is to link landholders with those who want to become urban farmers, and also to team up these people with those who can provide other necessary resources.

One of the most impressive urban-farm projects in Melbourne is one that resulted from a collaboration between FareShare and 3000acres. FareShare wanted to increase its access to fresh produce for its meal service, so they enlisted the expertise of 3000acres to create an urban farm near its kitchens in inner-city Abbotsford. Sponsored by the Royal Automobile Club of Victoria and Gandel Philanthropy, volunteers created 70 garden beds on land owned by VicTrack (the organisation that manages land for Victoria's public transport network), adjacent to Collingwood Football Club's famous Victoria Park. Where it was not possible to sow directly into the soil, raised beds were built to grow a range of crops including zucchini, turnips, carrots, silverbeets, capsicums, sweet potatoes, eggplants, beans and herbs.

Large compost bins were manufactured from recycled timber to provide fertiliser and soil-conditioning humus, while a couple of greenhouses were constructed for propagation needs. The freshly harvested produce goes directly to FareShare's nearby kitchens, with minimal delay between reaping and use as ingredients in the meals that FareShare makes and hands out on a daily basis.

This is a perfect example of how innovative organisations can coordinate and assist various stakeholders so they can take advantage of vacant community land in Australian cities. Urban farmers need resources other than land as well, and there is an increasing awareness in modern society of the opportunities that various corporate and philanthropic bodies can provide to the willing urban-farming workforce in our cities. The desire of budding urban farmers to grow more and more food plants is a powerful driver of these important initiatives.

CLOCKWISE, FROM OPPOSITE TOP
Capsicums are protected by a thick layer of straw mulch; raised beds that have been built from recycled timber look rustic and appealing; sunflowers provide both visual attraction and grain; large composting bays are made from leftover wood; an eggplant crop grows well in raised beds.

MULCHING

Mulch is a protective blanket of material that sits on top of the soil or growing medium. It acts as an insulating layer – keeping the soil cooler in summer and conserving the summer heat into winter – and, most importantly, it reduces evaporation and keeps the soil moist, which conserves precious irrigation water. By stopping temperature levels around the roots from reaching extremes of hot or cold, mulch promotes root growth and creates an environment where worms can thrive. Mulch also prevents or at least slows the growth of weeds, as it smothers their seeds and stops most (if not all) of them from germinating.

Plants always grow better with mulch than without it. We generally use mulch more for its physical effects than for its impact on chemical fertility; however, moist soil means better nutrient uptake, so mulch does have an indirect influence on a soil's chemical fertility. Some mulches can actually improve fertility by conditioning and/or adding nutrients to the soil. For example, lucerne hay is excellent mulch that stimulates worms and releases nutrients into the soil.

Usually, mulch should be coarse rather than fine, so that it rapidly admits water and does not soak it up. We also don't want rainfall or irrigation to sit on top of the mulch, where it will just evaporate – we need the water to run through the mulch easily and enter the soil below. The 'blanket' layer of air trapped between the mulch particles will then stop the water from evaporating. If you want to conserve moisture, it is not a good idea to use fine compost as mulch; however, if you've got plenty of water in the soil and/or a humid climate, this becomes less important – you can use fine mulch such as compost to insulate the soil and add nutrients.

Permanent vs seasonal

It's useful to divide mulches into two different types: permanent and seasonal (or one-crop). Permanent mulch is used for weed control and moisture retention around long-term perennial crops, such as fruit trees, vines, biennials and herbaceous perennials. In this case, you want

mulch that will last as long as possible and is usually topped up only once each year. These mulches should be woody (such as coarse pine bark or woodchips), or, for large-scale enterprises, they can be synthetic (such as weed mat or organic 'rolls' made from coconut coir, jute and paper/cardboard fibre).

Permanent mulches should be kept around 50–75 millimetres deep by adding new mulch each year as the bottom layer decays, but very woody and bark mulches will often last two years or more before they need to be topped up. Note that woody mulch often causes nitrogen drawdown (see the box on page 157 of the Fertilisers chapter). This can be overcome

ABOVE Sugar cane can be purchased quite cheaply, and it makes for an excellent temporary mulch for quick-turnover crops.

by applying nitrogen in solution over the mulch, or urea at 20 grams per square metre watered in lightly. The commercially composted woody mulches that come from the large-scale composting of garden green waste don't produce the same significant nitrogen drawdown as raw-wood mulches, and they are much more environmentally friendly because they comprise recycled materials. They are also cost effective.

Seasonal or one-crop mulches, as the name implies, are used on annual crops – such as most vegetables – where the growing cycle is usually 6–12 weeks. When we turn over the crops in a working vegetable-growing area, we often cultivate the soil as well. You don't want long-lasting woody mulches here, as they just get dug in and incorporated into the soil every time you replant. It's preferable to have readily decomposable mulches such as hay, straw, sugar cane and, where water is not a problem, fine compost.

It's not always necessary to mulch vegetable gardens. It can be very difficult, costly and time consuming to mulch very fast turnover crops such as coriander and lettuce, and downright fiddly with fine plants such as chives and spring onions. With the close spacing used between vegetable crops, and the shade cast by taller crops such as tomato and eggplant, the benefits of mulching are marginal if the soil is composted regularly and fed properly. It is important to water appropriately in such situations, so the surface soil does not stay permanently wet.

Types of mulch

There are many different materials that can be successfully used as mulch. Organically derived options include leaves, straw, hay, chipped bark, woodchips, newspaper and cardboard. Inorganic materials, such as gravel or synthetic weed mats, can also be useful for certain applications. Small, decorative stones are utilised mainly for moisture retention rather than thermal insulation (although the white ones do reflect heat) – but they are only suitable for use as permanent mulches. They are most effective in formal gardens, such as parterres and Italian- or Greek-themed gardens; keep in mind that formal gardens can be both beautiful and very productive. Here is a list of commonly available materials for use as mulches.

♦ **Lawn clippings** Many gardeners have access to a regular supply of freshly cut grass, either from their own lawn or from their neighbours. Green clippings have a fairly high nutrient content, but they are rather fine so it is a good idea to mix in some dead leaves or other coarse material, such as chopped straw (run over the straw with your lawn mower to shred it). This will help to open out the mulch and stop the lawn clippings from matting down and

BELOW Lawn clippings can be used as mulch if they are mixed with coarse leaves and twigs. If they contain weeds, the clippings should be composted.

becoming impervious to water. There are many advantages to using lawn clippings: they are free, they do not need to be transported, and they will help add nutrients to your growing beds. Ensure that there are no weeds going to seed in the lawn being mowed. If you do have a lot of weeds in the lawn, the clippings are best composted.

♦ Homemade compost Making your own compost from various organic materials is a fantastic way to generate mulch that has the potential to both feed and insulate your soil (see the Compostable Materials table on page 182). It's important to note that when using homemade compost as mulch, the larger the particle size, the better. We recommend sieving your compost into two particle sizes: coarse (preferably several millimetres in diameter) and fine (all the tiny particles). The coarse-grade compost can be used as mulch, while the finer particles can be dug in as fertiliser or soil conditioner. Homemade compost mulches are free to make, and you can be sure that they are 'organic' because you know that they do not have any artificial chemicals. They also add nutrients to the soil

if you have properly composted them, and thus your garden beds will not usually require the application of additional fertilisers.

♦ Raw woodchips Mixed tree loppings can often be obtained cheaply (or for free) from tree-lopping crews working in your local area. They must be composted first to get rid of weeds and to allow any natural toxins, such as tannins, to break down and dissipate. There is usually enough leaf material to promote composting, otherwise add some green matter to help the composting process. Wet the material up in a heap, and allow it to break down for a month or so before use. Woodchips are also available commercially as forestry residues, both as pine and hardwood chips and flakes, and these do not have weed or disease problems. Woodchips are good as long-term mulches for permanent plantings, such as fruit trees. All uncomposted woody mulches will cause nitrogen drawdown, which is overcome by applying some nitrogen (commonly urea). Blood and bone and other organic sources of nitrogen can also be used. Alternatively, you can compost them before use by adding urea at 100 grams per 100 litres, wetting them up and letting them break down for a month.

◆ **Composted, screened, recycled woodchips** This is the coarse fraction (usually > 20 millimetres) of composted green waste from kerbside collection and drop-off at waste recycling stations. It is usually well composted in large heaps, so it has been through the heating process and is thus free of weeds and pathogens. A low-cost and excellent long-term mulch, it can be a bit dull coloured for decorative use – but that's not our primary interest on urban farms. Since it's composted, this mulch does not generally cause nitrogen drawdown.

◆ **Newspaper and cardboard** This is waste paper and cardboard that is either shredded or unshredded. It can pack down and exclude air and water, so the shredded form is best for thermal insulation. Flat sheets of cardboard are excellent for suppressing weeds around tree crops (such as citrus), provided that there is adequate air and water movement through the holes in the cardboard created for your plants. In the past, this mulch was often obtained from office waste, but these days most of that goes to the paper recyclers – so you might have to make your own. Shredded paper and cardboard can blow around and look trashy; cover the mulch with another decorative and heavier material (such as woodchips) to solve this problem.

◆ **Pine bark** This is the most common decorative mulch available in the landscaping industry, and it comes in various sizes (just don't use the fines for mulch). A recycled forestry residue, it is both sustainable and renewable. It makes for excellent long-term mulch (especially around fruit trees) as it does not have excessive nitrogen drawdown, but it is more expensive than woodchips.

◆ **Sugar cane** The remains of sugar cane after the juice is squeezed out, it is present in abundant quantities in sugar-growing regions and is exported in compressed bales as mulch. It's a very good thermal insulator and does not create excessive nitrogen drawdown, so it makes for a good short-term mulch around vegetable crops.

SOIL AS MULCH

A layer of dry soil on the surface acts as mulch, especially if it is light and airy. Farmers will often cultivate the top 50 millimetres of the soil just to fluff it up and let it dry. This is also why watering deeply and less often is better for the garden. It allows the surface soil to dry out and conserve moisture at depth. A constantly wet surface acts like a wick, conducting water from below.

Blanching is a form of mulching where soil is used around plants to stop sunlight from turning stems green. Commercial asparagus growers use a 'hilling' plough to build up the soil around the crown of the plants. Pickers then harvest the white asparagus spears by utilising a chisel-pointed knife to cut the stems off below the ground.

◆ **Gravel** A decorative option, gravel is available in a wide range of colours and rock sizes. The best gravel for mulching purposes is 10–20 millimetres in size, and it should be applied to a depth of 50–75 millimetres. Only use it in permanently mulched areas, such as orchards, where the appearance of mulch is as important as its practical considerations.

◆ **Crop residues** These include straw as well as maize and sorghum stover, and are usually high in carbon. They are ideal for annual crops such as vegetables, as they decay quickly and add valuable organic matter to soils. However, they often cause nitrogen drawdown; this can be overcome by applying nitrogenous fertiliser, such as urea or chicken manure, to the soil surface before putting the mulch down, and then watering thoroughly.

◆ **Lucerne hay** This is the premium 'mulch and feed' material, and it stimulates both root growth and worm activity. This is not surprising really, as this stock feed is high in the nutrients and protein that plants and worms love. Unlike other carbon-based mulches, which can cause nitrogen drawdown, lucerne hay is quite high in nitrogen and actually adds this nutrient to the soil. It is especially useful for really fast-growing annual crops, such as tomatoes and root vegetables.

♠ Landscape fabrics Plastic weed mats and cellulose (coconut coir) mats are excellent for long-term weed control, and they provide some moisture conservation but not much thermal insulation. This is not a problem if you want to warm soil (they are often black, so they absorb heat), but it can be counterproductive if you want to keep the soil cool. They are also very cheap, unlike woven and matted fibre products (such as jute matting), which provide excellent weed, water and heat management, but are costly. Historically, these latter products were developed for erosion control.

Selecting mulch

The choice of mulch material will be influenced by a number of factors, such as the kinds of plants you are growing. Other factors include:

- The availability of materials – you might have your own source, such as lawn clippings mixed with dead leaves, or there may be a ready source of recycled or free material available locally. For example, some councils give away chipped green-waste mulch. However, always compost 'giveaway' chipped green waste for at least six weeks, as it will contain weed seeds and plant pathogens that can only be destroyed during a period of hot composting. Screen out the coarse fractions for mulch and use the fines as compost, or just put the whole lot on the garden as a 'mulch and feed'.
- The need for weed control – for the most effective weed control, it is best to create a continuous barrier (perhaps using cardboard sheets from recycled boxes). These mulches are very effective for new ground that is full of weed seeds, but they do exclude water so you will have to adapt your watering to suit (for example, don't use a sprinkler – place drippers next to the plant instead). Weed-free composted woodchips and bark are also very effective weed-control mulches.

- The wish to control water and temperature – for water efficiency and the moderation of temperature extremes, a thick layer of coarse, chunky organic materials will give the best results. Straw is very effective here, as its low density and coarse nature traps air for maximum insulation.
- The desire to feed plants – if you wish to fertilise your plants at the same time as gaining the other benefits of mulching (which is known as 'mulch and feed'), use a material that has a relatively high nutrient level, such as lucerne hay, pea straw or a mix of woody and nutrient-rich compost.

ABOVE Cereal straw or hay is a low-cost mulch that is easy to apply over large areas, but it can cause nitrogen drawdown.

NEXT PAGES A carpet of mulch insulates the soil, protecting the fragile roots of these seedlings from extremes of temperature.

WATER AND DRAINAGE

10

A DELICATE MOISTURE BALANCE

One of the keys to successful food production is a continuous supply of water that is of sufficient quality for the plants that are being cultivated. Water for crop irrigation does not necessarily need to be of the same standard as drinking water, so it can be derived from a variety of sources. It is important to explore the best way to supply your water needs in terms of quantity, quality and cost. Equally vital is to ensure that your soil does not become waterlogged, as this will kill plants if it continues for too long. Creating a growing environment that is well drained yet holds enough moisture for crop growth is a major part of urban farming.

WHAT ARE YOUR WATER RESOURCES?

Most urban areas will be connected to a town water supply that provides a source of more or less unlimited water, but this will often come at a substantial monetary cost so it is obviously advisable to not rely solely on it if possible. It is therefore worth exploring alternative water sources that may provide a lower-cost option. The capital cost may be significant when setting up systems such as rainwater tanks or bores, but you are likely to save an enormous amount of money in the long term, as well as reduce your dependence on expensive town water, which may be of variable quality.

Your water supply must be of appropriate quality if sustainable crop production is to be achieved. The most critical point is that salinity (the concentration of dissolved salts in the water) must be within the limits of the species you want to grow. The salinity level varies depending on the source of your water. Rainwater will generally have negligible salinity, and town water in most areas will not be a problem; however, bore and recycled water can both contain significant salt levels that may damage plant growth, and can cause the build-up of salts in the soil over time. If you are in any doubt about the quality of your water, then you should get it tested by a reputable laboratory that can hopefully also advise you on any treatment measures that may be needed to improve the quality.

Background salts can also be an issue if you liquid feed your plants, as fertilisers (both organic and inorganic) will further elevate the salinity of your irrigation water. If you have a salinity problem, then it is worth learning more about this topic and perhaps investing in a salinity meter so that you can monitor your soil and water.

HOW MUCH WATER WILL I NEED?

If you do not have access to town water, then it is critical that your water-storage facility – whether it is a small tank or a large dam – is

BELOW Roof-water harvesting and storage tanks are a practical way of reducing your dependence on purchased town water for your urban farm.

FAR LEFT Plants grown in terracotta pots need to be watered often, as water is lost through the porous pot. This does not occur with plastic pots.

LEFT Inexpensive timers take much of the work – not to mention guesswork – out of irrigation, especially during drought periods.

sufficient to get your urban farm through dry spells or droughts. The amount of water you will need depends on the size of your growing area and how intensively you are using it throughout the year. Other considerations include whether you are growing outdoors (and therefore utilising rainwater when it falls) or under some sort of cover, such as a greenhouse; soil type (how much water does your soil store?); and crop types (some will use much more water than others).

HOW OFTEN SHOULD I WATER MY CROPS?

The water requirements of any given crop on your urban farm are constantly changing. Your plants will obviously require much more water on hot or windy days, when they are actively growing and flowering, and when they are growing in soils that do not store moisture well. The depth of a plant's root system will also affect its ability to extract moisture. Plants will extend their root systems to seek out moisture in the subsoil, and we can encourage this through deep watering every few days to a week if there has been no additional moisture through rainfall or run-off.

At any time in Australia – summer or winter – harsh drought conditions can overtake us. This results in local authorities imposing strict restrictions on when and how we water our gardens and urban farms. If you are in any doubt about this issue, it is best to check with your local council or water authority, as fines for breaking the rules can be substantial. At times like these, an additional water source such as a tank or dam will be worth its weight in gold.

Plants in containers will usually need to be watered more frequently, as less water is stored in the limited volume of potting mix than in a garden bed. Your choice of soil or growing medium (such as potting mix) also impacts on watering frequency due to variations in water-holding capacity.

HOW MUCH WATER DO I NEED TO APPLY?

The amount of water to apply when you irrigate your crops will depend on your soil depth and type as well as the variety of crop that you are growing. A practical way of telling how much

FAR LEFT A granular wetting agent dug in to the surface of your soil will help reduce water repellence.

LEFT Using light-coloured mulches, such as white pebbles, on your garden beds will keep soil cool and conserve precious moisture.

water is needed is to apply a set amount of water over 1 square metre – or leave the sprinklers on for a known time – then wait 24 hours before digging a hole to see how far down the soil profile or potting mix the water has reached. If it has only penetrated 100 millimetres, then you know that to penetrate 200 millimetres (which is about right for vegetables) you will need to use twice as much water, or to water for twice as long. The depth of the wetting front (or depth of penetration) is seen more clearly if the soil is a bit on the dry side to start with. It is particularly important in saline soils that you irrigate deeply each time you water, as this carries the salts down the profile so they are not in range of plant roots.

WHEN SHOULD I WATER MY CROPS?

It is often stated that you should not water plants during the heat of the day. This is not necessarily true. It you water as we suggest – watering deeply but less often, rather than doing it lightly and frequently – then the evaporative losses are negligible. We agree that on hot, windy summer days, a lot of water can be lost by evaporation. However, when plants are highly stressed on very hot days and start to wilt, our advice is to cool them down with a big watering, just like you would hose the kids or the dog.

Watering plants very early in the morning during autumn and winter will help prevent frost damage to your crops. If you don't relish getting up before the sun, use an irrigation timer – set it to start at 3 am, and to turn off and on for the next two hours.

WATER-REPELLING GROWING MEDIA

Some soils (especially those that are very sandy) and even potting mixes actually repel water – water droplets form little spheres on the surface of the growing medium, and they enter only after minutes or hours, often resulting in erosion problems. Water is often channelled down cracks, leaving the growing medium totally dry in parts even after a considerable amount of water has been applied to the surface.

If you believe that your growing medium is repelling water, there are two remedies:

1 **Soil-wetting agents** There are a number of products available, such as Wettasoil®. These are made up in a watering-can and showered over the affected growing medium as required. After their use, water is attracted to the growing medium rather than being repelled. SaturAid® is another wetting agent, but in this case the product comprises granules that are mixed through the growing medium.

2 **Mulches** Water repellence is at its worst when a susceptible growing medium becomes very dry. Applying a suitable mulch will conserve moisture, greatly reducing the possibility of the growing medium drying out and subsequently being difficult to re-wet. Light-coloured inorganic mulches, such as white gravel, are ideal because they do not heat up as much as dark mulches; they also let in the maximum amount of water, because they do not absorb moisture as it flows through (unlike organic mulches, such as woodchips). On sloping sites, where water can run off and cause erosion, mulches are particularly important because they help to hold moisture on top of the growing medium while it gradually soaks in.

TYPES OF WATERING SYSTEMS

There are many different types of watering systems. Choose the one that best suits the size of your urban farm, the crops you are growing as well as your budget and time constraints.

♦ **Drip irrigation** Small emitters that release droplets of water at regular intervals are inserted into flexible plastic pipes, which are then laid along the ground close to the plants. Various emitters are available, depending on how many litres per hour are required. If you have extensive areas to water, then they often need to be divided up into sections that are watered consecutively; in this case, you will want to release water more quickly. Smaller areas can be comfortably watered more slowly. Drip irrigation is the most efficient watering system, as the water goes directly into the soil

and there is no chance of it evaporating into the atmosphere (which happens with sprinkler systems). It is also particularly well suited to plants that do not have extensive root systems, such as annuals and vegetables.

♦ **Sprinkler systems** These systems have outlets that spray water into the air, and the water then falls to the ground like gentle rain. Significant amounts of water are lost to evaporation, particularly on hot and/or windy days. However, the advantage of sprinkler systems is that very large areas can be blanketed with water at any one time. This makes them particularly suitable for lawns,

ABOVE Drip-irrigation systems are ideal for the water-conscious urban farmer, as they direct the moisture straight into the soil.

for instance. There are various options, from the familiar moveable sprinklers to fixed sprinklers that sink down into the soil when not in use (known as 'pop-up' sprinklers). Another extremely useful variation is the micro sprinkler. A number of these can be plugged into a flexible pipe (in the same way that drip emitters are installed), and they can be used to water intermediate areas (such as the drip line of trees and shrubs) without losing too much water to evaporation.

♠ Capillary watering (wicking beds)

You may have heard about wicking beds as a way of growing edible plants. They allow us to water plants from below; water rises towards plant roots because its attraction to soil particles outweighs the force of gravity trying to carry it downwards. The distance that water can rise depends on how fine the soil particles are – water can rise much further in a clay soil than in a sandy one. Thus, if you want to use this form of irrigation, it is vital to understand how it works and to design a system that will supply the amount of water that is needed.

Capillary watering has several advantages over watering from above:

- It keeps the foliage dry, so it is less prone to diseases.
- Plant roots are trained to go down to where the water and nutrients are.
- Plants can take up as much water as they need to grow at their maximum rate.
- It is much harder for plants to dry right out.

However, it is important to have a water supply that is free of pathogens, as problems such as root rot can spread very easily from plant to plant in the shared water of a capillary system.

ABOVE LEFT When using drip irrigation, it is essential that you install a filter to prevent blockages.

ABOVE Watering by hand is labour intensive, but it is often necessary to allow you to target new transplants.

OPPOSITE You can set up neat rows of Vegepods, with each one growing a different crop.

In addition, fertiliser salts can build up because there is no flow of water through the growing medium to flush any excess salinity away. If plants start to show symptoms such as burning on the margins of the leaves, then it is time to renew the growing medium. An alternative is to install a plughole in the base of the system that allows you to flush out the growing medium every few months or if a salt build-up becomes apparent.

⬥ **Hand-watering** The time-honoured method of standing with a hose and watering your garden is always an option, but of course it is very labour intensive. There is also a tendency to not apply enough water when we use a hose, as it takes quite a number of minutes to deliver enough water to most soils so that it reaches right down to the bottom of the root zone. One big advantage of hand-watering is that we can use the so-called 'weed and feed' method; a clip-on container is attached to the hose that allows you to easily liquid feed and apply herbicide to very large areas, particularly lawns, as you water them.

ENSURING YOUR IRRIGATION SYSTEM IS SAFE

Do-it-yourself irrigation systems for the garden are readily available, and they usually come with step-by-step installation instructions that any average home handyperson with a modest toolbox can follow. Some manufacturers have even produced videos to help you through the whole process. If you have any concerns or queries, distributors of irrigation equipment – such as hardware stores and garden centres – are excellent sources of advice and information.

If you are installing a permanent irrigation system that will be left constantly attached to a water outlet, then special precautions need to be taken to prevent the possibility of what is known as backflow. This can occur if broken pipes or other problems interrupt the mains water supply. If there is water in your irrigation system, it can flow back into the pipes and contaminate the mains water supply. Manufacturers of irrigation equipment can provide useful information and hardware to help you avoid this problem, or you can seek specialist advice from a plumber.

CASE STUDY: VEGEPOD

The Vegepod is an innovative Australian-designed growing system that is perfectly suited to urban farming, as it uses a capillary watering system in a lightweight and transportable unit. It is covered with a 'greenhouse' frame that both shields the crops inside from any climatic extremes and protects the plants from the ravages of pests and diseases. A large reservoir of water situated beneath the plants is accessible to the roots at all times, which is particularly handy as the plants grow bigger and thirstier or if you accidentally forget to water the plants for a few days.

It is certainly possible to make your own capillary system (wicking beds) from recycled materials, such as corrugated iron tanks or old fruit-picking bins; however, if you are not a handyperson, then a ready-made unit such as the Vegepod provides a practical alternative.

Bonbeach Primary School Garden

The proliferation of school gardens around Australia has been an incredibly important part of the urban-farming movement in recent years. Primary-school children are particularly receptive to learning about the basics of growing their own food and keeping chooks. Many city children live in medium- to high-density housing where opportunities for gardening are often very limited or even non-existent, so school grounds are one of the few places where they can get stuck into some serious food production. As many parents and teachers have found, however, the challenge is not so much in creating a school kitchen garden as it is in maintaining the necessary level of care and enthusiasm in the years after a project has been launched.

Bonbeach Primary School is located on Port Phillip Bay, in the south-eastern suburbs of Melbourne. The school's garden and its associated parent-led garden group, the Growing Green Thumbs, run by Amy Dowling and Jade Kavanagh, provide an excellent model for creating a sustainable school-based urban farm that successfully engages with the local community on an ongoing basis. Amy and Jade also run workshops for students and the wider community on a variety of topics beyond food gardening, such as nature-play structures, worm farms, teepees, frog bogs and mud pits.

The garden has largely been created on areas of asphalt within the school grounds by the construction of raised beds. A conscious decision was made to publicise the project and seek community help, and this has led to many donations of materials (such as potting and soil mixes), equipment (such as worm farms and wicking beds, including the Vegepod system) and expertise in the form of professionals donating time for education and input into the garden.

The school has balanced the need for security in the school grounds with the concept of a community garden by placing some garden beds outside the school grounds – families can access these outside school hours. It also invites locals to the Bonbeach Farmers' Market, which is held at the school on the second Sunday of every month. The market raises funds for the school and its garden by selling the produce from the school as well as other novel products, such as 'Worm Wee' fertiliser sold in recycled 2-litre milk bottles.

The Bonbeach Primary School Garden is just one example of a school-based urban farm functioning successfully within an Australian city, and its website (www.bonbeachpsgreenthumbs.weebly.com) is full of useful information and ideas for those who might like to start a similar project at their school. There are, of course, other highly successful models, with perhaps the best known being the Stephanie Alexander Kitchen Garden Program, which links cooking with the production of fresh fruits and vegetables. In our observation, the leadership of fully committed parents, teachers and other professional staff greatly enhances the chances of success of whatever style of program is chosen. A succession plan to ensure that leadership is passed on as students and parents graduate from the school is also highly advisable.

CLOCKWISE, FROM OPPOSITE Fruit trees combine beautifully with ornamentals in above-ground timber-edged raised beds; a wide variety of vegetables, grains and herbs is grown at Bonbeach Primary School; community spirit and shared endeavour is an important ingredient in urban farming; children learn about all aspects of planting out and garden maintenance.

CAN I REDUCE THE NEED TO WATER MY GARDEN?

Using less water on the garden can save us plenty of money. However, more importantly, there is an obvious need for society as a whole to take responsibility for conserving our planet's dwindling supply of fresh water. To decrease the amount of water you use in your garden, it is a matter of applying some very simple principles.

◊ Make appropriate plant choices

Plants from drought-prone climates can survive and even thrive on very little water. Australian native plants (with the exception of rainforest plants) and succulents (such as cacti) from various parts of the world are very adaptable to low water levels. It should be said, however, that drought-tolerant plants respond to higher water levels with more luxuriant growth, which will suffer if the extra water is suddenly withdrawn. It is a good idea to deep water all new plantings for the first few months to encourage an extensive root system, but then to gradually wean the plants off the extra water over a period of several months once they are well established.

◊ Use mulch

A 5–10-centimetre layer of coarse, chunky materials placed over the growing medium drastically reduces water loss due to evaporation. The best mulches for water conservation have particles that are at least 20 millimetres in diameter, and can be either organic (such as pine bark chunks or eucalypt chips) or inorganic (such as scoria or other types of gravel). See pages 204–9 of the Composting and Mulching chapter for more information.

◊ Improve water-holding ability

Well-rotted organic matter (ideally, compost made from manures and garden waste) can build up a soil's water-storing capacity. Simply dig as much compost as you can afford into the top 15 centimetres of your soil. This will reduce the amount of water lost through run-off and drainage, and hence conserve water in the soil where plants can use it.

LEFT Scoria is an excellent choice as a permanent water-saving mulch for perennials and pots, and it looks appealing, too.

OPPOSITE Hose wands extend your reach into the garden when watering, and help you to direct water to specific plants.

RETHINKING RUN-OFF

Many urban centres spend vast amounts of time and money ensuring that rainfall run-off is diverted quickly into rivers and oceans. What a waste of water! Sydney's CBD and surrounds, for example – where run-off is in excess of 90 per cent due to hard surfacing – encompasses an area of about 6 square kilometres, or 600 hectares. With an average rainfall of 1200 millimetres per year, this represents a total volume of about 7200 million litres of water that heads straight into the harbour. If each square metre of urban farm requires about 300 litres of supplementary irrigation water to fill the gaps between rainfall events, then Sydney's run-off would irrigate about 24 million square metres (or 2400 hectares) of highly productive land.

If each hectare of this productive land generated around 20 tonnes of produce per year, this equates to 48,000 tonnes of food – enough to feed just over a quarter of a million people for a year, assuming they consume around 500 grams per day of fresh fruits and vegetables.

At a smaller level, if the average house with a roof area of, say, 100 square metres is located in an area with an average annual rainfall of 1000 millimetres, then the total amount of stormwater that can potentially be collected in a year is 100,000 litres. This is a significant amount of water in relation to the needs of crops on an average suburban block, and would likely be enough to irrigate a garden of 300 square metres for a whole year in the complete absence of any rainfall.

DRAINAGE

Plants need a constant supply of moisture, or they will wilt and eventually die. However, plant roots also need oxygen, or they will suffocate. Ironically, wilting is the first sign of waterlogging, as the roots are suffocating and cannot function to support the plant. The ideal soil for plants provides a balance between air and water – it must be well drained, but retain plenty of moisture.

So, how can you achieve this balance? At first glance, it seems impossible to have both good drainage and good moisture levels in the same soil. The answer lies in ensuring there are differently sized pore spaces within your soil. Sandy soils have large pore spaces through which water flows very freely, with little of it being retained. Clay soils have much smaller pore spaces that hold water against the force of gravity, and therefore they tend to not be free draining. Loamy soils are a mixture of sand and clay; consequently, they usually have a balance of small and large pore spaces. This gives us the best of both worlds – that is, good drainage but also adequate water storage. The perfect loam will form a ball when the moist soil is squeezed together, but this ball will break apart fairly readily when it is dropped onto a hard surface.

The effect of slope on drainage

Obviously, water runs down a slope and collects at low points. For most soil types, the greater the slope the better the drainage will be, while drainage will be poorer at the bottom of the slope. Allow for this when selecting plants for a given area of your garden or deciding whether drainage is needed.

You can use surface-drainage techniques to distribute stormwater advantageously on your urban farm – it may be possible to landscape areas such as orchards in such a way as to divert stormwater across the property. Small mounds (swales) created along the contour lines of slopes will collect water behind them, giving the water time to slowly soak into the soil and irrigate your crops.

Conversely, it is not uncommon to find areas where run-off of water occurs after rainfall, especially where there are a lot of paved surfaces, and this leads to excessive wetness in the soil. Where this happens, an interceptor drain is required. This is a simple V-shaped open trench or gutter placed between a garden bed and an upslope area that directs the water from the slope away from the growing area. The trench only needs to be shallow to divert quite a lot of water to a stormwater drain or into tanks.

Choosing plants for drainage level

Some plants have evolved in the wild to cope with poorly drained soils, but most plants are the opposite – they require a soil where water drains away within a few hours. You can save yourself an enormous amount of trouble by determining how well your soil drains and then choosing crops that will adapt to the specific conditions on your urban farm.

At one extreme are plants that grow in coastal sand dunes or deserts – they will survive and even thrive in very free-draining soils. Such species are able to cope extremely well with drought. At the other extreme are aquatic species, such as edible water lilies, which need soil that is constantly saturated. Most crop plants lie somewhere in between these extremes. By heeding the helpful advice of gardening books and magazines as to the drainage requirements of a particular species, you can avoid having to do a lot of costly and unnecessary drainage work.

WHAT CAN I DO ABOUT POOR DRAINAGE?

When we talk about poor drainage, we really mean poor soil aeration. The usual cause of poor drainage within a soil profile is an impeding layer with no air pockets, such as compacted fill, rock, poor-quality clay at shallow depth or some other impermeable barrier. If your soil is poorly drained, then there are many different interventions that can be undertaken, from the simple formation of raised beds to the more complex – and hence expensive – installation of subsurface drains.

Improve texture and structure

The first and most cost-effective choice is always going to be using and improving your own site soil. Perhaps the easiest way to make either sandy or clayey soils more loam-like and thus well drained is to add organic matter, such as well-rotted compost. Apply a layer up to 10 centimetres thick on top of the soil, and dig or fork it into the upper 15 centimetres of topsoil. Gypsum may also be required in heavy, dispersive clays.

TEST FOR DRAINAGE

Dig a hole in your soil that is 200 millimetres deep, then fill the hole with water and let it drain away. Fill it again, and time how long it takes for the water to completely drain away.

< 5 minutes = the soil is very freely drained, no action is required

5–15 minutes = the soil is moderately well drained; hilling up may help

15–30 minutes = the soil is moderately to poorly drained; raised beds are needed

30–60 minutes = the soil is very poorly drained; subsoil drainage is required

> 60 minutes = the soil is impermeable; work on soil structure, and install subsoil drains

However, even when texture and structure are close to ideal, soils can still hold too much water for a variety of reasons, such as run-off from upslope areas. In this case, you need to think about creating built-up beds or perhaps an underground drainage system.

Make raised beds

Lifting the level of the soil above the surrounding area will help get the surface soil above any poorly drained lower layers. Cultivate your soil and at the same time mound it up to whatever height is feasible; 100–200 millimetres higher than the ground level is a good start. Even digging a compacted soil with a spade or fork can often be enough to provide suitable drainage for shallow-rooted plants, such as annuals, low-growing perennials and vegetables.

Simply hilling up the soil on the ground may not be adequate for some urban areas, and you may need to create deeper raised beds that are 300–500 millimetres in height to further improve soil drainage. In this case, it will be necessary to construct some kind of retaining wall to hold the soil, using materials such as timber or masonry. Prefabricated containers, tubs and corrugated iron structures are also available for purchase from garden centres.

Raised beds are usually placed on the existing soil, and they connect to the soil layers below. From a plant-growing point of view, it's not necessary to make raised beds any deeper than 300 millimetres – and in many cases less than this would do. However, sometimes we like to elevate the beds for convenience, so that we don't have to break our back bending over to weed and prune plants. In this case, the bottom of taller raised beds can be filled with existing site soil to save money on purchasing high-quality ingredients.

Garden centres and landscape suppliers sell natural topsoils, as well as 'garden mixes' that are created by blending topsoil with compost. Either product is suitable for creating a raised bed, although it is prudent to examine a handful of any purchased topsoil to ensure that it is sandy to loamy in character, and hence will drain well.

Install subsurface drainage

Sometimes poor drainage occurs when water is trapped at the boundary between the topsoil and the subsoil, especially when the subsoil contains a lot more clay than the topsoil. This can be problematic for plants, as waterlogged soil surrounding the roots can lead to root or collar rot, and plant death. Loosening the subsoil with a pick or mattock will provide temporary relief, but the long-term solution is to provide subsurface drainage with pipes.

Doubtlessly, the best strategy is to install subsurface drainage before any new growing areas are created and sown, as it invariably requires extensive soil disturbance that will be very harmful to established plantings. It is also important to recognise that subsurface drainage is a rather technical subject that may be best left to professionals such as engineers and landscape contractors, especially if the project is large or it involves sensitive areas (for example, steep slopes or unstable soils). It is also essential to check with relevant authorities (such as the local council, as well as gas, water and electricity suppliers) if you will be digging any holes that may disturb existing underground services or change current drainage patterns.

HERRINGBONE DRAINAGE

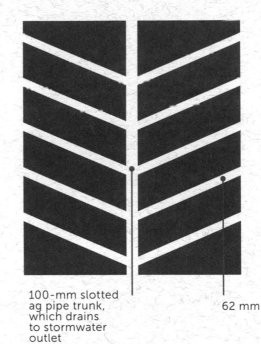

100-mm slotted ag pipe trunk, which drains to stormwater outlet

62 mm

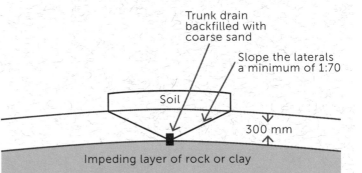

Trunk drain backfilled with coarse sand

Slope the laterals a minimum of 1:70

Soil

300 mm

Impeding layer of rock or clay

DO I NEED TO WORRY ABOUT SUBSURFACE DRAINAGE?

If your topsoil becomes waterlogged for more than a few hours during wet weather, then it is worthwhile to spend some time investigating your soil. In several parts of your garden, dig holes that are approximately 50 centimetres deep, as this is usually the depth at which topsoil changes to subsoil, and problems can occur. Fill each of the holes with a bucket of water, and observe how long the water takes to disappear into the subsoil. If it takes more than a few hours for the water to dissipate, then subsurface drainage is highly desirable.

There are a couple of choices when it comes to diverting any excess water collected in subsurface drains. Given that water is a valuable commodity, it is a good idea to retain as much as possible on-site, particularly if you have a large garden with lots of greenery — such as deep-rooted trees and shrubs — that can use the extra water. The option here is to install an absorption (transpiration) pit similar to those that were used extensively in the past with septic systems. Dig a trench that is several metres long, a metre wide and up to a metre deep (it must be lower than the level of your subsurface drain). This trench is filled with coarse gravel, such as blue metal, and then covered with a plastic semi-cylindrical trench liner that is perforated to allow the entry of water but not sediment. The water from subsurface drains is retained in the trench during periods of heavy rain, and it gradually seeps into the subsoil when things dry out.

The second option is to divert the excess water into a stormwater outlet, if one exists on your property — check with your local council. Not every property has a stormwater outlet (for example, old inner-city properties or those that are lower than street level often have no need for one). In such cases, an absorption (transpiration) pit is the only viable option. In either case, it is important to seek advice from a plumber or landscape contractor to ensure that your system is adequately designed. If you have insufficient fall to carry the subsurface water away, then installing raised beds that are up to 500 millimetres deep may be your only choice.

The most effective and easiest-to-install option for subsurface drainage is corrugated plastic pipe, sometimes known as 'ag pipe', which is readily available from both hardware stores and garden centres. It has slots in the corrugations to allow easy entry of drainage water, and it usually features a filter sock made from fine plastic fabric to stop dirt entering and blocking the pipe over time. Unless the drainage system is likely to carry huge volumes of water, the 62-millimetre diameter pipe will be sufficient. With larger systems, these pipes join up to a 100-millimetre trunk drain in a herringbone pattern.

For general garden beds, each drain needs to be installed 500–600 millimetres below the surface. If you are going to mound the soil into raised beds, you should install the drains 300 millimetres below the surface, and then hill up the soil on top of that. For fruit trees, 700–800 millimetres below ground level is more desirable. The drains should have a slope of at least 1:70 (in other words, a fall of 1 metre for every 70 metres of length). With very heavy clay soils, the drains may need to be as little as a metre apart; if the soil is lighter, they can be up to 5 metres apart.

It is extremely important that the pipe is surrounded by a granular material – such as coarse sand, pea gravel or 10-millimetre crushed rock – to prevent it clogging with silt (even if it has a filter sock). Place a 50-millimetre layer in the bottom of your trench before laying the pipe, and then cover the pipe with a further 50 millimetres of coarse material. A useful tip in very poorly drained soils is to backfill over the gravel with sand right up to the soil surface, which will help get the excess water into the pipe more efficiently.

ABOVE LEFT It is best to install subsurface drainage before planting out your urban farm, as digging the trench will disturb the plants' growing environment.

INSECTS AND ANIMALS ON THE URBAN FARM

11

PEST AND DISEASE MANAGEMENT

FAR LEFT Regular inspection of damage to plants and identification of the cause are vital to pest and disease control on the urban farm.

LEFT Weeds can harbour harmful insects and deadly plant diseases, so keep your garden plots as free of weeds as possible.

OPPOSITE The 28-spotted ladybird is a serious pest of cucurbits, but most ladybirds are beneficial, feeding on insect pests.

It would be hard to find a farmer who likes using poisonous chemicals to control pests and diseases; however, on the flip side, an environmentally friendly solution must provide adequate control, or the problem can get much worse. Harsh chemical solutions usually rely on a rapid 'knockdown' of pests, and they often appear to solve the problem once and for all. However, this can be very misleading – the chemical often also kills beneficial predators, and this can lead to pests suddenly flourishing in the absence of their natural enemies.

Integrated Pest and Disease Management (IPDM) is a scientific approach to managing various plant problems in an environmentally sustainable way that minimises the use of toxic chemicals. The underlying principle of IPDM is using a wide variety of methods to combat a problem, so that you keep pest populations and disease damage to an acceptable level. For many pests and diseases, it will not cause too much harm to your crops if you allow some damage to occur – the trick is to stop the problem spiralling out of control. Careful

monitoring is the only way to really know whether pest population levels are at stable, non-threatening levels. The bottom line is that you must learn all about the pest and utilise a variety of methods to break its life cycle if you are going to manage the problem in a sustainable way.

BEGINNING THE PROCESS

The first step in IPDM is to develop the habit of looking at your crops closely on a regular basis. Watch for any visible signs of damage or discolouration of the leaves, flowers and fruits, and then identify any insects, fungi or other pests that are lurking near the scene of the crime. Once you have identified the cause of a problem, you can then research all the ways you can stop it from multiplying and causing unacceptable damage to the crop.

◆ **Cultural methods** of pest and disease control are non-chemical farming practices carried out before, during and after cropping to minimise losses. These include the removal

CHEMICAL CONTROL

Organic farming is growing in popularity, because using toxic chemicals to control pests and diseases can have all sorts of risks, both obvious and unforeseen. Careless or negligent use of chemicals can result in acute toxicity, which can cause poisoning as well as allergic reactions. With some chemicals, long-term problems – such as carcinogenic side effects – often do not show up for decades. In addition to the risks to human health, toxic chemicals can also cause collateral damage on the urban farm by killing beneficial insects that happen to get in the way when chemicals are being applied.

However, if you are practising urban farming with a view to making a living from selling produce, then the time may come when you have to make the difficult choice to turn to chemical pest or disease control to protect your investment. It is absolutely vital that you strictly observe occupational health and safety precautions when handling and applying chemicals, particularly in urban areas where the surrounding population is also profoundly affected by the way you conduct your operation.

of non-crop host plants (such as nearby weeds) that harbour pests or diseases, quarantine practices to exclude pests and diseases from the farm, selection of pest- or disease-resistant crops, and choosing disease-free propagation material such as virus-free seed potatoes. There are many other examples, but the underlying principle is that thoughtful preventative planning and action can greatly minimise the risk of economic losses.

♠ **Biological methods** of control include introducing beneficial organisms – such as bacteria, fungi and predatory insects and arachnids – into the crop environment to bring and keep pest populations and diseases into balance. Examples include the bacterium

Bacillus thuringiensis, which infects and kills the caterpillars of various moths and butterflies; beneficial fungi, which live in mycorrhizal associations with certain plant roots and help to prevent root-rotting fungi from invading plant root systems; and predatory mites, which are used to control the devastating pest known as red spider mite.

FOREWARNED IS FOREARMED

Many pests are ubiquitous, and particular ones are almost certain to affect specific crops. For instance, two-spotted mites almost inevitably attack beans, while cabbages often succumb to – you guessed it – cabbage white butterflies. If you know that an attack by a certain pest is likely to happen, then you can plan your counterattack

ABOVE Cabbage white butterflies have green caterpillars. Despite their name, these butterflies will be attracted to any brassicas.

SOURCING GOOD BUGS

accordingly. Sticky traps (cardboard impregnated with adhesive goo) are a fantastic and inexpensive way to see what pests are sniffing around and therefore what sort of preventative measures you need to take to be ready for them.

You can identify a wide variety of pests and diseases on various free websites, such as www.abc.net.au/gardening/factsheets/pests_diseases_weeds.htm. Common pests that will almost certainly find their way onto your urban farm include:

- **aphids,** which are small sap-sucking pests that attack the new shoots of a wide range of garden plants, usually in spring. Mites and thrips are microscopic pests that also suck sap. As well as the physical damage these three pests do by robbing the plant of nutrients, they can also spread viruses if they move from an infected plant to a healthy one.
- **bronze orange (stink) bugs,** which are very damaging to all citrus plants.
- **fruit flies,** which lay eggs that hatch into small grubs (larvae). These grubs eat the interior flesh of many fruits, such as tomatoes and stone and citrus fruits.

There are many Australian companies that can supply a range of beneficial insects to control two-spotted mites, mealy bugs, citrus gall wasps, scale insects and other pests. Visit www.goodbugs.org.au to find a list of these suppliers. The Queensland company Bugs for Bugs (www.bugsforbugs.com.au) is a great example of the sort of resource available to urban farmers – the company not only supplies the helpful organisms, but also tells you how to successfully utilise them. While purchasing beneficial insects is not necessarily a cheap option, it is feasible for large urban farms and community gardens where the expense of losing enormous numbers of crops outweighs the cost of the insects. Alternatively, you may simply be prepared to pay a premium for the principle of having truly organic produce from your urban farm.

FAR LEFT, ABOVE
Voracious leaf-eating caterpillars of various species of butterfly cause incredible damage to a wide range of vegetables.

FAR LEFT, BELOW
Mites are usually seen on the underside of leaves. Check carefully, as they can be quite small.

LEFT If you see snails on your crops, they are best controlled by picking them off by hand.

OPPOSITE A physical barrier such as netting may be required if your plants are constantly being nibbled by rabbits.

- **caterpillars,** which are the voracious larvae of many butterflies and moths, such as the cabbage white butterfly.
- **African black beetles,** which are shiny beetles that lay eggs in the soil. Destructive curl grubs (which look like witchetty grubs) emerge from the eggs, and can devastate the root systems of a wide range of edible plants, particularly fruit and nut trees, but also vegetables.
- **scale insects,** which attack a wide range of edible plants, particularly citrus trees. They look like little scabs on the leaves and shoots, and can be rubbed off between the finger and thumb.

Equally important is identifying the beneficial insects that play an enormous role in creating a balance in your garden. If they are present, they will often breed up rapidly and control pest species. There are also specific predator insects available for certain pests. Fighting pests with their natural enemies means that you can avoid the use of toxic chemicals on the urban farm, safeguarding not only yourself but also your children and pets from the risk of inadvertent contact with chemicals. Some of the key insects to look out for are:

- **lacewings,** which eat aphids and thrips
- **dragonflies,** which will devour various small flying insects
- **praying mantis insects,** which feed on a wide variety of pest species.

PREVENTATIVE MEASURES

There are many simple things you can do in your garden to minimise the risk of damage from pests and diseases. For instance, you can exclude a pest by placing a protective barrier around your plants. A ring of coffee grounds or sawdust around your vegetable seedlings deters snails and slugs, as they dislike sliding over the jagged particles. Placing some chicken wire over the top of newly planted seedlings will protect them from a variety of large leaf-eating pests, such as rabbits.

In other cases, certain plants can be used as decoys to protect other species around them. For instance, I had an issue with a rather ravenous swamp wallaby in my vegetable garden. I loved watching this marvellous marsupial munching away, but I didn't enjoy the damage he did to my plants. Having worked out that his favourite food is the lush foliage of the sweet potato, I planted swathes of this easily propagated root vegetable. Since the crop is underground, I can afford to lose some of the foliage and still get a good crop – plus it keeps the wallaby away from my other vegetables!

TAKE ACTION

Cabbage white butterfly caterpillars can quickly decimate a cabbage crop, but they can be easily controlled by the regular use of a bacterial pathogen, *Bacillus thuringiensis*, which is readily obtainable as a product called Dipel. This bacterium is totally non-toxic to all but the caterpillars of a wide range of moths and butterflies. As the caterpillar must ingest the bacterium, it is important to spray the Dipel over as much of the foliage as possible. Also, be prepared for the fact that it takes a few days to kill the caterpillars – do not expect an instant 'knockdown'.

Another problem area in the garden is the damage caused by various fungi, such as those that cause leaf spot in lettuce and brassicas, or powdery mildew in peas and pumpkins. These fungi spread by microscopic spores that land on the leaves, fruits and flowers, and they start as small spots that gradually radiate out until they cause extensive death of plant tissue. There are a couple of environmentally friendly mixtures that can be sprayed on plants to minimise the damage caused by such fungi. Mix 1 tablespoon of bicarbonate of soda (also known as baking soda) with 2 litres of water, or one part fresh full-cream milk with five parts water.

Half the fun of growing food is getting out among your plants every day and watching them grow and develop. If you nurture this habit and really look hard at the web of life in your urban farm, you will be a long way down the track to preventing pests and diseases from building up and causing major damage.

COMPANION PLANTING

We have never seen any convincing evidence that companion planting works as a way of controlling pests and diseases. Garlic, for instance, reportedly repels pests from nearby plants, but it also attracts its own insect pests, such as aphids and thrips. In our experience, following evidence-based approaches to the management of pests and diseases is a far better policy. This is not to say that we should dismiss companion planting for other reasons. Interplanting nitrogen-fixing legumes such as beans with hungry plants such as corn or potatoes is always useful.

TOP These cabbages have not been damaged by hail – hungry caterpillars of cabbage white butterflies are the culprits.

ABOVE LEFT Mite damage caused underneath the leaf shows through as light spots on the upper surface.

ABOVE RIGHT Peach leaf curl is caused by a fungus. It can be controlled but seldom eliminated.

INTEGRATED URBAN FARMING

FAR LEFT Chooks are easy to keep, and they regularly provide food (in the form of eggs), even in very small urban spaces.

LEFT With a little knowledge and experience, you can obtain quality honey from bees housed on your urban farm.

Prior to the mid-twentieth century, animals were traditionally part of urban farms. Milking cows, pigs, goats, sheep, ducks and geese were all likely to be found on small acreages outside of towns and cities. Higher population densities in the modern era make it impractical to keep larger animals on most urban farms; however, there are two smaller creatures that are ideal for anyone who wants to extend their urban farm beyond simple crop production: bees and chickens.

Beekeeping is a particularly useful activity, as not only is it a potential source of honey, but it is also an excellent insurance policy to ensure that your crops are well supplied with pollinators. Although common honey bees are most popular, there has been a recent surge of interest in Australian native stingless bees. They do not produce anything like the yield of honey that their exotic cousins do, but they are very good pollinators that come without the risk of bee stings. The second activity that is highly compatible with many urban farms is keeping chooks. They turn kitchen scraps into valuable edible protein and useful manure, and they can also keep pests and weeds under control if they are carefully managed.

BEES
Written by Elke Haege, President of the Sydney Bee Club and breeder of native stingless bees in Sydney (www.elkeh.com.au)

Keeping honey bees is a very rewarding experience, but it is a lot more involved than keeping Australian native stingless bees, and the decision to get into honey bees should not be taken lightly. You may want to start by visiting a beekeeping club in your local area to see if keeping honey bees might be for you.

To be a beekeeper in Australia, you must register with the relevant state government department – even if you have as little as one hive (and even if you are a hobbyist).

- In New South Wales, it is the Department of Primary Industries.
- In Queensland, it is the Department of Agriculture and Fisheries.
- In Victoria, it is Agriculture Victoria.

- In other states, check with your state agricultural department or equivalent as to administrative requirements.

You must follow specific legal requirements and a Code of Practice if you own and manage bees. Regulation helps reduce the spread of pests and diseases that have the potential to quickly spread from colony to colony. It also controls and promotes responsible management with regard to both the public and any neighbouring lands and land uses.

A learning curve

Before actually getting bees, however, it is recommended that you do a hands-on course in beekeeping. These courses should be able to point you in the right direction with regard to equipment and bees, and advise you on the costs involved. Purchase a practical guidebook such as *Bee Agskills*, which is a good reference for beekeeping tasks such as performing brood inspections, identifying and managing diseases as well as recognising various behaviours and traits of honey bees.

Beekeeping clubs are very useful for not only new beekeepers but also experienced beekeepers to discuss local conditions and experiences. You can ask for, share and compare advice, as there is much more to beekeeping than just honey (in fact, honey is a very, very small part of beekeeping). Some beekeeping clubs – such as the New South

ABOVE One of the most riveting parts of beekeeping is watching individual bees hard at work gathering pollen and nectar from various flowers.

BEEKEEPING COURSES

Your local beekeeping club or association will be able to guide you towards a reputable and practical beekeeping course (and some clubs even conduct their own courses). The following websites also detail useful courses:

- www.dpi.nsw.gov.au/content/agriculture/ profarm/courses/beekeeping
- www.training.gov.au/Training/Details/ AHC32010
- www.theurbanbeehive.com.au/courses-2/

Wales clubs, under the Amateur Beekeepers Association – also offer affordable beekeeping third-party liability insurance. Being part of one of these associations will keep you abreast of beekeeping news (such as outbreaks of pests and diseases that may need careful attention when doing your brood inspections); help you share and gain information on requeening, swarm collection and control, and local bee behaviour at various times of the year; and provide tips on hive assembly and many other components involved in the gentle practice of managing honey bees. Clubs are also a good place to learn about and discuss with other beekeepers the issues bees are facing across Australia and around the world.

When you become a beekeeper, you are likely to also become more acutely aware of the natural landscape around you (such as what plants are flowering in your area, and when the wet and dry seasons are) – as this

significantly affects bees. As you perform regular brood inspections in your hive, you'll also start to become aware of the bees' cycles, smells, sound changes and collective behaviour traits, which I find the most rewarding part of beekeeping.

More than just honey bees!

Australia has more than 1800 different species of native bees. Most of these are solitary, but there are a few species that are social like honey bees (which were introduced to Australia in 1822). There is untapped potential in our Australian native bees.

One social species, which is naturally distributed in coastal Queensland and New South Wales (including Sydney), is particularly worth looking into if you are interested in bees. The native stingless bee (*Tetragonula carbonaria*) is a small (3-millimetre long) mostly black bee that is an efficient pollinator. Dr Anne Dollin's website (www.aussiebee.com.au) is a great

resource on this and many other native bees. If you want to keep bees but you only have a balcony or small garden, or you don't have the time needed for honey bees, then this is the place to start looking. You will soon learn how to manage a colony of native stingless bees or create a habitat for solitary bees.

CHICKENS

The red junglefowl (*Gallus gallus*), along with the dog, is among the earliest creatures that were domesticated by humans. About 7500 years ago, very soon after humans first settled in hamlets and villages in Southeast Asia, the red junglefowl – an omnivorous offshoot of the theropod (a three-toed dinosaur, nowadays called a bird) – learned that there were always rich pickings around human habitations. An inquisitive bird with a social disposition, it quickly became a favourite food source of humans, as it had the unusual habit of laying eggs constantly throughout its breeding season, unlike most birds that have a pronounced laying 'window' (which is usually only a few weeks in spring).

At first it was, without a doubt, pleasantly surprising to find a freshly laid egg in the morning, just in time for breakfast, and their habit of one rooster dominating and driving off the spare ones meant cockerel for dinner. The other unusual and highly desirable habit was that the hens laid perfectly good but sterile eggs in the absence of a rooster. Today there are varieties that still have the ancient habit of laying their eggs only in the warmer months, but most have been bred for constant year-round laying with hardly a pause at all. Bred in England, the Orpington was one of the first to lay throughout most of the cold English winter, which was quite a breakthrough. Some, like the ISA Brown, have had this seasonal tendency completely bred out of them, and they lay all year round, in any climate, if they have access to good food, water and comfortable surroundings.

Picking your chickens

Chickens are among the easiest and cheapest animals to keep, even in the smallest of areas. Their ability to eat almost anything – including garden and kitchen scraps, insect pests and even snails – while producing eggs and valuable fertiliser explains their enduring popularity with urban farmers.

Chickens are kept for many reasons these days; some are just for show, and the curiosity of breeding them. For our purposes, however, the chief interest is obtaining eggs. When we were kids, the sound of roosters crowing could be heard all over the suburbs. Sadly, this is no longer the case. It is more difficult to breed chickens in urban environments these days, as neighbours are often intolerant of the noise that roosters make. Today, many local councils have ordinances preventing the keeping of roosters, but if you are lucky enough to live in the right area, breeding chickens is very rewarding and especially fun for kids. There is nothing cuter than a busy hen roaming around with a cloud of fuzzy chicks ducking under her at the slightest hint of danger.

Even if you can't keep roosters, you are usually allowed to keep hens. Vaccinated hens can be purchased with little effort. The best egg-laying breeds are ISA Brown, Orpington, Australorp, Sussex, New Hampshire, Rhode Island, Leghorn and Plymouth Rock – all are large birds with large eggs. Hybrids are also available. There are many other breeds, but most are just for show. The Silkie, for example, is fun to look at and makes a good pet, but it is not useful as a layer. Many Bantams – often just mini versions of the common breeds – actually lay very well, but their eggs are just too small. However, they are an excellent choice for very small spaces.

ABOVE This portable coop can be placed over garden beds once the edible plants have been harvested, allowing chicken manure to fertilise the soil.

Safe as houses

Chickens need a secure, lockable henhouse at night-time (as there are many creatures, such as foxes, which like to eat them); the structure should be dry (as chooks become very miserable when wet), well insulated, out of the wind and protected from extremes of weather. They can be permanently cooped up as long as they have access to patches of sun and shade – so they can regulate their temperature – and a snug, dry perch or enclosed laying box at night. A laying box is handy – otherwise the chickens will lay their eggs anywhere, often secreting them from you.

It is much more fun, however, if chickens are allowed out to browse freely during the day. Fresh plant matter means chlorophyll in their diet, and this leads to golden yolks with higher omega-3 levels. Grazing on insects provides both protein and occupational therapy for a constantly busy animal, not to mention free pest control for your garden. Free-range birds are happy birds, but you do have to protect young seedlings from being scratched or pecked by hungry chickens. Use chicken-wire 'cloches'.

Chicken food

Pure grain is not a well-balanced diet for chooks, and it leads to wan, pale yolks (caged birds are fed colouring agents to disguise this). It is possible to feed free-range birds that have a large territory some wheat, as it supplements their diet. However, wheat and most other grains are deficient in calcium, so make sure your chickens have access to shell grit (calcium carbonate) as well.

Choose the larger size shell grit wherever possible, as it provides not only calcium content but also the grinding grit for their crop. This is the organ, just before their stomach, that stores the grit and, using a constant pulsing muscle action, grinds up even the toughest fibrous foods. It is an ancient organ. Fossilised piles of stones have been found with dinosaur skeletons in exactly the same position, at the bottom of the neck, as the crop is in chickens.

ABOVE Free-range chickens can be integrated with urban farming. They eat kitchen scraps and insects, and produce useful eggs and fertiliser.

It's one of the main reasons chickens are such efficient converters of low-quality feed into high-quality protein.

Most commonly, hens are fed pellets that have been specially formulated for egg laying. These pellets have a mix of grains, including high-protein pulses, and supplementary minerals such as calcium and phosphorus. Laying birds need plenty of calcium and phosphorus, or they deplete their own stores and their bones become brittle. Layer pellets are cheap and ensure a basic nutritional sufficiency. The free-range diet is a bonus on top of this, but chickens can be kept on just pellets and kitchen scraps. Make sure any kitchen scraps are fresh, as rotting food is not good for them. Chickens will eat almost anything from the fridge, but not too much all at once. They love old butter, for example, but don't give them the whole block!

Sure as eggs

Remember that egg production peaks in the first couple of years. It slowly declines until the poor old hen is just worn out, usually around the ten-year mark. In the good old days, hens would become 'boilers' – making excellent soup and stock – after about five years. We'll leave it to you to decide if you are a pet owner or a farmer.

Many hens go 'broody', that is, they will jealously guard and sit on their eggs if the eggs are not collected. Although the hen will peck you and try to stop you, it's important that you remove the eggs at least every second day or the hen will go broody and set. When they set (usually once they have six or more eggs), hens will not get up – they do not eat properly, they lose condition and they stop laying. The only way to stop this is to take their eggs away. You have to be tough with brooders.

Breeding chickens

Chickens are very easy to breed – all you need is a rooster. Actually, if you have a very broody hen, you can buy fertile eggs and be a breeder without having a rooster. Many people keep 'brooders', hens whose sole job is to raise the next batch of fertile eggs into chicks, rather than laying the eggs themselves. This is an

excellent choice if you live in an urban area where you are not allowed to keep roosters.

Where you can keep roosters, it is always a delight to watch their antics as they corral their hens, tease the dog and strut around. Remember though, one rooster to a minimum of about six hens – otherwise the rooster bothers the hens too much. If you have too many roosters, they will cause the hens to lose condition and reduce laying – and the roosters may even kill the hens. Keep only the best and most vigorous roosters to continue the line, and sell the unwanted ones at local poultry auctions and sales. Don't release them into the wild, as they just become a pest or get taken by predators. Transport them to your local market in strong cardboard or wooden boxes with the opening covered in chicken wire. Don't be surprised if people are not buying them as pets, but do make an effort to ensure the roosters will be treated humanely.

ABOVE This small, low-cost yet dry and secure house is big enough for half a dozen hens, which will produce plenty of eggs for an entire family.

OPPOSITE For larger urban farms, a solid wooden henhouse for two dozen free-range hens is ideal. It's important to lock them up at night to protect them from predators.

CONCLUSION: THE FUTURE OF URBAN FARMING

12

FARMING FOR TOMORROW

Everything old is new again. Agriculture and horticulture were the things that made urban life possible in the first place, and now many urban dwellers living in the concrete jungle of high-density housing yearn to reconnect with nature as well as the production of their food. Urban farming will never provide all your food needs – either now or in the future. However, what we are developing is a profound appreciation of what is involved in producing healthy and organically grown food (in the sense of it being free of toxic chemicals), and the ability to reconsider its value and necessity.

As well as doing our own urban farming, we can support farmers' markets and community gardens, which will encourage more local and sustainable food production. The move back to 'heritage' food plants is starting to happen all over the Western world. In the next decades, urban farmers will be growing a greater variety of food plants – both heirloom species and modern hybrids – than ever before, ensuring that we preserve crop biodiversity for future generations.

DESIGN AND TECHNOLOGY

As more and more rural land on the edges of cities is consumed by urban development, it is vitally important that planning authorities consider mandating community green space so that developers leave enough land for not only green landscapes but also urban farms. Some developers get it, but many others don't. When a landscape architect friend suggested the incorporation of a community garden for food growing, the astonishing reply was, 'We want them shopping in our supermarket, not growing their own food!' Obviously, it is up to councils to ensure that these kinds of developers don't get their own way.

There is usually a divide in landscaping: ornamental plants over here, and crop plants over there. The Salad Bar by Turf Design Studio (see page 127) is a sensational example of how productive gardens don't need to be simply

utilitarian in nature – they can be integrated into modern garden design. We are starting to see food plants being used in landscaping more and more, and this trend will continue to gain popularity into the future. For example, many councils plant parsley and ornamental brassicas together in patterned beds, while fruit and nut trees make excellent park trees in towns and cities.

The continuing evolution of cultivation technologies means that we can grow food across all sorts of urban environments – both

ABOVE Planting heritage varieties helps preserve vital food-crop biodiversity, which would otherwise disappear.

OPPOSITE Mixing urban greening with food production can improve the environment and create a serious amount of food.

horizontal and vertical – using fertiliser that we generate from our own organic wastes and stormwater that we harvest from our roofs and other hard surfaces. Recent Australian inventions such as Composta (see page 117) and the Vegepod (see page 219) make the most of very small spaces such as apartment balconies, ensuring that everyone can grow something – even if it's just a bunch of culinary herbs. Enterprising urban farmers build their own systems, often from recycled materials, and these creations are the basis for the next generation of innovative growing systems.

THE ONLY WAY IS UP

Vertical gardens (also known as green walls) are attracting a great deal of interest from urban farmers, as they utilise often-empty walls and take up little ground area. However,

in researching this subject, it has become apparent to us that this method of food production is still a work in progress. There are many commercial growing solutions, but every system that we road-tested required a large input from the grower. Based on recycled plastic PET bottles, the vertical food garden (see pages 128–9) designed by Sydney horticulturist Mark Paul is the most user-friendly system we have come across. We certainly see green walls overflowing with edible plants as one of the key directions for the future of urban farming, particularly as urban farmers work out new and clever ways to streamline the application of water and liquid fertiliser via drip-irrigation systems and worm farms.

Taking worm farms and urban farming to the next level – quite literally – we believe that in the not-too-distant future liquid fertiliser

ABOVE As high-density housing becomes a reality for more and more people, it's great to know that even small balconies can produce significant fruit and vegetable contributions for the table.

from large-scale worm farms could be used to feed rooftop hydroponic systems located on city buildings. Simple, lightweight plastic greenhouse structures could be erected to protect the cropping areas from wind-tunnel effects, climatic extremes and intense weather events, such as hailstorms. Operations such as these would overcome the current engineering problem of trying to accommodate and service garden beds comprising heavy soil or potting mix.

Another trend that is on the increase is the integration of crop growing with small animal husbandry, particularly chickens and fish. Horticulturist Mark Paul is working on a way to combine his renowned green-wall systems with fishponds. Water from the pond is pumped up and over the green-wall panels or pillars, and the plants actually clean the water as it trickles down and back into the pond. The plants use the nutrients that the fish excrete, while the fish enjoy clean water. On a small scale it certainly provides a very pleasing spectacle, but there is no reason it could not be expanded into a highly productive system featuring edible fish and plant cultivation.

PLANNING AHEAD

When Simon's father was a child in South Perth, the river flats alongside the Swan River were occupied by Chinese market gardens. He often describes the utopia of vegetable gardens nestled among mulberry and fig trees, apricots, loquats and twisting vines; water-filled channels dug to the freshwater table for irrigation were filled with fish that the men fed and then caught for the pot. Guinea fowl had escaped from the nearby zoo and bred up into big flocks; Simon's dad and his mates would catch them and take them home along with fresh vegetables they obtained from the gardeners in exchange for crabs they had caught in the river.

We don't have to imagine such an Eden. With the right planning laws and an urban population determined to return to an idyllic life, such a place could exist again. We need to re-imagine green space in our cities, turning away from the current 'turf and trees' model and towards a botanic paradise of productive integrated gardens that cool our cities, recycle wastes, occupy people's senses and reward urban farmers with fresh, healthy food.

As more and more people move to the world's cities, more and more pressure is placed on our agricultural soils to feed them – and this is not sustainable as we march into an uncertain tomorrow. Put simply, urban farming is the only way to rebalance this equation – it allows us to produce valuable food while also keeping us in touch with the natural and agricultural world. It is essential that we plan for our future food needs and make space in our cities for urban farming in all its forms.

ABOVE Urban farmers are starting to think outside the box, looking for new ways to make the most of vertical space in small gardens, on balconies and on rooftops.

BIBLIOGRAPHY

Roofs and Balconies

Dunnett, N. and N. Kingsbury, *Planting Green Roofs and Living Walls, 2nd Edition* (Portland: Timber Press, 2004).

Hopkins, G. and C. Goodwin, *Living Architecture: Green Roofs and Walls* (Melbourne: CSIRO Publishing, 2011).

Plant Varieties

Arthur Yates and Co. Pty. Ltd., *Yates Garden Guide, 44th Edition* (Sydney: HarperCollins Publishers, 2015).

Blazey, C., *All about Tomatoes and Potatoes, Peppers and Other Relatives* (Dromana: Digger's Club, 2011).

Davidson, A., *The Oxford Companion to Food, 2nd Edition* (Oxford: Oxford University Press, 2006).

Hedrick, U.P. (ed.), *Sturtevant's Edible Plants of the World* (New York: Dover Publications, 1972).

Roberts, J., *Cabbages & Kings: the origins of fruit and vegetables* (London: HarperCollins Publishers, 2001).

Soils and Fertilisers

Blake, C.D. (ed.), *Fundamentals of Modern Agriculture* (Sydney: Sydney University Press, 1976).

Craul, P.J., *Urban Soils: Applications and Practices* (New York: John Wiley & Sons, 1999).

Craul, T.A. and P.J. Craul, *Soil Design Protocols for Landscape Architects and Contractors* (New York: John Wiley & Sons, 2006).

Handreck, K.H., *Gardening Down-Under: A guide to healthier soils and plants* (Melbourne: CSIRO Publishing, 2001).

Handreck, K.H. and N.D. Black, *Growing Media for Ornamental Plants and Turf, 4th Edition* (Randwick: UNSW Press, 2010).

Hazelton, P. and B. Murphy, *Understanding Soils in Urban Environments* (Melbourne: CSIRO Publishing, 2011).

Leake, S. and E. Haege, *Soils for Landscape Development* (Melbourne: CSIRO Publishing, 2014).

Urban, J., *Up by Roots: Healthy Soils and Trees in the Built Environment* (Champaign: International Society of Arboriculture, 2008).

Plant Propagation

Hartmann, H.T., D.E. Kester, F.T. Davies and R. Geneve, *Hartmann & Kester's Plant Propagation Principles and Practices, 9th Edition* (Harlow: Pearson Education, 2017).

Stewart, A., *Let's Propagate! A plant propagation manual for Australia* (Sydney: Allen & Unwin, 2012).

Cultivation Techniques

Burnett, J. and S. Leake, *Making Your Garden Grow: A Guide to Garden Soils and Fertilisers* (Port Melbourne: Lothian Books, 1990).

Deans, E., *Esther Deans No-Dig Gardening and Leaves of Life* (Sydney: HarperCollins Publishers, 2001).

Glowinski, L., *The Complete Book of Fruit Growing in Australia* (Sydney: Hachette, 2008).

Gouldstone, S., *Growing Your Own Food-Bearing Plants in Australia* (South Melbourne: Pan Macmillan Australia, 1983).

Horsfall, M., *Fabulous Food from Every Small Garden* (Melbourne: CSIRO Publishing, 2009).

Maynard, D.N. and G.J. Hochmuth (eds), *Knott's Handbook for Vegetable Growers, 5th Edition* (New York: John Wiley & Sons, 2007).

McMaugh, J., *What Garden Pest or Disease Is That? Organic and Chemical Solutions for Every Garden Problem* (Frenchs Forest: New Holland Publishers, 2002).

Royal Horticultural Society, *RHS Allotment Handbook & Planner: What to Do When to Get the Most from Your Plot* (London: Octopus Publishing Group, 2015).

Wilkinson, J., *Nut Grower's Guide: The Complete Handbook for Producers and Hobbyists* (Melbourne: CSIRO Publishing, 2005).

Worms and Compost

Handreck, K.H. and N.D. Black, *Growing Media for Ornamental Plants and Turf, 4th Edition* (Randwick: UNSW Press, 2010).

Murphy, D., *Earthworms in Australia: A blueprint for a better environment* (Flemington: Hyland House Publishing, 1993).

Murphy, D., *Organic Growing with Worms* (Hawthorn: Penguin Books Australia, 2005).

Wilson, E., *Worm Farm Management: Practices • Principles • Procedures* (Essendon North: Pennon Publishing, 2002).

Watering and Irrigation

Handreck, K.H., *Good Gardens with Less Water* (Melbourne: CSIRO Publishing, 2008).

Handreck, K.H. and N.D. Black, *Growing Media for Ornamental Plants and Turf, 4th Edition* (Randwick: UNSW Press, 2010).

INDEX

ACKNOWLEDGMENTS

I would like to thank the farmers of the world for their ingenuity and inspiration. My grandfather, Tom Wood, was one of those special farmers. My other grandfather, Roy Stewart, was a magistrate who moonlighted on weekends as the best urban farmer I have ever known. I would also like to thank my mother, Audrey Turner, for her support and gardening inspiration. Thanks also to our intrepid photographer Brent Wilson and the excellent people at Murdoch Books including Diana Hill, Madeleine Kane, Emma Hutchinson, Dannielle Viera, Justin Thomas and the recently retired Sue Hines.

I would also like to thank my great friend and colleague A.B. Bishop for her inspiration and encouragement, and for her wonderful work on the case studies from around Melbourne for the book. The following people and organisations also gave generously of their time and knowledge, and helped with locations for our case studies: Amy Dowling and Jade Kavanagh from Bonbeach Primary School Garden, Simon Holloway of Vegepod, Mark Paul of The Greenwall Company, Wendy Siu-Chew Lee, Sue Turner of Swag Industries, Nigel Nattrass and Chris Quoyle of Reln, Julie and Brad from Composta Australia, Helene of Berowra Heights, Tim and Liz Johnstone of Johnstone's Kitchen Gardens, Wes Death and Richard Thomas of Wormlovers Pty Ltd, Ben Bell of Low Impact Pty Ltd, FareShare and 3000Acres.

Finally, I would like to thank my wonderful co-author Simon, who has shared many valuable horticultural insights with me over the many years of our friendship.

Angus

I would like to thank my university teachers: Professor N. Collis-George, Hal Geering, Dr Brian Davey and Gottfried Scholz for the quality of their teaching; Neil Black of TAFE NSW and Dr Stuart Miller (formerly of Environmental Geochemistry International) for their early encouragement. Most of all, thank you to Dr Colin Mansfield for all your help and support to establish the SESL laboratory, and for providing me with the benefit of your years of experience in the use of commercial scientific analysis to diagnose pathologies in living things.

Simon

IMAGE CREDITS

Brent Wilson, Front cover, back cover, inside cover and author portraits credits: Also 4–12; 16; 22; 24–7; 37; 43 top r; 44; 45 top l; 50; 62–3; 65; 70 2nd; 72–3; 84–5; 95 [1–4]; 97; 104–9; 115; 118–19; 126; 132–3; 146; 150–1; 153; 155; 165–6; 168; 174–7; 189; 204; 207; 212–13; 215 l; 219; 223; 228–9; 237 r; 238; 239 r; 244–51; 253; 260–3

Joel Barbitta, D-Max Photography 13
A.B. Bishop 202–3; 220–1
Luisa Brimble 3; 210–11; 240
Jesse Fenn 125
Joe Filshie 76; 79; 80; 86; 91; 98; 117 top; 157–8; 160 l; 184 r; 205–6; 216–17; 218 l; 222; 224

Dr Larry Ho 36; 47 l; 110
Ian Hofstetter 20; 74; 82; 100 l; 103; 112 l; 131 r; 135; 145; 183; 184 l; 190; 214; 215 r; 218 r
iStock: David A'Vard, the_apostrophe 29; kevinruss 45 top r; Birute 58; 190
Madeleine Kane 117 btm
Simon Leake 18; 32; 70 4th; 83; 111; 120-1; 162; 188; 192; 199; 237 l; 242
Marla Moore 31; 113
Murdoch Books Photo Library 43 l; 152
Robin Powell 40
Lorna Rose 14; 48, 234 top l; 241
Shutterstock: Molotok 289 30; Luka Balkovic 57; Miyuki Satake 67 btm r; Darknezz Skiez 124; Rainer Fuhrmann 179 top

Angus Stewart 15; 17; 19; 21; 23; 28; 33–5; 46; 47 r; 49; 52–6; 59; 66; 67 top l & r; 68; 70 top, 3rd & btm; 71; 88; 94; 95 top l; 103 r; 120; 121 top l, btm l & cnt r; 122–3; 127 r; 128–9; 134; 147; 149; 179 btm; 180; 185; 193–195; 197; 201; 227; 231–2; 233 top l & btm r; 234 r; 235–6; 239 l; 243
Sue Stubbs 38–9; 42; 51; 78; 89; 100 r; 148; 159; 163; 169 r; 170 l; 187
Mark Winwood 81; 87; 93; 112 r; 127 l; 130; 131 l; 136–144; 154; 160 r; 161–2; 164; 167; 169 l; 170 r; 172; 178; 181; 186; 209; 230; 233 top r; 234 btm l

Diagram credits
iStock: 41; 61; 91
Justin Thomas 64; 75; 92; 96 98

The publisher would like to thank the following individuals and organisations, who kindly allowed their gardens to be photographed for this book:
Pocket City Farms
Coal Loader Community Garden
John and Susan Hutchinson
Wayside Chapel
Marrickville West Community Garden
Mort Bay Community Garden
The Buckle family

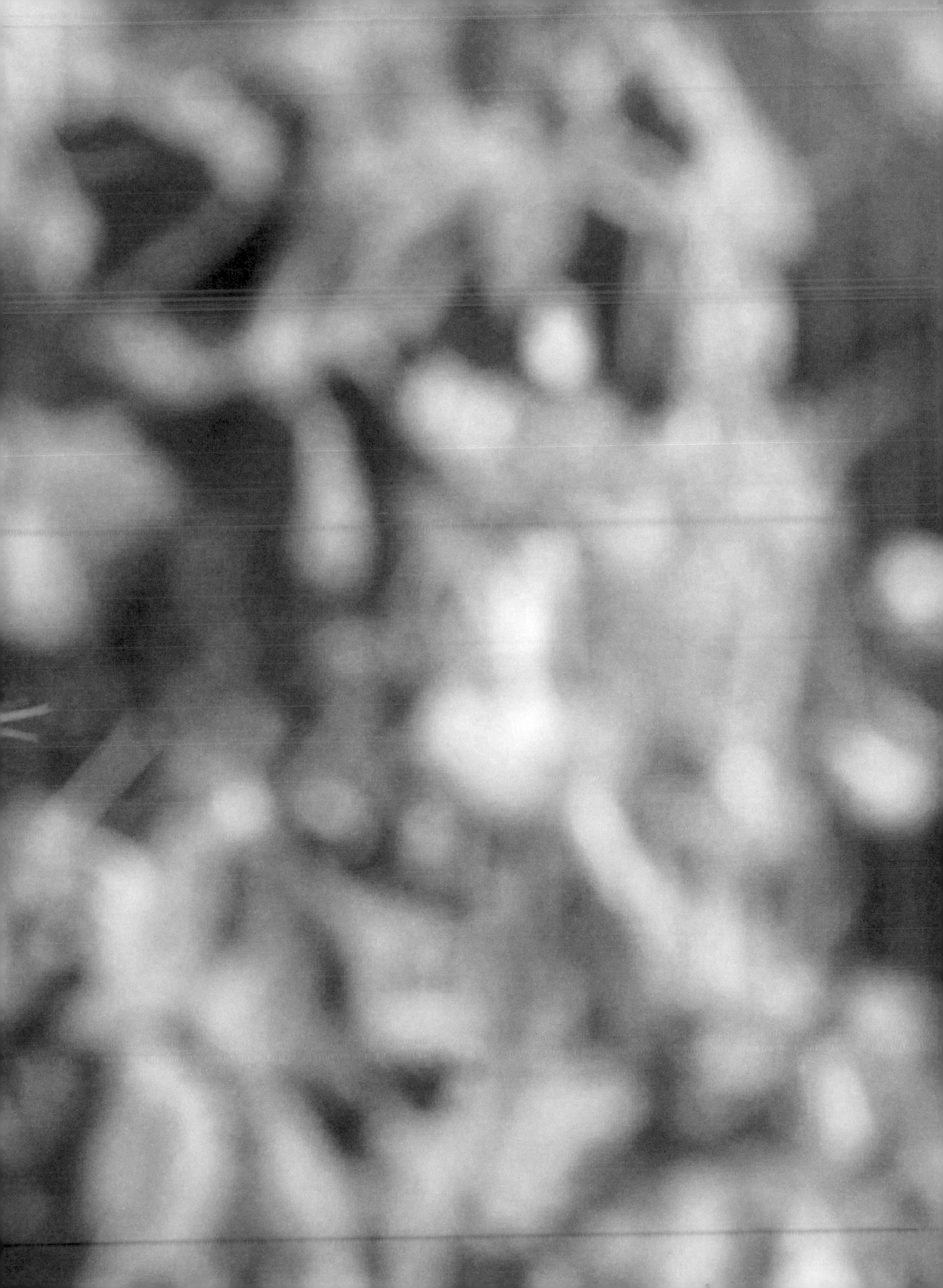

Published in 2017 by Murdoch Books,
an imprint of Allen & Unwin

Murdoch Books Australia
83 Alexander Street
Crows Nest NSW 2065
Phone: +61 (0)2 8425 0100
Fax: +61 (0)2 9906 2218
murdochbooks.com.au
info@murdochbooks.com.au

Murdoch Books UK
Ormond House
26–27 Boswell Street
London WC1N 3JZ
Phone: +44 (0) 20 8785 5995
murdochbooks.co.uk
info@murdochbooks.co.uk

For Corporate Orders & Custom Publishing,
contact our Business Development Team at
salesenquiries@murdochbooks.com.au.

Publisher: Diana Hill
Editorial Manager: Emma Hutchinson
Design Manager: Madeleine Kane
Designer: Justin Thomas
Project Editor: Dannielle Viera
Production Manager: Lou Playfair

A cataloguing-in-publication entry is available
from the catalogue of the National Library of
Australia at nla.gov.au.

ISBN 978 176052 262 9 Australia
ISBN 978 176052 764 8 UK

A catalogue record for this book is available
from the British Library.

Colour reproduction by Splitting Image Colour
Studio Pty Ltd, Clayton, Victoria
Printed by C & C Offset Printing Co. Ltd., China